Creating Postcolonial Literature

Creating Postcolonial Literature

African Writers and British Publishers

Caroline Davis

palgrave
macmillan

Softcover reprint of the hardcover 1st edition 2013 978-0-230-36936-8

First published 2013 by
PALGRAVE MACMILLAN

Palgrave Macmillan in the UK is an imprint of Macmillan Publishers Limited, registered in England, company number 785998, of Houndmills, Basingstoke, Hampshire RG21 6XS.

Palgrave Macmillan in the US is a division of St Martin's Press LLC, 175 Fifth Avenue, New York, NY 10010.

Palgrave Macmillan is the global academic imprint of the above companies and has companies and representatives throughout the world.

Palgrave® and Macmillan® are registered trademarks in the United States, the United Kingdom, Europe and other countries.

ISBN 978-1-349-35051-3 ISBN 978-1-137-32838-0 (eBook)
DOI 10.1057/9781137328380

A catalogue record for this book is available from the British Library.

A catalog record for this book is available from the Library of Congress.

Contents

List of Illustrations

List of Tables

Acknowledgements

I would like to acknowledge all those who have helped me during the research and writing of this book. I would like to thank David Johnson and Robert Fraser at the Open University for their immensely generous support, advice and encouragement at every stage of this study, from Ph.D. thesis to book manuscript. I am also most grateful to Isabel Hofmeyr, Stephanie Newell and Shafquat Towheed for their kind and constructive help and advice.

I would also like to thank my colleagues in the Oxford Centre for International Publishing Studies at Oxford Brookes University for their support, in particular: Jane Potter, Chris Fowler, Sally Hughes, Angus Phillips, Beverley Tarquini, Nicola Timbrell, and my former colleagues, Paul Richardson and Sue Pandit. I would like to acknowledge the generous research funding I received from Oxford Brookes University.

In carrying out this research, I have received extensive help from Martin Maw, Head of OUP Archives, who first alerted me to the existence of Three Crowns. I would also like to thank the archivists at Cape Town University Library, at the National English Literary Museum in Grahamstown, at The Cape Town Archives Repository and at Leeds University Library Special Collections. My thanks in addition to those who agreed to be interviewed for this project, namely, David Attwooll, James Currey, Ron Heapy, Marie and David Philip, Jon Stallworthy, Randolph Vigne and Dennis Walder. I am grateful to Valery Rose for proof-reading an earlier draft of this manuscript. I would also like to thank Ben Doyle and Monica Kendall at Palgrave Macmillan for their excellent editorial work.

A much earlier version of Chapter 5 appeared as 'The Politics of Postcolonial Publishing: Oxford University Press's Three Crowns Series 1962–1976', in *Book History*, 8 (2005), and a version of Chapter 4 was published as 'Histories of Publishing under Apartheid: Oxford University Press in South Africa', in *The Journal of Southern African Studies*, 37:1 (2011). A shorter version of Chapter 8 was published as 'Publishing Wole Soyinka: Oxford University Press and the Creation of "Africa's Own William Shakespeare"', in *The Journal of Postcolonial Writing*, 48:4 (2012), and a case-study within Chapter 9 appeared as 'Publishing Anti-Apartheid Literature: Athol Fugard's *Statements* Plays', in *The Journal of Commonwealth Literature*, 48:1 (2013). I am grateful for permission from these journals to reprint extracts here. Archival references, quotations and illustrations relating to Oxford University Press are reprinted here with the kind permission of the Secretary to the Delegates of Oxford University Press.

Finally, I am very grateful for the constant help and encouragement of friends and family, especially that of my father, Ian Davis, and my late mother, Judy Davis. I also owe special thanks to Sheila Clayton. Most of all, however, I would like to thank my husband, Andy Clayton, and my children, Joseph, Ellen and Jude. This book is dedicated to them.

List of Abbreviations

AOUP	Archives of the Oxford University Press, Oxford
CTAR	Cape Town Archives Repository
CTU	Cape Town University Libraries
LUL	Leeds University Library Special Collections
NELM	The National English Literary Museum, Grahamstown
OUP	Oxford University Press

Introduction

To represent Africa is to enter the battle over Africa.
– Edward W. Said, *Culture and Imperialism*, p. 80

This is a book about a largely forgotten series of postcolonial literature, Three Crowns, which was one of the earliest attempts by a British publisher to establish a list of African creative writing. Established by Oxford University Press in 1962 and continuing until 1976, it was the vehicle for the international publication of Wole Soyinka and Athol Fugard as well as Lewis Nkosi, John Pepper Clark, Obi Egbuna, Oswald Mtshali, Joe de Graft and Léopold Sédar Senghor, amongst other African writers. Although small, controversial, financially unsuccessful and short lived, the series provides a unique insight into the process of postcolonial literary production and transnational cultural relations.

While the main focus is the Three Crowns series, it also raises important questions about the history, politics and economics of publishing postcolonial literature in general. In the 1960s and 1970s, the publication of African literature in English was dominated by British commercial publishers. Faber & Faber published novels by Amos Tutuola, Peter Abrahams and Ezekiel Mphahlele in the 1950s. Heinemann published Chinua Achebe's *Things Fall Apart* in 1958 and, through Heinemann Educational Books, founded the African Writers Series in the same year as Three Crowns, which quickly became the market leader in the field, publishing 360 titles in total.[1] In the early 1960s, many other British publishers were keen to obtain manuscripts from novelists, poets and playwrights from the newly independent states now emerging in Africa. The London office of André Deutsch published several works of African literature from 1964, and in 1967 went on to become a partner in the East Africa Publishing House in Nairobi, which published African literature for the Kenyan market through its Modern African Library. Longman published the work of several African authors from 1965, including Mbella Dipoko, Ama Ata Aidoo and Efua Sutherland, and then established the Drumbeat series from 1979 to 1985, in which they published the work of Ben Okri and Miriam Tlali amongst others. By the late 1960s there was a growing trend for African literature in many London publishing houses: Allen & Unwin, Cape, Collins, Evans, Gollancz, Hutchinson, Macmillan, Murray, Methuen, Michael Joseph, Museum Press, Nelson, Penguin, Thames & Hudson and the University of London Press.[2] This study aims to contribute to two broader questions: how did Britain impose and maintain its cultural dominance over anglophone African literature beyond the end of formal colonisation in the continent; and what role was played by British publishers in the creation of African literature in this period of decolonisation?

The literature of the Three Crowns series exemplified the 'literary activity of self-making and nation-building', which was described by Elleke Boehmer as a response to decolonisation: 'Writers ... were involved as the beacons, soothsayers, and seers of political movements. It was seen as a writer's role to reinterpret the world, to grasp the initiative in cultural self-definition.'[3] Part of a wider intellectual search for an identity independent of the European colonial powers, these new African authors in the series narrated the new nations and sought to modify, subvert or reverse the prevailing discourse about Africa. They readdressed African history and culture, and focused on the formerly silenced and marginalised from a wide variety of perspectives: Nkosi, Mtshali and Fugard dealt with the struggles and oppression of black and coloured South Africans; Egbuna wrote of the cultural dislocation of colonialism, in terms of religious conflict, disputes over medical practice and conflicts caused by white settlers in East Africa; de Graft explored intergenerational conflicts in Ghanaian society; Clark wrote of cultural transitions in rural Nigeria, while Kimenye wrote of village life in Buganda; Easmon satirised postcolonial elites in decadent, independent West African society; Soyinka assumed a lead role as critic of his new nation, denouncing the regime's betrayal of the ideals of the national liberation movements. The literature in the Three Crowns series was part of an intellectual process of resistance against colonialism and apartheid, as well as a critical engagement with the post-independence nations. However, it was mediated by a British publisher which not only had a long history of colonial publishing, but also had a continued commercial involvement with the postcolonial African governments as well as the South African regime under apartheid. This study investigates how this paradoxical situation came about, and what its implications were for African literature. It explores the nature of the publisher's interventions in the literature of this series, both institutionally and in terms of the text and paratext of the published books.

Constituting African literature

There are two prevailing models that have been used to explain the relationship between the Western publisher and the African writer: one which presents the publisher as a benign influence, 'a necessary mid-wife to the author's prose' to use the metaphor employed by Juliet Gardiner,[4] and another that presents the publisher as an agent of cultural imperialism.

In the first model, the residual rhetoric of the 'civilising mission' persists. The European publisher is depicted as an important patron, offering vital support for African writers and bringing books, and thereby education and enlightenment, to the continent. Publishers' official histories tend to celebrate their achievements in disseminating books throughout Africa whilst underplaying the economic significance of these markets to themselves as publishers, for example in the official histories of Heinemann Educational, Longman and OUP.[5] In addition, Charles Larson argues that European publishers were crucial in supporting African writers in the late twentieth century, and considers that authors in former British- or French-ruled countries were given far more opportunities to be published than those in countries without a colonial history, for example, Liberia.[6] Phaswane Mpe's review of the African Writers Series also reflects on the positive benefits of the European–African literary interchange, in particular in providing a means of publication to authors whose work would be censored in their own countries.[7] Hans Zell regards publishers' investment in literature and books for the general market as compensation for their involvement in the 'lucrative educational book market'. He credits Western publishers, and Heinemann in particular, with the development and growth of a literary culture in Africa.[8]

However, a second, contrasting view of postcolonial publishing has been expounded by African Marxists. It identifies enduring structures of cultural domination in postcolonial literary institutions. For example, although Chinweizu, Onwuchekwa and Ihechukwu's critique relates specifically to Western critics and academics rather than publishers, they maintain that African literature was expected to conform to European literary canons and that African writers sought to supply the European literary tourist with 'new supplies of exotica'.[9] Similarly, Aijaz Ahmad writes, again in very broad terms, of the impact of Western literary institutions on postcolonial literature:

> Third world literature ... comes to us not directly or autonomously but through grids of accumulation, interpretation and relocation, which are governed from the metropolitan countries ... it has been selected, translated, published, reviewed, explicated and allotted a place in the burgeoning archive of 'Third World Literature' through a complex set of metropolitan mediations.[10]

It is my intention to test some of these more abstract models and speculations that cast Western publishers as either agents of a 'civilising mission' or agents of 'cultural imperialism' with reference to a detailed case-study of the publishing strategy of the Three Crowns series. Based on evidence from previously unexplored archives and extensive oral testimonies, I seek to understand how the literature in the series was selected, which literature was excluded and how the texts were produced, marketed and disseminated.

This investigation is related to the tradition of 'the sociology of the text' formulated by Don McKenzie and Jerome McGann, by which texts are studied in relation to the social conditions of their production, circulation and consumption.[11] Robert Darnton's influential model of the 'Communications Circuit' is adopted, and adapted, here, whereby the role of each agent in the life-cycle of the book is considered in turn. Darnton argues that, 'Book history concerns each phase of this process and the process as a whole, in all its variations over space and time and in all its relations with other systems, economic, social, political, and cultural.' This is, as Darnton concedes, a 'large undertaking', but he argues that 'the parts do not take on their full significance unless they are related to the whole'.[12] Yet, Darnton's model does not register the hierarchies and power relations that define each stage in the communications circuit, although these seem fundamental to an understanding of colonial and postcolonial book production. In examining these various stages in the communications circuit of postcolonial African literature this book aims to foreground the impact of the globalised publishing industry on literature and authorship and address the role of the publisher in the commodification of postcolonial literature. My investigation is particularly concerned with the production end of the communications circuit and with the effect of local and international literary marketplaces on the creation of the literature in the series; a detailed investigation of the reading and reception of the literature in Africa is, however, beyond the scope of this study.[13]

Concerning authorship, I examine the patterns of assimilation and resistance in author–publisher relations, and propose that an understanding of the publisher's interventions in the other stages of the circuit shed light on the relationship between the African author and the British publisher. This relates to the long-standing debate about the 'profoundly complicit and compromised figure' of the postcolonial author,[14] a debate that dates back to the writing of Frantz Fanon, Amilcar Cabral and Albert Memmi during the anti-colonial struggles of the 1950s.[15] In a postcolonial context, Ngũgĩ reflects on the alienating impact of international publication for the African writer. He argues that they face the dilemma of being cut off from their communities when they adopt European languages, or marginalised if they choose to write in their mother tongue.[16] Chidi Amuta also identifies the exclusionary practices in Western literature, the pressure on African writers to produce African exotica and the collusion of the writer in the process.[17]

The current critical consensus continues to suggest that assimilation is inevitable for African authors seeking acceptance in a globalised media industry. Pascale Casanova, in *The World Republic of Letters*, defines literary assimilation as 'a process of fusion and integration',[18] and contends that it as an intrinsic aspect of international literary relations, which may be taken as 'applying to the artistic and cultural productions of all colonized or otherwise dominated regions'.[19] For her, assimilation 'often represents the sole means of access to literature and literary existence'.[20] Similarly, Graham Huggan's *The Postcolonial Exotic* argues that: 'African writers through their dealings with western "agents of legitimation" are inevitably compromised, suckered into successive reinventions of an Africa that the white man has known all along.'[21] Brouillette's recent study, *Postcolonial Writers in the Global Literary Marketplace*, proposes that contemporary postcolonial authors no longer resist or oppose the process of commodification by publishers, but consciously interact with the interpretation and reception of their texts. She argues that 'strategic exoticism and ... general postcolonial authorial self-consciousness' now function as literary strategies and as marketable commodities in the global literary market.[22] I intend, through an investigation of the exact negotiations between Three Crowns authors and OUP, to reappraise these arguments in the light of close attention to publishing histories.

In terms of the editorial strategy for Three Crowns, my intention is to establish how OUP assumed a role as both gatekeeper and 'consecrator' of African literature in this period of decolonisation: how it attained the power to confer value on the literature, and what the implications of this were for the literature that was published. This study draws on Pierre Bourdieu's sociology of the literary field and specifically his study of the role of the publishing industry as a cultural agency, as outlined in *The Rules of Art*, and in his essay 'The Production of Belief'.[23] I analyse the institutional framework around postcolonial literary publishing, using original archival evidence to examine the strategies involved in the symbolic production of the literature, the publishing systems of exclusion and inclusion, accreditation and textual circulation, and the means by which cultural and economic capital was conferred.[24] Although Bourdieu's theory of cultural production forms an important part of the theoretical background for this book, my aim here is to examine the relevance of his model (which was based on French literary publishing practice) to the specific circumstances affecting British publishers and African writers in the second half of the twentieth century.

To understand the nature of the postcolonial symbolic economy – specifically the cultural hierarchies operating in the UK and Africa in this period – I turn to Pascale Casanova's theory of international literary production. She proposes a helpful revision of Bourdieu's model in the form of the 'literature-world': an international literary space, in which literary domination is exerted by 'consecrated' nations upon other nations which are normally – but not exclusively – in an economically subservient position. Making the important point that a nation's position in the literary hierarchy can be gauged according to its level of autonomy in the production of literature, she argues that a text's symbolic value is dictated by its place of publication.[25] However, the hierarchies identified by Casanova in relation to literary production might also be extended to literary consumption: the value of postcolonial literature was evidently determined by its destination market. I examine how the racially and geographically 'segregated readership', to employ Shafquat Towheed's term, affected the editorial strategy for the literature of the series.[26]

With respect to the design, production and publicity processes in Three Crowns, I consider the ways in which ideological and economic structures are manifested in the books' paratext – what Gérard Genette describes as the *peritext* (the publisher's interventions within the books themselves) as well as the *epitext* (the publicity and marketing matter circulating beyond the printed book) – to appraise how the material form of the books and the accompanying publicity influenced the interpretation and reception of the Three Crowns literature.[27] I examine how Three Crowns texts were shaped by OUP by means of filtering through the publishing apparatus and how the extra-textual elements of this postcolonial literature created specific forms of meaning. Through case-studies of the publication of Soyinka, Fugard and other Three Crowns authors, I chart the negotiations between authors and publishers that were manifested in the books' paratexts, and compare the texts and paratexts of their printed books, and the reception of the plays as performances and as published products, to explore some of the contradictions and ambiguities that emerged.

Regarding the sales and distribution strategy for Three Crowns, I question the widely held assumption that the Western market was, and is, the only significant market for postcolonial literature. Graham Huggan's thesis rests on the assumption that the main market for African literature was in the West, in his depiction of the Western publisher as an intermediary between the African writer and the Anglo-American marketplace, who is complicit in reinforcing 'stereotypical views of a romantic Africa of "primitive", even primordial tribal existence for the Western touristic reader'.[28] In his study of literary prize culture, James English writes that 'global markets determine more and more the fate of local symbolic economies'.[29] Casanova makes no mention of the significance of the markets in the 'literarily dominated nations' – the assumption being that only the markets of the 'centres of consecration' (in her terms, New York, London and Paris) are worthy of consideration.[30] Sarah Brouillette examines the impact of local readers on the development of postcolonial literature, but she still situates the 'global literary marketplace' predominantly in the West. She argues that, 'It remains the case that the expansion of the market for English literatures has been mainly an Anglo-American phenomenon. Products from a plurality of locales are incorporated into the central metropolitan locations of New York and (decreasingly) London.'[31] There seems, therefore, to be a general assumption in postcolonial literary criticsm that the most significant readers of postcolonial literature are situated in Europe and the United States. This study aims to examine this assumption more closely, and to pay attention to the impact of readers of African editions of African literature in African schools and universities in this particular period. For, as Nourdin Bejjit's research on the African Writers Series also demonstrates, the African educational marketplace had a decisive influence on the emergence of African literature.[32]

In its concern to move beyond an exclusively textual reading of African literature, this book is thus part of a broader critical movement concerned with the institutions and processes behind postcolonial literary production, which seeks to reinsert the publisher as an essential part of the context for understanding postcolonial literature. Previous studies of publishers' interventions in the creation of African literature have, however, centred on the larger, more successful and enduring African Writers Series, for example by Bernth Lindfors (1995), Loretta Stec (1997), Camille Lizabarre (1998), Phaswane Mpe (1999), Graham Huggan (2001), Gail Low (2002) and James Currey (2008). Three Crowns, its poor relation, has been largely ignored.[33] This study demonstrates that the problems that inhibited the development of this parallel, albeit much smaller, series of African literature are themselves revealing, and in particular its turbulent editorial history offers an important insight into the pressures and constraints on African writers during this period. By focusing upon the publishing process for this series, the intention is not to diminish the agency of individual authors, or the influence of the individual literary texts. Instead, I aim to draw attention to the negotiations between African authors and their publishers, and the influence of transnational cultural and economic relations on the constitution of their literature.

Culture and commerce

Publishing is an industry that operates at the juncture between culture and commerce, or at the 'intersection of two axes of value', in Janice Radway's terms.[34] An essential and preliminary concern of this study is the relation between the commercial and the cultural in the work of Oxford University Press, and specifically in the Three Crowns series. How did the inherent tension between the literary expectations of the series and the economic imperative of OUP in Africa define the series?

Pierre Bourdieu's distinction between economic and cultural capital provides a useful vocabulary for understanding the work of the Press in respect to the 'culture/commerce dichotomy'. According to Bourdieu, publishers operate in one of two distinct fields: the restricted field of cultural production, 'oriented to the accumulation of symbolic capital', or the large-scale field of economic production, which confers 'priority on distribution, on immediate and temporary success, measured for example by the print-run'.[35]

However, a more complex relationship between different markets, or hierarchies of value, is usual in British publishing practice, where both strategies tend to be integrated within a single company: large commercial publishers have traditionally supported their prestigious, uneconomical lists through their mass-market commercial lists.[36] This study charts the way in which OUP developed an interdependent system of generating economic and cultural capital, involving the subsidy of the academic, Oxford-based Clarendon Press by profits from the London-managed educational publishing wing, which sold large numbers of school textbooks to African and Asian markets.[37] The principle was gradually established that the centre would be economically supported by the periphery.

Alongside this commercial imperative for its colonial expansion, I attempt to discern the nature of OUP's cultural mission in Africa. I examine how, under British colonial rule, OUP's mission was aligned to the Native Education agenda to 'enlighten the native about Western civilisation'.[38] This 'civilising mission' is regarded by Edward Said as an intrinsic part of the imperial process:

> inscribed within the humanistic enterprise itself ... is the idea of Western salvation and redemption through its 'civilising mission'. Supported jointly by the experts in ideas (missionaries, teachers, advisers, scholars) and in modern industry and communication, the imperial idea of Westernising the backward achieved permanent status worldwide, but ... it was always accompanied by domination.[39]

How, then, was this 'civilising mission' altered after decolonisation in Africa? I propose here that it was ostensibly modified into a duty to support African literature, scholarship and education, for the success of OUP in the independent African states relied to a great degree on the successful presentation of itself as an investor in the new nations rather than as a commercial enterprise. To protect its position in the independent states, OUP engaged in a publicity campaign, constructing narratives of redemption to describe its cultural mission in Africa. Thus, the London Publisher of OUP, John Brown, announced in 1970: 'The Oxford University Press has one purpose only, to advance scholarship and education. It publishes works of learning, and educational books, in order to achieve this purpose.'[40] In Said's terms, such narratives serve to disguise or obscure economic and territorial domination, thereby creating 'a justificatory regime of self-aggrandising, self-originating authority'.[41]

This study examines how Three Crowns was positioned within this 'culture/commerce' dichotomy in OUP. The Three Crowns editor, Rex Collings, conceived of Three Crowns as a 'new departure' for OUP. Arguing his case for venturing into the publication of African literature in 1962, Collings described his cultural ambitions for the series: 'Why should we publish?

We should publish because we want to expand our list to include original work of merit by local authors.'[42] The ideological and public-relations function of the series is addressed, and there is a discussion of whether African literature was envisaged as a means of deflecting charges of neo-colonialism. Collings aspired to challenge the existing strategy in Africa, and argued that literary publishing was necessary to compensate for OUP's lucrative educational publishing programme: 'I am convinced also that there is still a place for us in African publishing if we can plainly show that we are not in fact only interested in selling enormous quantities of primary schoolbooks by expatriate authors. Politically therefore it is also important that we should publish.'[43] The suggestion here is that culture should offset commerce in OUP's Africa publishing programme, and Collings envisaged Three Crowns as a series of high-brow literature that would operate in an international literary market. I question here whether his ideals were realised in practice: to what extent did the series have to function within the enduring colonial-style book-distribution channels in Africa? In examining how the Press represented its literary and economic enterprises on the continent, I aim to shed light on the strategic role of Three Crowns for OUP in Africa.

Researching publishers' archives

An array of accessible primary resources associated with the Three Crowns series enables a unique understanding of the economics of literary production, global copyright arrangements and privileges, political restraints and transnational author–publisher relations. The OUP archive is the most important source of information for this project. Editorial files contain author–editor correspondence, readers' and editors' reports on new manuscripts, author contracts, new title proposal forms, together with related internal memos, production schedules and print-run information, promotional materials associated with the individual books, copies of book and play reviews, and sales information. The Three Crowns series files also include financial records of the series and information about the strategy for Three Crowns, as well as details of debates about its continuation and the series reviews.[44]

However, an array of exclusions and occlusions is also evident in the OUP archive, governed as it is by commercial, legal and practical restrictions.[45] Most problematic for the researcher is the significant metropolitan bias of OUP's archival records, for the archives of the African branches have not been kept as assiduously as the Oxford archive: little remains in the OUP archive in Nairobi; nothing remains in Ibadan, and the Cape Town archive is not open to outside researchers. A selection of 'branch accounts' files in the Oxford archive, which relate to OUP's work in East, West and Southern Africa, provides limited information about the branches' publishing finances and annual reports, but offers limited insight into local editorial, marketing and distribution strategies. Editorial files exist only for the books published in the UK, and there are no files relating to the Three Crowns books in the series published in the Ibadan or Delhi branches or the literature published in other series from African branches. Ann Laura Stoler describes the colonial archive as a 'cross-section of contested knowledge' that signals 'the very substance of colonial politics'.[46] Calling for a reading of the archive 'along the archival grain', Stoler writes, '[w]e need to read for its regularities, for its logic of recall, for its densities and distributions, for its consistencies of misinformation, omission, and mistake'.[47] This study has attempted a reading of the OUP archive 'along the grain', by considering which commercial and political agendas were served (and continue to be served) both through these records and through the omissions. However, the most significant challenge of this project has been to conduct research 'against the grain of the archive': to investigate the areas that are hidden from the official records and to draw on alternative accounts by authors, publishers, critics and, where possible, readers of this literature.

This study draws on alternative accounts by publishers in archives in Cape Town and Grahamstown, where two former editorial managers of OUP in Cape Town deposited their own records and correspondence. Leo Marquard's papers are stored at the University of Cape Town Library and David Philip's papers have been preserved in the National English Literary Museum (NELM) in Grahamstown, and include some additional papers entrusted to him by Leo Marquard. The National Archive at Cape Town includes important records relating to many of OUP's titles in South Africa, in particular those submitted to the Publications Control Board. In addition, this research has been informed by the West African theatre archival collection at the University of Leeds Library, deposited by Martin Banham, which is a rich source of records relating to the local production and reception of drama in Nigeria in the late 1950s and 1960s. Of particular relevance are the collections of correspondence, journal articles, theatre programmes and reviews relating to the English Literature Department in the University of Ibadan in this period, and the correspondence between Soyinka and Collings during and immediately after Soyinka's imprisonment.

This study has also used oral histories to help provide insights into the history of Three Crowns and of OUP in Africa. These include interviews with the surviving former editors of the series: James Currey, Jon Stallworthy and Ron Heapy, and with David Philip, former editor of the Cape Town branch, and David Attwooll, former editor of the Ibadan branch and editor of some of the later Three Crowns texts. Randolph Vigne gave a very interesting perspective on the publishing industry in 1960s South Africa, and email correspondence with James Gibbs has helped shed light on aspects of Collings's life and work. An email interview with Professor Dennis Walder provided important insights about the publishing of Fugard by OUP.

Outline

This book has two parts, and Part I seeks to survey the wide-ranging historical and contextual background to postcolonial literary publishing in Africa. This unfolds in four chapters that chart OUP's strategy in colonial and postcolonial Africa. It assesses how the Press balanced cultural capital and economic capital in their work, and how this tension was manifested as an opposition between literary and scholarly publishing versus educational publishing. The main objective of the first part is to review the effect of OUP's Africa strategy on the institutions of African literary publishing in general and on Three Crowns in particular. Part II is a detailed case-study of the Three Crowns series, which addresses its history and editorial strategy. It includes detailed chapter-length examinations of the publishing of the two major authors in Three Crowns: Wole Soyinka and Athol Fugard, and shorter case-studies of many of the lesser-known authors in the series.

Chapter 1 charts how British publishers established a 'hand-in-glove' relationship with the British Colonial Office throughout East, West and Southern Africa in the early twentieth century: how publishing accompanied and supported British imperialism in this period. In addition, it reviews how the literary publishing strategy of OUP in British colonial Africa was embedded within its English-language teaching agenda through supplementary readers. The chapter concludes with an overview of OUP's policy for the independent African nations, to explore how the Press adapted its cultural and economic strategy in Africa after the end of British rule.

In Chapter 2 there is an examination of the economic significance of the postcolonial West African market for British publishers in the 1960s and 1970s. The chapter questions how the Nigeria branch of OUP managed to navigate its way through the conflicting demands of London and the local markets by reconciling two imperatives: the need to adapt to the new African nationalism to survive and prosper in the independent state, and the commercial imperative to provide unprecedented profits for the London business. There is attention to the literature produced for the African educational market, in order to understand the specific limits and pressures influencing the 'literary' publishing of Three Crowns.

Chapter 3 considers the publisher's articulation of its 'civilising mission' in Africa, with an exploration of the continuities between the work of the Christian mission presses and the work of the OUP branch in East Africa. There is a discussion of the way in which OUP's 'narratives of redemption' were reworked for a secular and postcolonial context, and the success of its mission is assessed, with reference to the branch publishing programme and to the literary output from Nairobi. There is an analysis of the hierarchies of postcolonial literary production that were established in the region, where OUP was a dominant publisher in the 1960s and 1970s.

Chapter 4 explores OUP's work in apartheid South Africa. Here, the tension between cultural and economic capital took the form of a conflict between scholarly publishing for the white liberal academic establishment and schoolbooks for Bantu Education. The chapter is framed in the broader question of the role of the publisher's history in South Africa as an aspect of its ideological positioning. It also touches on the implications of these developments for Three Crowns, which was used by editors as a means of continuing a liberal and anti-apartheid publishing tradition beyond South Africa.

Part II, Chapter 5 addresses the history and editorial development of Three Crowns. The series was the site of conflict within the Press, and its turbulent history was marked by a succession of financial reviews: this chapter considers how the inherent tension between the cultural expectations of the series and the economic imperative of OUP in Africa was manifested in the history of the series. The series was, as a result, rapidly deemed to be a financial failure, leading to a halt in acquisitions and the ultimate closure of the series. The chapter concludes by examining the ways in which, despite a lack of investment in its development, the series was an integral part of OUP's cultural mission in Africa.

Chapter 6 is concerned with the role of the publisher in judging postcolonial literature. It examines how the Three Crowns series editors grappled with creating a new African literary list, charting the editorial and managerial deliberations over the selection criteria for the series, and examining how the aesthetic and commercial value of the texts was negotiated. The chapter is illustrated by three case-studies drawn from the series: Léopold Sédar Senghor, Raymond Sarif Easmon and John Pepper Clark.

Chapter 7 examines the relationship between the editor and author in Three Crowns, and the processes of literary production. The chapter analyses various constructions of the Western editor of African literature as, for example, 'champion' or 'supporter' of the African writer or conversely as an agent of neo-colonialism. It then reviews the copy-editing of the series, the design and production stages, the marketing and promotion processes, with reference to four case-studies of the publishing history of Tsegaye Gabre-Medhin, Barbara Kimenye, Obi Egbuna and Oswald Mtshali.

Chapter 8 is a longer case-study of Wole Soyinka's early plays, which concentrates on the deliberations surrounding each stage of the publishing process, as well as the author–publisher relations that developed between Soyinka and Collings. It assesses the impact on Soyinka's books of OUP continuing to operate under colonial modes of publishing in the immediate post-independence period, and considers the ways in which the African educational marketplace had a decisive influence on the publishing of Soyinka, and how the racially and geographically stratified readership dictated the editorial strategy for Soyinka's plays. The chapter analyses the different paratextual elements created by the publisher – within the book and beyond – that influenced the reception of his works.

The final chapter addresses the creation of Athol Fugard's plays not as performances or as texts, but as material objects. It charts the debate surrounding the decision to publish Fugard in the Three Crowns series, and assesses the various transactions over 'Athol Fugard' as an increasingly valuable piece of intellectual property. The chapter draws attention to the sharp distinction in the way that Fugard's performances and published plays have been received, most acutely in respect to the plays published as the trilogy *Statements: Three Plays*.

In summary, this book aims to examine OUP's literary endeavour to 'represent Africa' and the commercial, ideological and discursive 'battle over Africa' that ensued. It examines the institutions of postcolonial literary publishing on both a macro- and micro-level, by combining an analysis of the historical, political and economic context of British publishing in Africa in the immediate postcolonial period with author case-studies. These case-studies explore the construction of literary value, the relationships between British publishers and African writers, and the critical importance of the African market for one of Britain's leading publishers. With regard to the book as a physical product, this volume addresses the ways in which ideological and economic structures are manifested in the paratext of the individual books. The main aim, then, is to address some of the broader concerns of postcolonialism through a study involving the precise methodology of book history.

Part I
Oxford University Press in Africa, 1927–80

1
The Vision for OUP in Africa

> I have a vision ... of Oxford African Primers in the hands of these squatting boys, in mission schools, in town and village, in bush schools far out in the blue where native teachers, only a little less heathen than their pupils, are struggling to make a greater Africa. This is not only 'uplift', it is also a sound business proposition, because each book will be paid for!
>
> – Letter from Eric Parnwell to Kenneth Sisam, 1928[1]

Eric Parnwell, 'Expert in Overseas Education' at OUP, first visited Africa in 1927 with the mission to seek out new markets for OUP and to identify the new direction for the company on that continent. Parnwell's account of his 'African tour' is an illuminating document, which articulated his plan for a racially stratified publishing policy. His vision was for OUP to undertake mass publishing of schoolbooks for African children across the continent: a combination of a vision of a 'greater Africa' and a 'sound business proposition'. This chapter examines how Parnwell's cultural and economic strategy unfolded in South Africa and in the African colonies in the twentieth century, and examines how OUP's strategy was modified in the postcolonial period.

The British Empire was a captive market of vital significance to the British book trade in the late nineteenth century.[2] The imperial book trade served two distinct markets with separate sales channels: firstly, trade to the settler colonies, which consisted largely of trade books for the white settler populations of Australia, New Zealand, Canada and South Africa, and, secondly, trade to the occupied colonies, which was predominantly in the form of schoolbooks for the colonial education system. As the settler colonies became self-governing dominions in the early twentieth century, British publishers moved in to protect these markets and several larger publishers established publishing branches in these countries: indeed, in the first half of the twentieth century, the prosperity of British publishers came to hinge on these special commercial relationships with Britain's so-called 'free empire'. Most significantly, British publishers moved in after self-government in Australia in 1901, to ensure a continued commercial advantage: Macmillan led the way, opening a branch in Melbourne in 1905, and OUP swiftly followed in 1908. This business was dominated by colonial editions, which were series of mainly new British novels published in conjunction with UK editions and sold by British publishers to exporters throughout the empire and dominions.[3] OUP opened a branch in Toronto in 1904, and was followed, after self-government in Canada, by Macmillan in 1906. Publishers then, with varying degrees of success, attempted to follow a similar model in the other British dominions of New Zealand and South Africa.

The book trade to the occupied colonies was also significant for British publishers in the early twentieth century. British publishers enjoyed the protection of copyright legislation: the 1842 and 1911 Copyright Acts applied throughout the colonies, with the result that any book published in Britain was automatically entitled to be published in the empire. India, at the heart of the British imperial strategy, was the major book export market for British books. Priya Joshi describes the Indian book market as 'massively profitable' in the nineteenth century, and writes that 80 per cent of Macmillan's foreign book sales were to India in 1901.[4] The most commercially significant trade in schoolbooks was dominated by Macmillan, Longmans, Green and OUP. Macmillan opened branches in Bombay (1901), Calcutta (1907) and Madras (1913), and OUP followed suit, establishing a branch in Bombay in 1912 to produce Indian schoolbooks in the vernacular, and subsequently opening branches in Madras and Calcutta in 1915.[5]

In the early twentieth century, OUP also established itself as a major publishing authority on the British Empire. Rimi Chatterjee's detailed study of OUP's publications for and about India identifies the 'saleability of the other' at this time: 'the Press made its money interpreting other civilisations for the West'. She notes how OUP continued this tradition until the end of British rule in India: 'The old pattern of "India experts" in England writing books from the English point of view continued to be followed in London as the norm.'[6] Similarly, OUP played a significant role in what Said terms the 'codification of difference' about Africa in this period.[7] It was involved in the task of categorising and systematising the continent through amassing empirical knowledge: ethnographic, economic, scientific, geographic, linguistic and historical. OUP published such seminal works as Eric Walker's *Historical Atlas of South Africa* (1922), *The African Research Survey of Science in Africa* (1935), Evans-Pritchard's *Witchcraft, Oracles and Magic Among the Azande* (1937) and *The Nuer* (1940), C. G. Seligman's *Races of Africa* (1939), T. R. Batten's *Africa Past and Present* (1943), Elizabeth Colson and Max Gluckman's *Seven Tribes of British Central Africa* (1951) and the *Handbook of African Languages* (1956).

Alongside this role in supporting the creation and circulation of Eurocentric discourses on Africa, OUP began to establish a commercial empire in Africa from the early twentieth century. A sales office was opened first in Cape Town in 1915 and trade to the British colonies in Africa began in the late 1920s. This was followed by the establishment of sales offices in Nairobi, Ibadan, Accra, Dar es Salaam and Addis Ababa during the 1940s and early 1950s. The Press was not a commercial institution: it was, and remains, an arm of the University administered by the Delegates – appointed academics within the University – and managed by the Secretary, a full-time manager relieved of academic duties. However, it was supported by the commercial London-based business of Oxford University Press, which had been established in 1896 under the management of the Publisher to the University, with the primary purpose of serving the Clarendon Press by promoting, distributing and selling the publications of the OUP throughout the world.

The principle was thus established that the cultural and scholarly endeavours of the Clarendon Press should be funded by the profits from colonial markets. According to Bourdieu's analysis, this is an economy of cultural production that contains inherent contradictions. In *The Rules of Art* he sets out a model of cultural production in which the fields of restricted and large-scale production are polarised, and while he acknowledges that it is possible for a publishing house to have 'two different economies coexisting within it, one tuned to production and research ... the other orientated toward the exploitation of assets', in his opinion this is an irreconcilable position: 'one can easily conceive of the contradictions that result from the incompatibilities between these two economies'.[8]

This chapter assesses OUP's enterprise in order to understand the interplay of cultural and economic capital between London and the African branches: it examines how OUP's system of cross-subsidisation of different areas of its publishing list was carried out, and asks whether this strategy led to 'contradictions' and 'incompatibilities'. In addition, it charts the relationship that was established between OUP and the British colonial government, and considers the impact of this on the educational and literary texts that OUP published for Africa. This overview of OUP in Africa is followed in the three subsequent chapters by a closer examination of OUP's strategy in West and East Africa after independence, and in South Africa after 1946.

OUP in South Africa, 1927–46

As the London Publisher from 1913, Humphrey Milford authorised OUP's early expansion into Africa. Five years after the Union of South Africa was founded as a dominion of the British Empire, in March 1915, Charles Mellow was appointed as OUP's representative in Cape Town, and he acted as an agent for OUP and other publishers.[9] However, the South African market proved to be particularly challenging to British publishers in the first half of the century due to local competition and strong anti-British sentiment: Macmillan, OUP, Blackie and Longmans, Green all struggled for a share in the book market.

One of Parnwell's first tasks when he visited East and South Africa in 1927–28 was to investigate the situation in the Cape Town branch in person. He rapidly came to the conclusion that the publications of the Clarendon Press would be suitable only for the white English-speaking minority, and that the 'European' educational market was saturated by local publishers. He felt that the main area for expansion in Southern Africa would be the provision of books for the South African and British colonial government's Native Education programme, identifying 5.5 million Africans in the Union and one million in Southern Rhodesia. However, despite Parnwell's enthusiasm to enter this market in South Africa, there is no archival evidence that the plan was successful. On a return trip in 1943, he wrote that the 'Native and European' trade in South Africa was being surpassed by the trade in West Africa.[10] Both OUP managers and Parnwell agreed that the Cape Town branch development was hindered by its failure to move rapidly into Native Education.[11]

The Press had difficulty entering this market in South Africa due to the lack of funding and central organisation of the African schools. Elsewhere in British colonial Africa, OUP worked closely with the Colonial Education Department to supply schoolbooks, but as a self-governing dominion South Africa's education system was independent of the Colonial Office. Native Education in the Union was handled by the four provincial Education Departments, each of which worked independently. African education was seriously underfunded by the government from 1910 to 1948, with the result that only 30 per cent of African children received any schooling. Expenditure for white pupils was nearly ten times as much as for African pupils. Church groups and missions largely controlled African education, and, as Jeffrey Peires describes, they had their own printing presses for publishing textbooks, which restricted the opportunities for commercial publishers.[12] In 1926 in South Africa there were 2702 schools run by church groups and missions, and only 68 state schools for black students.[13] This situation continued into the early 1950s, when, for example, only about 1 per cent of schools in the Cape were state provided (24 out of 2296).[14] Jonathan Hyslop argues that the mission schools were incapable of meeting demand, and as a result 'failed both the potential pupils they excluded and the minority of actual pupils they took in'.[15] Parnwell thus anticipated the market for schoolbooks for Native Education as early as the 1920s, and the foundations were laid in the 1930s and 1940s. However, his strategy was slow to be realised, and it was not until the advent of Bantu Education that the Press was able to achieve mass publishing of schoolbooks for black South Africans.

'A hand in the game': OUP in British colonial Africa, 1927–45

In addition to developing a strategy for South Africa, Parnwell set out to develop the business of OUP in the African colonies. Indeed, the Overseas Educational department (OED) of OUP had been formed in 1926 expressly for the publication of books for schools in the empire.[16] Parnwell's first memorandum back to London in 1927 explains the process by which OUP negotiated this arrangement. Parnwell begins by describing how he got to work building up relationships with the colonial education officers to convince them to start adopting Oxford University Press textbooks in their schools:

> I had an interview this morning with S. Rivers-Smith, Director of Education in Tanganyika. He told me that he did a good business with Macmillan in Swahili readers and other books produced in India. There was no objection whatever to the employment of Indian labour on this work, in fact it was essential in order that the books should be cheap. Evidently Macmillan thought it worth their while, as they were keen on it, and he would like us to have a hand in the game.[17]

He then described how textbooks for the colonies were beginning to be organised centrally by the Colonial Office, specifically by the African Books Committee:

> The Committee also advises the local directors of Education and teachers in the choice of existing English and vernacular textbooks, and will arrange for the publication of manuscripts of which it approves. It may be predicted that any textbook approved by this committee will have a fairly wide sale. In the case of the standard series of English readers for African schools which is one of its first projects, the sale should start off by the hundred thousand, and in the end reach to millions.[18]

Parnwell's report describes how Major Vischer, the Central Education Officer for the British Colonies and Protectorates, was keen to get OUP involved: 'Major Vischer would welcome our cooperation and hopes very much that I will go to tropical Africa and in the light of knowledge gained work hand-in-glove with him.'[19] The only impediment to this relationship with the colonial establishment was the presence of rival British publishers, and in particular Macmillan: 'Always they are ahead of us, but by degrees I am beginning to pick up some of their methods – which are exceedingly good and thorough – and I hope to gain on them in time.'[20] In correspondence with the Bombay branch at the same time, Parnwell bemoaned the fact that Macmillan had beaten OUP in the East African vernacular market: 'I expect that Macmillan have already collared the vernacular market and their Swahili books are no doubt officially prescribed.'[21] However, Parnwell was confident of the potential in this area. He wrote, 'the more I go into the question of Native Education, the more I believe that there will be a big field for us if we tackle it straight away'.[22]

Parnwell was at first tentative about launching OUP in East Africa, however, for with Swahili as the lingua franca in East Africa, the market was considered to be much smaller. Initially, they simply sent catalogues to bookshops in Tanganyika, Kampala, Nairobi and Zanzibar.[23] He expected a market for schoolbooks amongst the Indians settled in East and South Africa, rather than with the Africans themselves, and the market was envisaged as an extension of the India branch market. However, he eventually acknowledged that there was a problem getting Indians in Africa to accept OUP books derived from India, concluding that they tended to look to Europe for their cultural identity, rather than India: 'I don't think we are going to get anyone this side of India to buy from India: anything of yours we want to sell e.g. in Africa should bear an English price, and be advertised by London.'[24] Evidently OUP publications for Africa had to be endorsed by London.

'Enlightening the native': implementing the Phelps-Stokes education policy

The Colonial Office introduced a policy of vocational education for the British African colonies in the 1920s, in a scheme first outlined by the Frazer Commission of 1911. The influential reports of the Phelps-Stokes Commission in 1922 and 1925, under the chairmanship of Thomas Jesse Jones, then recommended that education for Africans be adapted to their rural environment; they should adopt a manual and vocational training as had been developed for American ex-slaves in the southern states after the civil war.[25] The philosophy of Phelps-Stokes was taken up enthusiastically by the British Colonial Office's Advisory Committee on Native Education in Tropical Africa. Its first policy document, *Educational Policy in British Tropical Africa* (1924), emphasised the importance of a technical rather than an academic education:

> Education should be adapted to the mentality, aptitudes, occupations and traditions of the various peoples, conserving all sound and healthy elements in the fabric of their social life. ... Its aim should be to render the individual more efficient in his or her conditions of life ... and to promote the advancement of the community as a whole through the improvement of agriculture, the development of native industries, the improvement of health ... and the inculcation of true ideals of citizenship and service.[26]

OUP was then given instruction in how to adapt textbooks to suit this educational philosophy. In 1932, Parnwell met Dr Spenser, the Chief Examiner in Science to the Board of Education, and reported back that:

> He told me that I must not imagine that there was any intention to teach Primary School Africans formal Biology. The aim was to make science (as opposed to the classics, or literature) the vehicle for enlightening the native about Western civilisation, that is, as much of it as could beneficially be superimposed on his tribal life and traditions. What was to be taught was the biology, not so much of plants or animals as such, as of the community to which he belonged, the 'works' of his environment. Realisation of the scientific principles which lie at the base of all life would lead to a clearer understanding and appreciation of Western progress.[27]

OUP's textbooks for African colonial schools in the 1930s embraced these dual aims of assisting in the 'inculcation of true ideals of citizenship and service' and of imparting a 'clearer understanding and appreciation of Western progress'. *A First Course in Geography and History for African Schools*, published by OUP from London in 1931 for Anglo-Egyptian Sudan, sets out the practice and ideology of colonial citizenship. The textbook emphasises the necessity to pay taxes and to pay respect to the District Commissioner: 'The D.C. is the representative of the Government. He must be treated with respect. School-children should always salute him when they see him.'[28] Thereafter the book recounts 'how civilization came to Africa, for long ago, all people were ignorant and lived ... almost like animals',[29] whereas, 'Civilized people are those who practise reading and writing, wear fine clothes, build beautiful buildings and manufacture all kinds of things to make life more agreeable and more interesting.'[30] *A Practical Modern Geography*, a 1934 textbook for West African primary schools, reinforces this ethnic and racial stereotyping: 'The people of Africa are of many different tribes. Negroes are short, with thick lips, wide noses, and woolly hair. They have beautiful velvety skins. The people of the desert are much fairer. The people of the forest are very short, and are still very wild.' By contrast, the British are described as literate ('Everybody can read and write'), as 'great merchants' and interested in sport (to 'make them strong and fit').[31]

The Phelps-Stokes education policy, adopted so readily for British Native Education, was highly contentious at the time. The British educationalist A. V. Murray, for example, in *The School in the Bush* (1929) argued that the Phelps-Stokes Commission 'have dealt with education in the light of a hypothetical rural village. ... The establishment of happy self-sufficient villages, where each man lives quietly under his own vine and fig-tree, is a pleasing picture, but it is neither big enough as an aim of education nor is it relevant to the forces that hold Native life in their grip.'[32] The policy also met with significant resistance when it was introduced in the African colonies. According to Sybille Küster, proto-Nationalist African political organisations such the Southern Rhodesian Bantu Voters' Association (SRBVA) and the Industrial and Commercial Workers' Union (ICU) in Rhodesia in the 1930s regarded the education system as a means of 'perpetuating the socio-economic and political subordination of the African population at large'.[33] She argues that mission school enrolment decreased dramatically when this education policy was introduced, and that many schools reintroduced a more rigorous academic training in an effort to attract students back. Ruth Makotsi argues that Kenyans regarded this education policy as a measure designed to restrict them to jobs as farm labourers, craftsmen and junior clerks.[34] OUP's willingness to cooperate with the colonial government in the implementation of this vocationally orientated African education – described by David Johnson as 'utilitarian instruction for the masses'[35] – exemplifies the polarised publishing strategy in the Press at this time. Whilst the Clarendon Press continued to be engaged in what Bourdieu terms the 'production of "pure" works destined for symbolic appropriation', OUP's books for Africa were 'specially destined for the market',[36] in this case the colonial schoolbook market.

'Vast opportunities for the publisher': the development of the *Oxford English Course*

During his tour of Southern Africa in 1927–28, Parnwell came to the conclusion that there was an urgent need for suitable textbooks to teach children English as a second language. Initially, he tried to write his own materials; he wrote a little book for schools in Malta, and produced his own list of 2000 words as the basis of the *Pocket Oxford Dictionary*, which he intended to turn into an elementary English course for African schools. However, he soon realised the need for a more comprehensive course. In the 1920s, Longmans, Green was the market leader in the field of English Language Teaching publications, due to the success of Michael West's *New Method Readers*. Parnwell sought to find an author for the Press who could establish a similar reputation. He wrote, 'Evidently there were vast opportunities for the publisher if he could find the man to write the books that were so badly needed.'[37]

The man he was looking for turned out to be Laurence Faucett, who had, in fact, written an English-language course closely modelled on West's *New Method Readers*. Parnwell drew up a contract with Faucett in 1931, and his *Oxford English Course* became the foundation for OUP's publishing strategy throughout the empire.[38] The course was based on a structured and limited vocabulary that was divided into four stages, consisting of students' and teachers' books, together with graded supplementary readers. It was subsequently adapted and expanded for the African market, and included readers, science textbooks and English literature books. According to A. P. R. Howatt, this was 'the first multi-volume ELT "package" to reach the world market', and it was to become 'the standard model' for ELT course design.[39] During the 1940s and 1950s, there were few innovations in the course, although it was customised for the different international markets of the Press. The regional editions of the *Oxford English Course* were adapted only superficially for the local markets: there was no adjustment to the linguistic needs of the different mother tongues, and OUP simply capitalised on former investment and innovation. The main marketing strategy for the books was the association with Oxford University, resulting in, for example, the *Oxford English Course for Mauritius* (1948), the *New Oxford English Course for Southern Africa* (1952) and the *Oxford English Course for Bantu Schools* (1959). Further editions were published in the 1950s for the Gold Coast, Nigeria and East Africa. Despite the fact that they bore little relation to academic and scholarly texts, these elementary language teaching materials were deliberately marketed with the 'Oxford' brand name with its connotations of academic elitism and excellence.

In *The Rules of Art*, Bourdieu defines the length of the production cycle as the key determinant of the position of a published text in the cultural field. He argues that publishing enterprises categorised as commercial are characterised by a short production cycle and therefore high print-runs 'designed to ensure the accelerated return of profits by a rapid circulation of products which are fated to rapid obsolescence'.[40] However, the publishing strategy for the *Oxford English Course* indicates a different model: the course achieved very high print-runs over a long production cycle. In the period leading up to decolonisation in East Africa from 1957 to 1959, the average annual print-run for *The New Oxford English Course for East Africa* Pupil Book I was 115,000 copies, and for *The New Oxford English Course for Nigeria* in the same period the average annual print-run was 121,000 copies.[41] The initial investment in this course led to a product that was published worldwide over four decades, and which went through only minor adaptations for different regions. This illustrates well how OUP successfully exploited one product to obtain maximum profits with minimal outlay.[42]

Supplementary readers

The literary publishing strategy of OUP in British colonial Africa was embedded within its English-language teaching agenda; the dominant form in which OUP disseminated literature was the supplementary reader, which accompanied the *Oxford English Course* and its adaptations. The first supplementary readers were written by Laurence Faucett and his wife, M. G. Faucett, who had adapted and abridged numerous European and American classics (for example, Charles Lamb's *Tales from Shakespeare* in 1933, as well as John Bunyan's *Pilgrim's Progress* and Charles Dickens's *A Tale of Two Cities* in 1934).[43] The Oxford Story Readers for Africa were published in London from 1939 to 1955, and were an attempt to make the literature more suitable for the market.[44] Sister Isabelle Frémont, based in Tanganyika, was the main author. Her books included *Seven African Tales* (1939), *Parable Plays* (1940), *The Animals' Bond, and Other Stories* (1941) and *The Goat and the Hyena, and Other Stories* (1949).[45]

A further series of supplementary readers was the *Oxford English Readers Library* for older readers. The literature in the series served a didactic function to teach students English. The back cover pronounced that it was 'intended to fill the gap between "simplified" texts and the full range of original literature'.[46] Information on authors and titles was subsumed within the series design: books were published with uniform grey and white covers and an OUP crest with three crowns on the front cover. These included a selection of abridged literary texts, such as Trollope's *The Warden* (1950), Homer's *Odyssey* (1952), H. G. Wells's *Seven Stories* (1953) and *English Poems and Ballads* (1957). There was a limited attempt to Africanise the series, but the selected stories of African leaders perpetuated the assumption of African 'inadequacy to be independent, equal and fit', to quote Said.[47] An abridged version of Thomas Mofolo's *Chaka the Zulu* (1949) cast Chaka as 'a story of human greed and unchecked ambition, an ambition that masters its victim and leads to his downfall and to terrible punishment'.[48] *Moshesh, the Man on the Mountain,* by John Grenfell Williams, related the trials of Moshesh in leading the Basuto tribe through wars against the Zulus and the Boers, which left him in abject need of British salvation: 'Moshesh knew that what he had hoped for through all the bitter months had happened at last. The Queen would accept him and his people as her subjects, and his troubles were at an end.'[49]

OUP's supplementary readers were predominantly simplified tales based on African folklore and fables alongside abridged European classics: a 'canon of "reduced" novels for foreign readerships', in the words of Stephanie Newell.[50] There was a great deal of conservatism amongst teachers: even in the late 1960s there was still a tendency in schools to purchase texts first published in the 1920s and 1930s. John Nottingham later wrote: 'East African teachers are particularly conservative about supplementary readers and even in 1968 they are still ordering from Britain hundreds of thousands of readers first published thirty or forty years ago.'[51] The longevity of these publications meant that the readers formed a profitable backlist for OUP in Africa. It also meant that books published for the colonial education system remained, anachronistically, in the catalogues decades later.

I turn to two accounts by readers of these books in African colonial schools.[52] Firstly, Ngũgĩ wa Thiong'o relates the alienating experience of reading the *Oxford Readers for Africa* in a Kenyan school:

> In my primary school we were taught English from a text under the general series *Oxford Readers for Africa*. We used to read the story of a boy

> called John and a girl called Joan. And it thus came to pass that, while still in my village and before I knew the names of other towns in Kenya, I already knew about a town called Oxford where the two children were born and another called Reading, where John and Joan went to school. ... What has, for us from the former colonies, twisted the natural relation to languages, both our own and those of other peoples, is that the languages of Europe – here, English – were taught as if they were our own languages, as if Africa had no tongues except those brought here by imperialism, bearing the label MADE IN EUROPE.[53]

Secondly, Joseph Okpaku, the Nigerian author and publisher, describes the impact of the literature and textbooks published for the Native Education system in Nigeria:

> In Nigeria ... the educational propaganda of 'Humpty Dumpty had a Great Fall' and 'Cinderella' was imported through crown agents of the British government, administered by British educators in both secondary schools and at the universities, with Oxford University Press, Heinemann and Longman among those providing the logistics support. ... The European textbook publishers, as aliens, were regarded as 'impartial', a European euphemism for a whole chain of terms including 'Western', 'disinterested', 'purely commercial', or most important 'uncommitted'. ... Herein precisely lies the danger, or failure, from the African viewpoint, of present-day educational publishing in Africa.[54]

Okpaku goes on to argue that educational publishing in Africa 'has proved to be, ironically, the one most effective system of preventing the political and social education of the African people', and was designed in collaboration between the colonial education system and British publishers.[55] Thus, the seemingly innocuous supplementary reader was regarded by these former students of British colonial education as a significant medium of 'educational propaganda' and an intrinsic aspect of British cultural imperialism in Africa.[56]

'A bigger field': OUP's postwar expansion in Africa

By 1942, Parnwell identified West Africa as the most significant market for OUP in Africa and one of 'the most important areas for future development', mainly on account of educational reforms in the area: 'In West Africa there are 25 million Africans advancing rapidly with all the encouragement the British Government can vouchsafe them.'[57] The assistant secretary, A. Norrington, understood that the Press enjoyed a privileged position in the region: 'there is the very great advantage that there are few competitors, and we can get a far larger share of the market than in the UK'. Astutely, he anticipated how English Language Teaching would present a global opportunity for the Press beyond Africa and throughout the empire:

> For Africa, while it has its own immense intrinsic importance, is also part of a bigger field still, the publishing of educational books for foreign-speaking countries, especially tropical or sub-tropical countries, and especially such countries within the B. Empire. The root of the business is the world-wide teaching of English.[58]

After the war, Geoffrey Cumberlege became London Publisher and he continued to prioritise the expansion of OUP overseas; sales offices and publishing branches were opened throughout Africa to sell educational texts published in London. In South Africa an editorial department was added to the Cape Town office in 1946 in order to convert it to a publishing branch. In Nigeria, a sales office was opened in Ibadan in 1949. The East Africa sales office was opened in 1954, and in 1952 the Gold Coast office was opened in Accra under the management of C. O. Botchway. This expansion took place in the context of a programme of a limited educational investment implemented by the Colonial Office in the postwar period. The Colonial Development and Welfare Act of 1945 funded a development programme for the dependent empire.[59] As part of this new cultural investment, literature boards were set up throughout the African colonies: in 1948 the Northern Rhodesian and Nyasaland Publications Bureau and the East African Literature Bureau were established with the aim of 'furthering African authorship, African culture, and traditions through writing, and assisting in the campaigns against illiteracy'.[60] At this time, there was also a campaign in the UK to protect Britain's privileged imperial book markets, led by Stanley Unwin, as Chairman of the Publishers' Association. The result was the imposition of two trade agreements between US and British publishers: the British Commonwealth Market Agreement of 1946 and the British Traditional Market Agreement of 1947, which created two international cartels that carved up world rights. Under the terms of these agreements, British publishers acquiring rights to a book automatically acquired rights to its publication in the 56 British colonies and former colonies, and US publishers were in return entitled to expand into other English-speaking countries.[61]

OUP's profitable expansion into Africa was thus based on Parnwell's astute prediction of the nature and size of the potential market for OUP in the continent. OUP was invited to have a 'hand-in-glove' relationship with the Colonial Office in the administration of Native Education. He shrewdly predicted that educational publishing in Africa would be a 'good business' for OUP, and that sales of the English readers would reach millions of copies. The books were to be of low production quality: 'produced in India' and 'cheap'. The 'game' that Parnwell sought to have a hand in was at the profitable, commercial end of the cultural spectrum, in the 'big field' of mass production.[62]

This study turns now to a brief overview of OUP's policy for independent Africa, and in particular focuses on the extent to which it had to adapt its cultural and economic strategy after the end of British colonial rule.

The strategy for postcolonial Africa

The end of formal colonisation in Africa evidently gave British publishing companies the opportunity to become more, rather than less, deeply entrenched in the cultural life of the continent. Newly elected governments prioritised education, and their programme of school expansion led to new opportunities for British publishers, who rushed to meet this new demand.[63] Peter Sutcliffe writes: 'As the Old Empire dissolved, the Overseas Education Department set out to build a new one.'[64] Thus, the Ibadan office was converted into a branch in 1962, two years after Nigerian independence. OUP opened a publishing branch in Nairobi in 1963, as Kenya achieved independence, and the sales office in Lusaka was converted into a publishing branch in 1964, upon Zambian independence . A branch was opened in Addis Ababa in 1965, and finally, nine years after independence in Ghana, a branch was opened in Accra in 1966.

The International division was based in the London office of OUP and was the coordinating centre for the foreign branches, except for New York, which was independently managed. John Brown was the London Publisher during this period, and John Bell was the manager of the Overseas Education department. The main role of the branches continued to be the distribution and sales of London and Clarendon Press publications, but they were authorised, to varying degrees, to undertake local publishing. The branch had to inform London of each new publishing project, but it was not required to wait for its approval of each decision. The London business, in turn, was not required to get specific approval from the Delegates for each new title proposal.[65] Strict boundaries were set, however, on the type of permitted publication. Publishing in London and the branches had to be within the genres of religious, scholarly and educational publishing.[66] Branch managers were granted a degree of independence over decisions that affected their own markets, and increasingly managed their own publishing and production programmes for these markets, although all decisions affecting international markets were referred back to the centre.

A series of directives from Oxford reinforced the principle that the cultural and scholarly endeavours of the Clarendon Press should be funded by the profits from the postcolonial markets. By the 1960s, the overseas branches were required to adhere to the standing instruction from the Delegates that, 'the branches' obligation to be profitable overall remains and ... branch managers are controlled by a need for balance and restraint in branch publishing programmes'.[67] Devolvement of the publishing operation to the branches evidently raised concerns about local independence, and the Delegates wanted to legislate against ambitious and high-risk publishing endeavours.

In 1970 there was a parliamentary investigation into the workings of OUP, which became known as the Waldock enquiry. The resulting report described the Press as 'a leader among United Kingdom publishers and an instrument of learning, education, and culture of national and international importance'. The committee recommended that the press's world expansion should continue, 'not simply because of the financial rewards but because of the benefit to the spread of British culture and influence', and argued that, 'any general curb on the development of OUP could hardly fail to diminish the influence of English thought and culture in other countries'. This report also recommended a system of cross-subsidisation across the Press: that London and branch publishing should be strictly on a 'profit-making basis' to generate the 'financial resources of the Press'.[68]

However, by the 1970s tensions in OUP's overseas strategy were becoming apparent. As the Waldock enquiry revealed, the Press was financially dependent on its overseas income. There was also a growing awareness of OUP's need to protect its reputation as a charitable organisation. OUP had applied for exemption from UK Corporation Tax in 1952 and this had been granted on certain aspects of its income. The Waldock Report stressed the importance of OUP maintaining an image as a non-commercial publisher:

> The Press's high reputation in publishing circles and throughout the learned world depends not only on its own exceptional performance but also on the knowledge that, as an independent non-profit-distributing enterprise, it is free from domination by commercial considerations. The loss of that reputation might indeed be a serious matter.[69]

This 'high reputation' was particularly vital when OUP made a new application for exemption from UK Corporation Tax in 1977 on the grounds of being 'a charity, the purposes of which are the advancement of learning and education in the widest sense'.[70] In 1952 exemption had been granted to OUP's income from investments and capital gains, but not for publishing-related earnings. The new application in 1977 was for exemption on all its activities: 'We claim that ... the profits arising from the printing and publishing of the Press both in this country and in its offices overseas should be exempted from tax.'[71] In its application, the cultural function of the Press overseas was asserted: 'The Delegates further recognise the University's obligation to contribute to high standards of learning and scholarship throughout the world: works of distinction by authors of many nationalities are actively sought for publication either in the Branches, or in the Centre, for world-wide distribution.' In fact, the Three Crowns series was specifically cited as one of the cultural missions of the Press: 'It also publishes in the "Three Crowns series" original contributions to the English literature of their countries by writers of the "Third World".'[72] It was successfully granted exemption in 1977 on the conditions that surpluses should be ploughed back into non-profit-making publishing and that it should not become the source of revenue for the university.

Conclusion

This chapter has charted the way in which OUP managed to achieve significant success in the African colonies under British rule by cultivating close 'hand-in-glove' relations with the Colonial Office and creating publishing programmes supporting the agenda for Native Education. The conclusion drawn by this chapter is that, far from being an incompatible model of cultural production, as Bourdieu maintains, a complex relationship between different forms of capital was evidently fundamental to the OUP's colonial publishing strategy. OUP adopted a system of cross-subsidisation of cultural and economic capital that was global in scale: symbolic capital accrued by the academic, Oxford-based Clarendon Press helped sell educational textbooks throughout the colonies, whilst the economic capital generated at the periphery supported the cultural endeavours in the metropole.

Parnwell's vision for OUP was largely realised on the eve of decolonisation in Africa; Oxford primers were indeed widespread throughout schools in the African colonies, together with an array of supplementary readers. The literature that was circulated was subsumed within OUP's schoolbook publishing programme and was mass-produced in cheap paperback editions. The next chapters consider how this literary strategy was modified in the African branches after independence was attained, and seek to evaluate the wider impact of this publishing programme in the emergence of African postcolonial literary culture.

2
'The Obligation to Be Profitable': OUP in West Africa

Introduction

The Publisher of OUP, John Brown, visited the Nigeria branch in 1971 to attend a ceremony marking the opening of a new warehouse (Figure 2.1). The Western State Military Governor, Brigadier Adeyinka Adegayo, formally opened the warehouse, and Brown then gave a speech that celebrated OUP's programme and mission in Nigeria:

> The Oxford University Press is a department of Oxford University. It is not a company. It has no shareholders. It distributes no profits, not even to the University. Any surplus of income over expenditure, after the payment of taxes and of interest on money borrowed, is turned back into the business, so that it can carry on its work. The Oxford University Press has one purpose only, to advance scholarship and education. It publishes works of learning, and educational books, in order to achieve this purpose. Scholarship and education are essentially international and books cross many frontiers. Because of this the Oxford University Press has established branches in a number of countries. These branches sell and distribute Oxford books. But they also publish books in, and for, their local areas. Thus we sell books to Nigeria and we also publish books in Nigeria, books by Nigerian authors, printed in Nigeria. ... I would like to emphasise another fact about the Oxford University Press, and that is that we do not manage and run our branches from Oxford or London. It is the Manager in Nigeria who assesses the needs of Nigeria, deals with authors, decides what books should be published, how the staff should work, what numbers should be printed, and what prices should be charged. The Oxford University Press in Nigeria is our Nigerian Manager. We in England help of course with the technical advice, with experience gathered elsewhere and with money, particularly with money. But he takes the decisions.[1]

Figure 2.1 John Brown (the Publisher) and T. T. Solaru (Nigerian branch manager) at the opening of the new warehouse in Ibadan (1970). By permission of Oxford University Press

Brown's rhetoric suggests a one-way flow of money, skills and advice from London to Africa: OUP's mission is primarily charitable (it 'distributes no profits') and cultural ('to advance scholarship and education'); its purpose is to invest in African culture (publishing 'books by Nigerian authors, printed in Nigeria'). The function of the centre is simply to help branches with 'technical advice, with experience ... and with money'. I examine here Brown's claims in the context of the history of OUP in West Africa, to appraise whether this much-publicised speech was simply a 'gloss of altruism' on its work in the region.[2] This chapter explores the interplay of cultural and economic capital in West African literary publishing. It also seeks to understand the hierarchies of textual production that were instituted by the Press in the region, and to consider to what extent the branch exercised equality and autonomy over its publishing programme, as is suggested by Brown.

The *raison d'être* of the publisher is to add value at each stage in the book supply chain, not simply in monetary terms, but more significantly in symbolic terms.[3] According to Bourdieu, the symbolic value of literature depends on its autonomy from the marketplace, and 'disavowal of the "economy" is placed at the very heart of the field, as the principle governing its functioning and transformation'.[4] Thus, in his view, the prestige of a work of literature within the cultural hierarchy is defined by its dissociation from economic capital. This study aims to discern the 'logic' of the field of African literary publishing, by considering the implicit values that underpinned the field. With reference to OUP's work in postcolonial West Africa, I explore the part played by geography in constructing the symbolic value of a literary work: both in terms of its place of publication and in terms of its destination market. For, in this colonial and postcolonial context, the economic disinterestedness of a work of literature seems only partially to account for the complex ways in which symbolic value is constructed.

Pascale Casanova argues that a nation's position in the international cultural hierarchy depends on its level of literary autonomy and that 'the most independent territories of the literary world are able to state their own law, to lay down the specific standards and principles applied by their internal hierarchies'.[5] Autonomous literary spaces are those nations 'most endowed in literary resources', exercising linguistic dominance and strong publishing networks.[6] By contrast, nations subjected to or emerging from colonisation are described by Casanova as 'literarily dominated spaces',[7] characterised by several factors: economic or political domination; a tendency towards 'neo-naturalistic' and political concerns in literature; a newly established written literary history but strong oral literary traditions; and dependence on association with the specific power of an international literary capital.[8]

This chapter examines the 'global literary hierarchies' of literary production in the work of OUP, and extends this enquiry to the hierarchies of literary consumption. The main contention is that a notional hierarchy of the international literary marketplace operated in international publishing in this period, and that the value of a publication was defined not only by its place of publication but also by its geographical destination. British publishers evidently regarded the most prestigious market for African literature – at the apex of the hierarchy – as the Anglo-American literary marketplace. The African book market occupied a subordinate position, but within this marketplace there were also hierarchies of value. The general or trade market for literature was the most prestigious market in Africa, although this was also the most difficult to corner. The educational marketplace was of a lower standing, despite being the most profitable market for African literature.

This perception of a hierarchical literary marketplace can also be traced in scholarship and critiques of African publishing, in which there has been a tendency to privilege the Western market over the marketplace in the former colonies. As already alluded to, several prominent critics have failed to account for the significance of the African market in the development of African literature, for example Graham Huggan, who concedes that the African Writers Series 'catered for a sizeable African reading public' but argues that it was 'primarily an export product, aimed at a largely foreign audience'.[9] Bejjit contests, by contrast, that the African education market served as a rationale for the development of the African Writers Series. He provides a detailed archive-based account of the development of the educational book market from the 1950s to the 1970s, charting the impact of this developing schoolbook market as a stimulus for literary publishing in East and West Africa.[10] James Currey also stresses the importance of the African educational market for the series, noting the 'extraordinary sales, especially in Nigeria but also in Kenya and Zambia'.[11] His account contains important anecdotal evidence and archival detail about the sales strategy for the African Writers Series and sales figures for the books.[12]

It has become almost axiomatic in African publishing studies to refer to Africa as a 'bookless society', or as a continent suffering from 'book hunger', to use phrases coined by Philip Altbach and Hans Zell, respectively.[13] Privileging the trade market for books in Africa and disregarding the large educational and popular-fiction marketplaces, critics have concluded that Africa has no reading culture or literary marketplace. Stephanie Newell in *Ghanaian Popular Fiction* takes issue with this notion of Africa's book famine, and observes that the most important markets for literature in Africa have tended to be overlooked by critics.[14] Her study of popular literature and print culture in colonial Ghana in the 1940s describes a prolific reading culture of predominantly locally published books and market literature: 'A market exists for locally published literature, but it is not always visible in an urban bookshop. ... The dynamic "informal sector" is where much of West Africa's reading public can be located.'[15] She makes the important observation that 'many of the scholars ... have ignored the submerged but vibrant informal sector of the economy'.[16] Robert Fraser also emphasises the necessity of acknowledging local conditions in his study of print culture in West Africa. He counters Chinua Achebe and Wendy Griswold's arguments that Nigeria has no general reading culture and notes the development of a diverse literary culture in West Africa in the late twentieth century that resisted Euro-American literary genre classifications.[17]

The rest of this chapter seeks to examine how such cultural and economic hierarchies were instituted and reinforced by OUP after independence, and consider their impact on the metropolitan and West Africa branch literary publishing programmes. By focusing here on a much-neglected literary marketplace, the African educational market, much useful insight can be gained on the specific limits and pressures that influenced the 'literary' publishing of Three Crowns.

'To serve the interests of education overseas': OUP's establishment in Nigeria

Oxford University Press was the first publishing house to open an office in Nigeria. The Nigerian educationalist Chief T. Tanimonowo Solaru was appointed as the West African Representative in 1949, and five years later a new OUP office was opened at Oxford House in Iddo Gate, Ibadan, together with a warehouse at Apapa. A leaflet marking the occasion clearly stated the Press's mission in the region:

> The erection of 'Oxford House' may be regarded as a logical development of the policy of the Press, firstly, in setting up in London a department to serve the interests of education overseas, especially in the Colonies and, secondly, in appointing a qualified West African educationalist to develop its work there. It signifies, further, the firm intention of the Press to consolidate and extend the progress it has made in that region.[18]

In 1962, two years after the Federation of Nigeria attained independence, the Ibadan office was converted into a fully fledged publishing branch under Solaru's management. Reflecting the aims of the London business as a whole, the Nigeria branch had a three-point policy: firstly, to promote Oxford books published by the Clarendon Press and the London business; secondly, to adapt Oxford books to meet syllabus needs in Nigeria; and, thirdly, to publish 'local books in English and Nigerian languages for educational purposes'.[19]

In West Africa, educational expansion began in the 1950s under the British colonial government. In Ghana the 'Accelerated Development Plan of Education' was introduced in 1951 to increase state control of education. Four years after independence, in 1961, the Education Act stipulated free and compulsory education as well as the creation of local education authorities and the opening of mission schools to all, irrespective of belief.[20] In Nigeria, school expansion began during the Representative Government of the 1950s, and, following independence in 1960, secondary education rose sharply in Nigeria. At the point of independence there were 19,883 students in secondary grammar schools across the country, and this had risen to 448,908 by 1973. Overall school enrolments dropped during the civil war, but after the end of the conflict, there was again a rise in enrolment, reaching a total of 4.6 million pupils in 1973. The most phenomenal expansion occurred in 1976, when free universal primary education was launched throughout the federation. According to Victor Nwankwo there were 18 million school pupils registered in Nigeria in 1976, although this fell to 14.6 million by 1987.[21]

Schoolbooks were by far the most profitable sector of the OUP's Ibadan-based list. Initially, the most profitable educational texts originated from London, but the branch increasingly published texts locally, including literature in African languages to fulfil school syllabus and examination requirements; around 20 literary texts were published in the Nigerian languages of Igbo, Yoruba, Hausa and Efik. The branch also published language-teaching materials in Yoruba and Igbo, including grammars and dictionaries, as well as courses relating to the certificate examinations. The great majority of new educational titles published in the branch were, however, English-language teaching texts. Frederick French's *New Oxford English Course* (based on the *Oxford English Course* of the 1930s) was customised for Nigeria in 1967 and was published alongside other English-language teaching materials: dictionaries, comprehension exercises, workbooks and reading cards. During the period 1956–63, Book 1 in the series achieved sales of over £600,000 (with a profit of £574,000) while Book 2 sales reached over £1.1 million (with profits of just over £1 million). Similar profits were achieved for the other titles, although the major boom in educational sales in Nigeria occurred after 1976.[22]

In the 1960s and 1970s, schoolbook publishing in Nigeria was dominated by a handful of British publishers. Longman was OUP's main competitor and had an annual turnover of nearly US$4 million in 1972,[23] while Macmillan, Heinemann Educational Books, Evans Brothers, Thomas Nelson, Cambridge University Press and the University of London Press all had offices in either Ibadan or Lagos. The market was highly contested: Solaru writes in his 1970 Branch Annual Report of the 'fierce, and sometimes unscrupulous, competition by rival publishers'.[24] In addition, the ascendancy of British multinational publishers was increasingly contentious amongst the West African intelligentsia and publishers. OUP and other major educational publishers were publicly accused of cultural imperialism. A conference entitled 'Publishing in Africa in the Seventies' was held at the University of Ife in Nigeria from 16 to 20 December 1973, and the main verdict of the conference was that 'the time has now arrived for the book industry to become primarily indigenised'.[25] G. O. Onibonoje, for example, proclaimed that: 'The form of cultural revolution we demand must ensure that publishing in Africa is by Africans to disseminate and inculcate African culture and heritage and make the voice of Africa heard, clear and loud.'[26]

How, then, did OUP manage to protect its dominant position in West African educational publishing, in the face of such calls for an indigenised publishing industry? It appears that three factors were crucial: firstly, the branch's good relations with the Nigerian federal government, secondly, their association with the West African examination boards, and, thirdly, the branch's prominent investment in academic, scholarly and literary publishing by West African writers.

West Africa branch relations with government

As branch manager, Solaru sought to build up good relations with the Nigerian government, and was a strong supporter of the government during the civil war, which lasted from May 1967 until January 1970. In his Annual Report of 1968, Solaru wrote of the Biafra conflict as a 'rebellion' that was prolonged by 'external interference – whether humanitarian, from missionaries, or military, from the French'.[27] In 1968, he wrote to London that business had been good despite the 'disturbance of the civil war'.[28] Over a million died in battle or from starvation during the civil war, yet Solaru's Annual Reports suggest that OUP's business was little affected by the conflict. By 1970, he declared that 'the Nigerian Head of State, General Gowon, saved the country from further travails by proclaiming a general amnesty'.

From the late 1960s, the Nigerian government began to restrict the work of multinationals and to insist on the indigenisation of multinational companies. The first of the indigenisation Acts was the Companies Decree of 1968 (Part X).[29] The branch responded swiftly to political pressure to replace expatriate staff with Africans, and carried out an 'Africanisation' policy in the following year. Solaru's Annual Report comments:

> Long laid plans for training suitable Nigerian replacements for expatriates are proving successful. We have already dispensed with an English warehouse manager, this year will dispense with an English production manager and probably the sales manager as well, all replaced by promising Nigerians. There will always be the necessity for one or preferably two English editors.[30]

OUP was unusual amongst British publishers in Nigeria for localising the publishing process: books were taken through the editorial and production stages at the Ibadan office, whereas the other British companies sent their production work to Britain, with film positives being returned for printing in Nigeria.[31] Paul Sturges and Richard Neill regard this as a successful strategy for concealing the fact that OUP's profits continued to be repatriated to the UK: 'The only element which could not be said to have been localised was the resultant profit from these titles, which continued to be exported back to the parent company.'[32] It seems, however, that this strategy served to protect OUP from new indigenisation legislation. The First Indigenisation Decrees of 1971/72 ordered 'rapid compulsory transfer of foreign capital in the industrial, service and trade sectors into indigenous hands', while the 1972 Nigerian Enterprises Promotion Decree required businesses to be transferred entirely or in part into Nigerian hands, normally requiring between

40 per cent and 60 per cent of a company's equity to be sold to Nigerians.[33] Most multinational subsidiaries in Nigeria were forced to become minority shareholders, with the majority of equity transferred into local hands,[34] and Solaru questioned whether OUP would be able to continue to operate in Nigeria. However, the company found in 1973 that they had been granted exemption on the basis that they already ploughed back into the business over 40 per cent of their annual profits to meet expenses on local publishing and expansion.[35] This was a fortunate, if temporary, reprieve for the Press.

West Africa branch relations with examination boards

OUP's dominance of the West African schoolbook market was greatly assisted by its good relations with the local examination boards. A. B. Fafunwa, a specialist in Nigerian education, wrote that 'it is an educational truism that examinations control the curriculum and whosoever controls a country's examination system controls its education'.[36] The retention of a British-style educational system and continuation of British-staffed examination boards meant that British publishers were at an advantage in getting their books prescribed – as it was termed – for primary and secondary school syllabuses. After independence, the University of Cambridge Local Examination Syndicate was retained in West Africa. Although it was superseded by the West African School Certificate Examination, it still retained its strong links with the Cambridge system.[37] The Ibadan branch was given advance notice by the West African Exams Council of texts they wanted to prescribe, to give them the opportunity to publish them in time for adoption.[38] Zell describes the tendency of these examination boards to encourage and recommend the use of British-published schoolbooks: 'African primary syllabuses, for example, were drawn up by expatriate-controlled Ministries of Education, and the books written by expatriate teachers. The net result was rapidly rising sales and high profit margins for the few British publishers serving these markets.'[39]

Keeping 'local goodwill': Nigeria branch publishing 1962–78

Solaru wrote, in 1968, that he was keen to expand the list of the Ibadan branch, and to publish appropriate and locally written books for the Nigerian market: 'There is an increasing demand for our services and flow of publishable books. Our local goodwill is considerable. It is to be hoped that we can serve Nigeria by increasing the number of our local publications.'[40] Following independence there was an expansion of higher education in Nigeria: the University of Nigeria at Nsukka opened in 1960, the University of Ife in 1962 and the University of Benin in 1971.[41] A well-publicised local publishing programme was evidently a vital means of building up 'local goodwill' and countering the threat of Nigerianisation. The OUP branch turned its attention to developing a list to support the new Afrocentric academic discourse and meet the needs of the local higher education market.

The academic and scholarly texts published in Ibadan reflected a new concern to rewrite West African colonial history and to analyse models for nation-building and development. The majority were written by Africans and were specifically related to West Africa. Over 40 per cent of the new titles developed by the branch were academic and professional texts,[42] and the branch also published books and journals for professional societies and academic institutions (Figure 2.2).[43] Economics texts related principally to Nigerian economic development with, for example, the publication of A. A. Ayida and H. M. A. Onitiri's *Reconstruction and Development in Nigeria* (1971). Political texts included Janusz Zielinski's *Lectures on the Theory of Socialist Planning* (1968) and Francis Adigwe's *Essentials of Government for West Africa* (1974). The history list included general and regional histories of Nigeria, studies of Nigerian archaeology, the history of Islam in Nigeria and a re-evaluation of British rule in Nigeria.

In a study of OUP in India, Robert Fraser argues that the Press 'used the post-war decades gradually to renegotiate its relationship with all of its

Figure 2.2 Oxford University Press book exhibition, Ibadan (1970). By permission of Oxford University Press

offices overseas', and argues that its flexible organisational response to the needs of new markets helped it to flourish during this period, unlike its competitor Nelson.[44] The evidence of Ibadan's local publishing programme confirms a rapid adaptation to a new postcolonial context, and it represented a significant modification of the model of cultural production that had so successfully served OUP's interests over the previous four decades. Instead of the branches simply serving the centre by exclusively undertaking commercial educational publishing, a dual-economy of cultural production was also introduced at the branch level, and less-profitable academic and scholarly publishing was funded through the profits of the educational market.

'A "nursery" of literary talent': OUP's literary publishing strategy in West Africa

The literary publishing programme of the Ibadan branch in the 1960s was confined to literature for the educational market. The branch editor, Adam Buther, wrote to London proposing that the branch serve as a model for others in this area:

> If a branch wants to encourage writers of fiction, the best way may be that which we've adopted here. We have got a few young authors to try their hand at supplementary readers, which are short enough to be edited thoroughly and should be economically viable. In this way, we are doing what is expected of us both by the Delegates and by those who call for more local writing; we are also developing a 'nursery' of literary talent. For these purposes a branch should be able to find its own authors, actual or potential.

He continued that OUP was ill-equipped to enter the competitive field of literary publishing:

> We should, of course, be willing to consider novels and poetry that come our way, and stand a good chance of attracting work from new writers, but trying to capture established authors would be expensive and risky in view of the number of publishers ready to publish African material; in other areas the situation may be different. Further, many of the scripts published in, for example, the African Writers Series have to be edited with extreme thoroughness, and to operate on any scale one would need a specialised, and centralised, editorial department.[45]

Supplementary readers were the staple of the Ibadan branch's English literature list. These readers were published for all levels of the educational spectrum: at the primary level they were linked to the successful English teaching programmes, and at the secondary level they were the literary texts prescribed for school certificate examinations. In the period after independence in Eastern and Western Africa, from 1961 to 1967, the main supplementary readers were the *New Oxford Supplementary Readers*, which were published in London and, occasionally, reprinted in the branches. The branch also commissioned its own supplementary readers to augment the *Oxford English Course*, for example Morgan Kemi's *How the Tortoise Captured the Elephant* (1966) and *The Ungrateful Hen* (1966). By avoiding 'expensive and risky' projects and sticking to 'economically viable' supplementary readers the branch managed to reconcile the demands of the Delegates and 'those who call for more local writing'. As a result, literature in the branch was infantilised and the branch started to function as a '"nursery" of literary talent' for 'young authors'.

Under Bill Mitchell, branch editor in the early 1970s, there were attempts to recast OUP in Ibadan in the role of 'patron of the creative arts in general'. Together with David Attwooll, Mitchell sought to get local artists to produce cover designs for creative writing.[46] He was keen to expand the limited literary publishing strategy of the branch. In a letter to John Bell in 1971, he argued that the Press should adopt a strong internal policy in support of fiction publishing to compete with the other British publishers in this area:

> It seems to me that we will not get novels (which at present go straight to Heinemann) unless we have a positive internal policy to publish them, and unless this policy is clearly broadcast externally. If there is a definite and positive policy to publish novels ... I cannot see insuperable difficulties in our breaking Heinemann's monopoly in Africa. The niceties of the London fiction publishing scene are, happily, lost on most people here. Whereas everyone is aware that OUP is the leading publisher in Nigeria, and they rightly imagine it to be a considerably more significant force than the like of Heinemann in the world at large.[47]

However, there was an embargo on fiction publishing by the OUP Delegates, which was reiterated in a standing instruction from the OUP Delegates in 1969.[48] John Bell was not prepared to challenge the Delegates' standing instruction, and the prohibition on fiction publishing was retained.

The Three Crowns series was important to the Ibadan branch. The branch managers in the region on occasion helped with the acquisition of new manuscripts for the series – for example, in the case of Wole Soyinka and Joe de Graft. Other West African authors in the series were Raymond Sarif Easmon, John Pepper Clark, Léopold Sédar Senghor, Obi Egbuna, Davidson (Abioseh) Nicol and Ola Rotimi. Three Crowns books tended to be published in Ibadan in parallel with the London editions – especially in the case of Clark and Soyinka. Ibadan was the most important branch market for Three Crowns literature. For example, the vast majority of sales of Soyinka's texts were in his native Nigeria, in particular if they were prescribed by the West African Education Committee. Regarding Soyinka's bestselling play *The Lion and the Jewel*, for example, in 1970 a total of 18,421 were sold worldwide, 15,490 of which were sold in Nigeria. In the following year, 13,737 copies were sold in total, of which 11,302 were sold in Nigeria.[49] Similar sales were achieved for Clark's *Ozidi* after it was selected by the West African Education Committee in 1976/77.[50]

Despite being the major marketplace for African literature, a hierarchical relationship was instituted between London and West Africa with respect to literary publishing. John Bell, manager of the Overseas Education programme in London, specified that new literature in the African branches should be offered to Three Crowns in London before being adopted for the branch literary list. He suggested that 'all work in the field of creative writing which a Branch thinks worthy of publication should first be sent to Ely House for the Three Crowns editor to read. In consultation with the Branch he will decide whether or not the work should appear in Three Crowns.'[51] Building on the reputation of Three Crowns, the Ibadan branch set up a playwriting competition in 1969, with prizes for work in both English and Nigerian languages in order to encourage new drama and to acquire new manuscripts. However, the branch drama series, 'Drama in English', was deemed to be inferior to Three Crowns and was designed as a vehicle for publishing drama that was unsuitable for the international marketplace. The drama was targeted primarily at the schools market, but also at the West African universities.[52] Authors in the series (who, incidentally, went on to achieve considerable critical acclaim) included Ola Rotimi for *Ovonramwen Nogbaisi: An Historical Tragedy in English*, Nanabenyin Wartenberg for *The Corpse's Comedy* and Sonny Oti for *The Old Masters*.

Eventually, this rigid hierarchy began to break down. As editor of Three Crowns from 1971 to 1976, Ron Heapy encouraged the branch to publish new works for the series locally. Under the editorial control of David Attwooll in Ibadan, new titles were acquired specifically for the Nigerian market and titles previously published in the Drama in English series were incorporated into Three Crowns. Indeed, after the closure of Three Crowns as a London-based series in 1976, Ibadan took over the responsibility for the series, and published four new titles: Rotimi's *Our Husband Has Gone Mad Again* (1977), David Umobuarie's *Black Justice* and Rasheed Gbadamosi's *Behold My Redeemer* (1978), as well as republishing Wartenberg's *The Corpse's Comedy* in 1977. It was fitting that Three Crowns, with its roots in West Africa and its main market in the region, should in the end be appropriated by the branch in Nigeria.

The local publishing programme – literary, scholarly and academic – evidently served an important publicity function for the branch. As John Brown's warehouse speech exemplifies, OUP's cultural mission in West Africa was reiterated in public relations rhetoric, to explain and legitimise their material interest in the region. However, I now focus on the question of the economics of Nigerian publishing, to examine Brown's claim that OUP in London financially supported its programme in Nigeria.

Nigerian profits 1962–78

The Nigeria branch accounts detail the sales and overheads as well as the gross and net profit relating to the sales of books within the Ibadan branch. The accounts demonstrate a steady rise in net profits from a loss of £1221 in 1962 to a peak of over £9 million profit in 1977 (see Table 2.1). In the 1970s, the branch became the most profitable branch not only in Africa but worldwide.

The branch accounts are only part of the financial picture, however, as profits from the sale of London books were retained largely by the centre. There are unfortunately few records of the sales of books to Nigeria from London, although this was the mainstay of Nigeria branch publishing. In 1967, Solaru reported that the Nigeria branch had sold £140,000 worth of books from Oxford.[53] In June 1971 Philip Chester wrote that only 15 per cent of the titles of the Ibadan branch were London-originated, but qualified this by saying that 'By far the greater part of the turnover, however, must arise from these titles.'[54] At the opening of the branch, it was specified that the profits for Nigeria branch sales of OUP titles were to remain in

Table 2.1 Nigeria branch accounts, 1962–78 (income in £ on branch publications)

Year ending	Total sales (£)	Gross profit (£)	Net profit/loss (£)
1962	124,125	21,054	−1,221
1963	175,047	30,082	−4,835
1964	226,790	60,491	16,950
1965	298,385	113,573	70,989
1966	303,615	94,092	44,541
1967	344,101	100,730	37,473
1968	393,408	140,050	94,472
1969	422,845	116,770	20,636
1970	469,322	183,232	62,912
1971	735,119	245,543	85,156
1972	841,965	342,165	172,854
1973	1,123,780	329,286	134,756
1974	1,318,590	410,897	137,179
1975	1,769,453	486,189	176,490
1976	4,164,927	1,449,735	903,925
1977	9,004,661	3,626,255	2,161,268
1978	7,271,389	3,052,727	2,367,597

Source: Nigeria branch accounts, AOUP.

London: 'The terms on which London supplies the Branch have been set to allow only the minimum necessary gross profit to the Branch, the profit being retained in London.'[55] There would have been a number of reasons for this: to avoid punitive local taxation, to avoid handing over equity to the Nigerians and to avoid the negative publicity that might arise from being a highly profitable multinational business in Nigeria. The result is that the branch accounts evidently indicate only a small percentage of the profits that Nigeria was actually bringing into the Press at this time.

By the mid-1970s, it was hard to conceal the significance of the Nigerian market. The Annual Report of 1975–76 noted: 'Among all the overseas offices Nigeria had the most outstanding year; its sales more than doubled. Further dramatic increases are expected in the coming year as a result of universal primary education.'[56] This did indeed lead to a huge boom in book purchasing for primary schools after 1976. The economy was at this stage, according to Victor Nwankwo, 'flush with petrodollars'.[57] Nigeria became the single most important market to the Press, and the International division created its own UK-based Nigerian editorial unit. In 1976 the Nigeria branch turnover was over £4 million and the total OUP turnover was £35.1 million (see Table 2.1). Thus, Nigeria alone generated 11.7 per cent of the total income of the Press. By 1977, the branch turnover peaked at £9 million, representing over 20 per cent of OUP's total turnover of £46 million.[58]

The Annual Report of the Oxford University Press of 1977 acknowledged that a high proportion of the £6.58 million trading surplus was gained through the Nigeria branch, but expressed concern about the dependence of the Press on this market:

> A further qualification concerns the extent to which earnings are made overseas. Allowing for the effects of inflation, the trading surplus within the United Kingdom is still inadequate; it is not enough by itself to sustain and develop the activities that produce it. The Press, of course, is not the only publisher to be dependent on overseas earnings but the balance, although now better than during the last two years, needs somewhat to be redressed. ... Within some countries, notably Nigeria, the growth of sales has been remarkable, but it would be rash to expect all gains to be maintained; the risks in many areas are very high.[59]

The report was at pains to demonstrate that the relationship was mutually rewarding, although very precarious: 'Nigeria has contributed substantially to the prosperity of the Press and the Press has made an important contribution to the rapid expansion of education in Nigeria. ... The market, however, is volatile.'[60] Nigeria was, of course, a very significant market to British publishers generally during the early 1970s. Eva-Maria McLean Rathgeber noted that in 1971, 80 per cent of books and pamphlets imported to Nigeria came from Britain and £13 million in foreign exchange was spent in Nigeria on book imports.[61]

This boom in the Nigerian market was, however, short lived. Local ownership was brought in as anticipated in 1978, and OUP was forced by a change in Nigerian law to sell 60 per cent of its assets in the country: 'The ... divestment is being forced upon us by Nigerian law, we shall be a major shareholder in the new indigenised company and shall seek to play a full part in its development.'[62] The new company was named University Press Limited. Immediately following this, the schoolbook market in Nigeria collapsed. The federal government in 1978 ended its policy of purchasing textbooks for primary schools directly. Responsibility was passed to the state governments, and in turn to the local governments, which had no funds to buy books.[63] This marked the beginning of an economic crisis in Nigeria in the 1980s, which resulted from failing oil output and a sharp fall in the price of petroleum. Educational spending was cut, the government failed to pay the Press 'large sums of money', and there was a resulting drop in the price of the shares OUP were forced to sell on the open market.[64] Thus, the boom years were followed by forced withdrawal and then a calamitous collapse in the market, proving that this had been both a highly profitable but also a high-risk business for OUP.

In terms of literary publishing, an immediate consequence of these indigenisation policies was, as Bernth Lindfors remarked in 1985, a growth in local publishing: 'If this trend continues, truly autonomous national literatures could well begin to emerge.'[65] However, he and other critics and commentators criticised British publishers in Africa for their failure to cross-invest profits from the commercially lucrative educational market into the less profitable but more 'culturally significant' African general and trade market. In a series of donor-funded seminars on the African book trade from the 1970s to the 1990s, a prevailing argument was that the multinational publisher together with the state publisher had served to undermine the development of a general book market in Africa.[66] This was reiterated in a 1991 article by the Scandinavian publisher Per I. Gedin:

> While very much part of their own culture in their own countries, where they can support important non-profitable books, in developing countries profit is too often their sole criterion. ... Most of these profits either remain in the local branch or are sent back to the parent company. They are seldom re-invested in the developing country, and especially not in 'non-profitable' fiction.[67]

The British retreat from African literary publishing in the 1970s and 1980s was widely criticised, and British multinational publishers were blamed for the lack of a general book trade in Africa, and specifically the lack of a literary marketplace for 'non-profitable' fiction.

Conclusion

This history of OUP's branch in Nigeria provides an insight into the cultural and economic hierarchies that were implemented between London and the African branches after independence. OUP's academic publishing in the UK was supported by the profits of, and exports to, the Nigeria branch. The dual economy established under colonial rule was modified, however, as branch managers and editors had to navigate their way through the conflicting demands of London and the local markets.

At branch level, a careful balancing of non-commercial and prestigious local academic and scholarly publishing alongside the profitable educational publishing meant that the essential local 'goodwill' was retained. As a result, and contrary to widespread criticism, OUP cross-invested some of its profits in West Africa into the creation of diverse academic and scholarly lists. Rapid and efficient Nigerianisation of the office was carried out and the branch list encompassed locally authored academic, educational and literary titles relating to West Africa. However, these local publishing programmes were ultimately constrained by directives from the Delegates that the African branches should be profitable and should publish only within certain parameters; investment in local publishing was entirely dependent on a buoyant local book market. Thus, the branch successfully managed to adapt to the new African nationalism to survive and prosper in the independent state, whilst continuing to provide unprecedented profits for the London business. These profits were carefully concealed by means of specific accounting methods, and by the construction of public relations campaigns that focused on the cultural mission of OUP in West Africa.

The West Africa branch of OUP might be regarded as a 'dominated literary space',[68] which was obliged to follow guidelines from the metropole regarding literary publishing, and which restricted itself initially to mass-produced school literature. Ibadan was prohibited from entering fiction publishing, and drama publishing was only permitted for a regional market, after the branch became highly profitable. Although deemed inferior in terms of literary production, this was, however, the principal marketplace for the African literature published in London. West African readers functioned, in Edward Said's words, as 'people on whom the economy ... depend[s] but whose reality has not historically or culturally required attention'.[69] Paradoxically, this region functioned as the most commercially significant, but also the most culturally marginalised, marketplace for African literature.

3
'The Call to Duty': OUP in East Africa

Introduction

The first manager of the Eastern Africa branch of OUP, Charles Richards, wrote in his memoirs of the sense of vocation that inspired him to go to work in Africa: the desire to help 'those countries towards the development of literature through which the peoples of those countries could express themselves'.[1] Richards had worked in Nairobi initially as a Church Missionary Society bookseller and publisher from 1935 to 1948, and his rhetoric is heavily reminiscent of the nineteenth-century civilising mission – in Edward Said's terms, 'a "duty" to natives, the requirement in Africa and elsewhere to establish colonies for the "benefit" of the natives'.[2] Richards then went on to manage the East African Literature Bureau from 1948 to 1963, still inspired by a faith in the transformative power of books in Africa:

> I believe in what Churchill once said – 'Books in all their variety provide the means by which civilisation can go triumphantly forward'. ... I took on this work in order to help in the development of all aspects of the provision of the printed word.[3]

Upon independence in Kenya in 1963, Charles Richards accepted the proposal to develop OUP Eastern Africa from an office with a sales representative to a publishing branch of the Press. Charles Richards writes: 'OUP imprint had always been for me typical of all that was good and beautiful in printing and publishing.'[4] The Eastern Africa office had been founded in 1954 and it shared a building with the Church Missionary Society (CMS) bookshop.[5] Publishing branches were instituted in Dar es Salaam, Lusaka and Addis Ababa, while Kampala remained an office. After only two years in post, Richards was asked by the World Council of Churches, Geneva, to return to work in Christian literature, and he reluctantly left OUP. However, he wrote of the new empire he helped build for OUP in this region by founding 'a chain of local offices or connections from the Zambezi to the Red Sea, including the office at Addis Ababa'.[6]

A starkly contrasting verdict of Richards's mission and legacy is written by Henry Chakava in his history of Kenyan publishing.[7] He argues that Richards used his role in the Literature Bureau as a means of 'preparing the ground for the entrenchment of foreign publishers, particularly Longman, Oxford University Press, Macmillan and Nelson', and writes that he should have 'crowned his exemplary service to publishing in Kenya by spearheading, at independence, the establishment of a locally-owned firm'. Instead, he chose to become the manager of OUP. Chakava concludes his critique:

> However well intentioned Charles Richards may have been, he lost a major opportunity to leave a national monument behind after 30 years of credible service to Kenya, unleashing instead a multinational ogre that was to dominate the post-independence publishing scene for many years.[8]

Chakava argues that a combination of multinational dominance and state monopolies crippled the growth of an independent consumer publishing tradition in Kenya.[9] Ruth Makotsi and Lily Nyariki also attribute many of the long-term problems in the East African book trade to British monopolisation of the textbook market, in particular by Longman, Macmillan and OUP:

> the entrenchment of multinational publishers and state publishing houses curtailed the emergence and development of indigenous private publishing in Africa. The result has been the slow development of the industry as a whole, lack of a reading culture and inaccessibility of books published in African languages.[10]

This chapter addresses the disparity between the sense of mission articulated by Charles Richards and his successors in the OUP Eastern Africa branch, and these negative interpretations of OUP's impact on Kenyan book culture. I address the branch managers' objectives for their branch, how these were realised in the branch publishing programme and the limitations placed on their ambitions by London. The aim here is to consider the impact of OUP's work in East Africa on literary publishing in the region, and to evaluate the significance of the Nairobi branch in the history of the Three Crowns series.

'Ploughing back profits': the mission of the OUP Eastern Africa branch

Charles Lewis took over management of the Eastern Africa branch from Charles Richards in 1965, and in his first Annual Report he set out his mission statement for the branch. He argued that OUP had a duty to support 'locally needed books and scholarly journals' by cross-investing the branch profits from educational publishing into literary and academic publishing, encouraging local authors and recruiting and training African staff. These objectives he considered to be morally and politically necessary for OUP in postcolonial East Africa:

> I think it is true to say that the OUP in Eastern Africa is establishing a more acceptable image locally by providing books at all levels in response to local needs. This is important if the charge, commonly made, is to be refuted that expatriate publishers are simply yet another example of 'neo-colonialist exploitation' ... the OUP has a responsibility in developing countries to plough back some of its profits into local development, not only in the provision of locally needed books and scholarly journals, but also in the recruiting and training of African staff, and the encouragement of local authors, particularly in academic subjects.[11]

The branch went on to create a wide and diverse publishing programme relating to East African geography, cartography, anthropology, agriculture, architecture and law. The titles were drawn from the whole region, but the majority (80 per cent) of the new titles published from 1963 to 1980 originated from Nairobi.[12] Many titles in the branch reflected Lewis's own left-wing political interests, for example W. Friedland and C. Rosenberg's *African Socialism* (1964) and Dharam Ghai's *Portrait of a Minority: Asians in East Africa* (1965) and Josiah Kariuki's *Mau Mau Detainee: The Account by a Kenya African of his Experiences in Detention Camps, 1953–60* (1963). The list also included histories of Zanzibar, Zambia, Buganda, the Bunyoro-Kitara, the Baluyia and the Kikuyu. Evidently there was also a market for economics books that promised a quick transition from underdevelopment to affluence: Peter Teum's *From Poverty to Prosperity: An Introduction to Economics* (1969) and Malcolm Falkus's *Readings in the History of Economic Growth: A Study of Successful and Promising Beginnings* (1968). However, the overriding activity of the Eastern Africa branch was schoolbook publishing, in terms of both number of titles published and income obtained. OUP was the market leader in Kenyan book publishing and, together with Longman, dominated the profitable textbook market, which constituted 80 per cent of the value of the total book market in Kenya during this period, and which was totally dominated by British publishers during the 1960s.[13] How, then, was such dominance of educational publishing in East Africa achieved?

Educational expansion, 1963–69

After Kenya became independent in 1963, the new government promised investment in education. The 1964 Ominde Commission Report set out the new educational policies, and this was followed by the Education Act in 1968. This first wave of educational reforms concentrated on secondary education, which under British rule had been very restrictive: at independence only 1255 pupils had passed their school certificate.[14] The 1960s witnessed a significant increase in primary school enrolment from 870,000 in 1961 to 1.2 million in 1968, most of this expansion occurring in Standards 6 and 7 (for pupils aged 12 to 14 years old). Investment in universal primary education came later. By 1973, in response to public clamour in Kenya, the President decreed that there would be free education for all children in Standards 1–4 (for pupils aged 6–10 years old) throughout the republic. This led to a rapid expansion in primary school enrolment from 1.8 million in 1973 to 2.8 million in January 1974.[15]

In Tanzania the Arusha Declaration of 1967 established a seven-year programme of investment in rural education. The Second Five-Year-Development Plan of 1969 stipulated education for all, and Universal Primary Education was achieved in 1972. From 1970 to 1982 the records show that primary school enrolment increased by 63 per cent. However, this tremendous quantitative improvement in enrolment was unfortunately not matched by capital expenditure on education, which if anything declined from 1974 to 1978 due to a widescale collapse in the Tanzanian economy.[16]

In 1968, 50 per cent of the turnover of the branch was gained from primary school textbooks and supplementary readers, many of which were either printed in London and shipped to Nairobi, or reprints of London-originating titles.[17] By far the largest category of schoolbooks was English Language Teaching. The first book to be published in Nairobi was Frederick French's *New Oxford English Course* for East Africa Asian Schools in 1957, and, once the branch was opened, the most profitable London titles were transferred to Nairobi: the *New Oxford English Course for East Africa* and the *New Oxford English Course for Uganda*. OUP had major success in Kenya with the *New Peak English Course*, which was developed in partnership with Kenya's Education Department in 1965. The East Africa branches also published schoolbooks in a range of other subjects: geography, children's literature, history, French, science, study skills, music and civics.

British publishers in general – and OUP in particular – have been criticised for securing preferential treatment through their strategic associations with the examination boards and with the heads of state. The East African Examination Council was created in 1967 and a new examination system was devised, whereby the East African Certificate in Education (EACH) O-levels and A-levels replaced the Cambridge Certificate Examination.[18] John Nottingham, a former District Colonial Officer in Kenya, who became director of the independent East African Publishing House, complained that the education system was a British stronghold in the 1960s:

> There is still a deep attachment to the British educational legacy and British personnel in teaching methods, examination standards, curricula, course books, and the provision of teachers from schools and the Inspectorate.

> In 1965, when the East African Publishing House was founded, we faced a British monopoly publishing position securely rooted in a British-type educational system, which seemed almost impregnable.[19]

The Nairobi branch established good relations with the newly elected presidents: OUP was the chosen publisher of Tanzania's first president, Julius Nyerere, and Kenya's first president, Jomo Kenyatta. All of Nyerere's works were published through the Dar es Salaam branch of OUP: his Swahili translation of Julius Caesar in 1963 (Figure 3.1); *Freedom and Unity* (*Uhuru na Umoja*) in 1967; *Freedom and Socialism* (*Uhuru na Ujamaa*) in 1968, and *Man and Development* (*Bindamu na Maendeleo*) in 1974.

The Nairobi branch also published Jomo Kenyatta's speeches: *Harambee!* (1964), *My People of Kikuyu* and *The Life of Chief Wangombe* (1966). Gedin argues that this special relationship between OUP and the African presidents gave OUP an unfair advantage:

> Heads of state such as Kenneth Kaunda or Nyerere prefer being published in London to using publishers in their own countries – even those owned

Figure 3.1 Julius Nyerere (President of Tanzania) receiving a copy of his book *Uhuru na Umoja* from Charles Lewis (manager, Eastern Africa Branch) *c.* 1967. By permission of Oxford University Press

Table 3.1 Eastern Africa branch accounts, 1964–74 (income from branch publications in £ sterling, excluding sales of imported OUP books from Oxford and London)

Year ending	Total sales	Gross profit	Pretax net profit
1964	167,615	22,649	8,258
1965	262,848	76,349	30,916
1966	349,120	148,832	88,925
1967	363,493	110,003	23,967
1968	423,584	128,439	30,307
1969	522,939	152,194	9,811
1970	504,120	191,565	39,923
1971	580,407	205,354	41,797
1972	543,343	358,021	NA
1973	414,933	NA	NA
1974	485,229	NA	NA

Note: This records the profit-and-loss accounts for the total Eastern Africa branch, encompassing the head office in Nairobi, and the offices in Dar es Salaam, Lusaka, Addis Ababa and Kampala (until its closure in 1973). Profit-and-loss accounts have been retained until 1972, incomplete records exist from 1973 to 1974, and thereafter there appear to be no financial records available in the OUP Oxford archive.
Source: East Africa/Nairobi branch accounts 1966–75, AOUP.

> by the state. The first Kiswahili dictionary was published by OUP from its Kenya office. Since it had been prepared over many years by the Kiswahili Institute at Dar-es-Salaam University, I enquired why it was not offered to the state-owned Tanzania Publishing House. The answer was that OUP were specialists in dictionary publishing – but given this kind of competition, how do local publishers get started?[20]

The Eastern Africa branch was very profitable in the 1960s, and reported a rapid rise of sales from £167,615 in 1964 to £580,407 in 1971. The net profit to the branch rose from £8258 in the first year of trading (in 1964), to £41,797 in 1971 (see Table 3.1).[21] In the 1960s, the branch turnover and profits for OUP in East Africa compared favourably with those of the Ibadan branch.

State publishing, 1965–69

Despite OUP's good relationships with governments in East Africa, Lewis recognised the political vulnerability of the branch. Although there were no government initiatives to expel foreign companies in this region, as was the case in West Africa, the Annual Reports from the Eastern Africa branch from 1966 to 1973 reveal a constant anxiety about the branch's future.[22] Lewis was aware of political pressure to Africanise the branch: he wrote in 1965, 'there is certainly scope, and indeed pressure from Government, for further

Africanisation'.[23] This was carried out rapidly: in 1967 Lewis reported that the Nairobi office had African staff in the editorial, production, sales and accounts departments. By 1969 it was reported that 'the branch has effectively Africanised itself at almost every level'.[24]

Lewis was particularly concerned about the incursion of government into state publishing and state distribution of books.[25] In 1965, the Kenyan state began to take over educational publishing,[26] and Lewis was particularly anxious about Harold Macmillan's negotiations with the East African governments in 1965 to set up 'semi-state publishing houses with the intention of taking over the primary and secondary school textbook market'.[27] Macmillan successfully set up contracts with the governments across much of East and West Africa,[28] in which it held 49 per cent of the shares and the government 51 per cent. Hans Zell describes these agreements as 'lop sided ... partnerships, in which Macmillan had everything to gain and virtually nothing to lose ... it was the kind of commercial opportunism, coupled with an indifference in serving local needs, that brought the multinationals into general disrepute'.[29] OUP wrote a press release complaining about Macmillan's initiatives: 'We do not approve of such developments as they are retrogressive educationally in that they prevent the publishing of better books and the free play of competition, and in that they inhibit the growth of the local publishing industry.'[30] The UK Publishers' Association took up the issue and published articles in *The Bookseller* and *The Sunday Times* against state monopoly publishing and distribution in Africa.[31]

Much to Lewis's alarm, the argument then threatened to backfire against the work of OUP in Eastern Africa, and the Nairobi branch itself was singled out for attack. *The Bookseller* published statements by Macmillan's African partners and supporters. John Nottingham provided a characteristically biting critique on British publishing in East Africa, claiming that £40–50 million came to British companies through African textbook publishing and accusing the Publishers' Association of operating as a 'trade ring' that simply protected its own interests. He wrote that of the 300 supplementary readers for Kenyan primary schools, OUP published 100 while Longman published a further 100. Of the remaining 100, 84 were published by other UK publishers, and only 16 by the Kenyan publishers, that is the East African Literature Bureau and East African Publishing House, and argued that state publishing in the region was a means of encouraging indigenous publishing in East Africa and breaking the British monopoly over publishing.[32] Lewis responded with a press release defending the work of OUP in East Africa: 'We take African staff to Britain for training, and a large majority of our staff in Africa are themselves African. We look for African authors. We believe that books for Africa should be thought out and produced as far as possible in Africa.'[33]

By the late 1960s, state publishers in East Africa exercised a near monopoly on educational publishing, which meant that OUP could no longer depend on the profitable primary textbook market as they could in Nigeria. In the financial year 1967/68 there was a drop of £41,000 in sales in Tanzania and Uganda.[34] Gradually OUP's primary courses and supplementary readers, which had contributed around 50 per cent of their turnover, were replaced in East Africa by government publications.[35] For example, the Uganda Publishing House in 1968 was permitted by the government to appropriate OUP's main mid-primary textbook *New Oxford English Course for Uganda*. As such the branch was forced into higher risk publishing and the Nairobi branch became more dependent on the smaller secondary and tertiary educational markets than the Ibadan branch.

Uncertain markets, 1970–78

By the late 1960s, there were significant fluctuations in branch income, not only because of the new competition from state publishers but also because of the volatile economic conditions in the region. Lewis left Nairobi to become general manager of the India branch in October 1969, and was replaced by the more pragmatic Roger Houghton, former production manager of the branch. Faced with the imposition of price controls on books in Kenya and the potential cut of up to 50 per cent in the Kenya primary school orders, he was under pressure from London to keep a tight rein on expenditure and keep his credit position with London under strict control. He decided that the branch should tighten up on the publication of new books and cut back the publishing programme, particularly at the tertiary level.[36] In 1972, the decision was taken not to replace editorial and production staff when they left, and to concentrate on imported titles and backlist sales rather than new book publications.[37]

Competition from other British commercial publishers in East Africa was intense at this time. According to Chakava, by 1968, nearly 80 British publishers were present in Kenya in some form or other. Although some only had agency arrangements, others such as Nelson, Evans, Pitman and Cambridge University Press had representatives in place, whereas Longman and Heinemann Educational Books had publishing branches.[38] This forced OUP to diversify further, and to concentrate on promoting London books, and on the provision of books in local African languages, particularly Swahili for schools in Tanzania and Kenya.[39]

In the early 1970s, the Ethiopian school market was very profitable for a short period. The foundations for work in Ethiopia had been laid by Charles Richards, who had come to a gentleman's agreement with an old friend, a senior officer in the Ministry of Education in Ethiopia, that OUP would produce an English course specifically for Ethiopia. The Contact series was specifically developed for Ethiopian secondary schools, and was published in 1970. However, the overthrow of the monarchy in the 1974 *coup d'état* signalled the end of OUP's work in the country; the teaching materials produced under Haile Selassie's government were all destroyed, the office in Addis Ababa was closed and the staff dispersed.[40]

In 1971 there was a political and financial crisis in Uganda, after the assumption of power by the Ugandan army under General Idi Amin. The economy was devastated in 1972 following the expulsion of 80,000 Asian settlers, and the subsequent collapse of businesses, cement factories and sugar production. Tanzania's economy also collapsed in 1971 as it struggled with the expense of imposing rural development, *ujamaa,* on its mainland and annexing the island of Zanzibar. Its financial crisis was further exacerbated by the first oil shock of 1973 and the need to borrow from Western banks in order to meet the new fuel prices.[41]

The 1970s were marked by fluctuating sales in the Eastern Africa branch and profits plummeted in 1973, when the branch registered a loss of £51,331.[42] Decisions were taken to close the office in Uganda, cut down on Nairobi office staff and relinquish all but the most profitable publishing commitments.[43] The Nairobi office recovered briefly in 1975 with a large order of primary textbooks by the Kenyan government in the wake of free primary education, and achieved a profit of £87,105, but two years later this slumped to only £903.[44] There was no increase in the government book allowance for primary schools in Kenya from 1972 to 1988, despite the devaluation of the currency. In 1977, Tanzania closed its border with Kenya after the breakdown of the first East African Community, with the result that it was not possible to move books from one territory to another, and the branch lost a principal market, leading the branch to register a loss again in this year.

Thus, the Eastern Africa branch had a volatile history: it enjoyed rapidly rising fortunes in the 1960s and, together with Longman, became the foremost publisher in the region; it then suffered major contractions of the market in the 1970s, and experienced a significant overall decline in profit. I turn attention now to the branch's literary publishing programme, to investigate how the cultural mission of the branch was implemented, and how it was affected by commercial pressures from London.

Entering the field: literary publishing in OUP Eastern Africa

Richards and Lewis as branch managers were both committed to the development of a strong literary list that would feature publications in both English and East African languages. Lewis, in particular, campaigned for the development of new African writing. He was an ardent proponent of further investment in literary publishing, which he regarded as morally necessary as well as politically pragmatic. Jonathan Kariara was a Kenyan poet, novelist and editor appointed by Lewis in 1965 'to develop the creative African writing side of its list'.[45] Kariara started his career as editor for six years at the East African Literature Bureau, where according to Charles

Richards he 'made a distinctive contribution to East African literature and to the encouragement of local artists'.[46] This appointment was a departure for the Press: branch editors were normally British. Charles Lewis wrote a memo back to head office describing Kariara's plans for the East and West Africa branches to publish their own literary series, which 'would be less restricted in outlook than the London series and would certainly include plays, poetry and novels', and would 'open new fields for East/West African writers without exposing them to the rigorous standards of Ely house'.[47] Lewis emphasised that 'This should not mean a lowering of standards, but the branches would have a freer hand in publishing literature of an experimental nature.'[48] Under Kariara's direction, three new literary series were developed in the branch: New Drama from Africa, New Fiction from Africa and Poetry in English, and he also edited the literary journal *Zuka*.

New Drama from Africa was launched with Seydou Badian's *The Death of Chaka*, in 1968, in English translation by Clive Wake. Two plays by Murray Carlin were then published in 1969. *The Thousand* is set in a prison in a Congo-like country, Kurtzville; a white visitor claiming to be an Anglican bishop visits an imprisoned black nationalist leader to plead for the release of a thousand white women and children hostages. *Not Now, Sweet Desdemona* was first performed at the National Theatre in Kampala. Set in a theatre in England, it is a play within a play that concerns the off-stage love affair between a West Indian actor who is rehearsing the part of Othello and a wealthy white Johannesburg actress, who plays the part of Desdemona. As the back-cover copy suggests, the play seeks to explore the universal significance of the racial and sexual politics in *Othello*:

> *Othello* becomes the catalyst in bringing out the long hidden conflicts in their lives. The West Indian argues that Othello was the first racial play to be written, that Desdemona was the first white liberal – power-hungry and passionate. She hits back, and, as tempers rise, the rehearsal in hand gains momentum, giving relevance and meaning to Shakespeare's play in a modern situation.[49]

A rather lukewarm review of the plays was written by Austin Bukenya for the *Journal of Commonwealth Literature*. He judged that they did not class as African literature, written as they were by a white South African, and concerning 'elaborate thought and foreign topics', and concluded that the plays 'only emphasize the need for a specifically East and Central African body of dramatic writing'.[50]

The Plays from Africa series also consisted of drama in Kiswahili, including Ebrahim Hussein's historical play *Kinjeketile*, which was published in 1970, and which was immediately afterwards translated into and published in English, and S. S. Mushi's Kiswahili versions of Sophocles' *Oedipus the King*, *Mfalme Ediope*, in 1971. However, the most critically esteemed playwrights in the series were Robert Serumaga and John Ruganda. Serumaga was director of Theatre Limited in Uganda, whose play, entitled *A Play*, was published by the Uganda Publishing House in 1968. *The Elephants* was then published by OUP Nairobi in 1971. This comedy, in brief, explores the friendship between a British research fellow and a Ugandan refugee, which is disrupted after the arrival of an American girl. His plays were well received in East Africa: R. N. Ndegwa of Kenyatta University College considered him to be 'Uganda's leading playwright',[51] and Chris Wanjala rated him as 'East Africa's most popular dramatist ... his plays are hilariously funny and entertaining'.[52] However, OUP did not retain Serumaga for the series, and his subsequent play *Majangwa* was published in the African Writers Series. He died at a young age in 1980. John Ruganda's *The Burdens* was published in 1972: the playwright was OUP's editorial and sales representative in Uganda, and the play was first produced for the Makonde Group in January 1972 at the Uganda National Theatre in Kampala. The action of the play follows a government minister's fall from grace after plotting with foreigners to overthrow his government, his ensuing life of poverty and hunger, and his inability to meet family obligations. Again, OUP failed to retain the playwright subsequently, and his next play *The Floods* was published by the East African Publishing House in 1980. The Plays from Africa series was still in existence in 1993, with Alex Mukulu's *Thirty Years of Bananas* published in Kampala, but the series was evidently very slow to develop and reached only number 16 in 15 years.

Plays from Africa was regarded in London and the other branches of OUP as a subseries of Three Crowns, suitable for publishing local drama that was considered inadequate for international publication.[53] Kariara complained about the lack of interest in the series by other branches, in particular the New York branch.[54] Three of the plays in the series were first offered to Three Crowns, but were rejected: *The Death of Chaka* was declined, and the Carlin plays were rejected on the grounds that they were 'not quite good enough for Ely House publication', and because they were written by a 'European'.[55] The Nairobi branch objected to the policy of being required first to offer East African plays to London for Three Crowns before publishing them in the branch. Roger Houghton, branch manager from 1970, complained that this protracted process led to good plays being seized by others: 'we are not particularly keen to give London first option on the very few good plays that come our way, unless we feel that they really are of international stature and that we would be misleading our authors by putting them in our local series'.[56] He then protested in 1970 that 'London took so long to make up its mind about the Ethiopian play "The Marriage of Equals" that Macmillan stepped in and published it.'[57]

Charles Lewis engaged in a persistent campaign to expand the branch literary publishing programme. In 1966, he wrote to Jonathan Crowther in London that he would like to have more literary editors and talent scouts employed at the local level, to seek out new authors.[58] A letter written by Lewis to John Bell in 1969 was later referred to by colleagues as his 'call to duty'. In this he urges the press to develop further its African literature lists, and to seek an amendment to the Delegates' standing instruction:

> It would be good, therefore, to have an official O.K. from the Delegates that fiction publishing, particularly in the Branches, may now be encouraged, and that Ely House will support publication of novels by outstanding writers like Ama Ata and accept in principle the risk, if any, of the Branch or London not getting an adequate financial return on really worthwhile creative writing. ... If OUP is seriously going to enter the field of worthwhile novel publishing then the Delegates ought formally to declare OUP's interest in encouraging creative writing particularly overseas.[59]

The branch's attempts to 'enter the field' included attempting to publish Rebeka Njau, if Lewis could tempt her away from the African Writers Series, and also to acquire the latest novel of Aidoo's, *The Wild Cock*. This was part of a concerted effort on the part of Kariara and Lewis to acquire women writers for OUP, and indeed to secure them for Three Crowns. Lewis also suggested that Aidoo should be offered a retainer to report on new writing in Ghana, to make contact with promising writers and to advise on the publication of worthwhile manuscripts.[60] Bell replied to Lewis that he was 'not too happy' about what he proposed. He confirmed the need for 'balance and restraint' in the branch publishing programme, and cautioned Lewis against approaching Aidoo: 'I am afraid that general publication of novels in competition with established fiction publishers is not on at present.'[61]

The Poetry in English series was also established by Kariara. This included Marjorie Macgoye's *Song of Nyarloka and Other Poems*, Ruth Finnegan's *Oral Literature in Africa* (1976) and *An Introduction to East African Poetry* (1976) edited by Kariara and Ellen Kitonga (English language editor at the Nairobi office) for school use. A small number of literary texts in Swahili, Luo, Luganda and Kamba were also published from Nairobi, including drama, prose and poetry, short stories and novels. In Swahili, for example, there was N. H. Zaidi's *Hadithi Kutoka Nchi Mbali Mbali*, Shanwa's *Mutu Asiuye na Uso* and Katherine Arnott's *Ayo, Msichana wa Kiafrika*.

Despite the lack of support from OUP in London, Kariara persevered in trying to develop a thriving literature publishing programme. He created the series New Fiction from Africa which, as a series designed specifically for schools, was exempt from the usual OUP injunction against fiction publishing. In 1969 four new titles were brought out in the series. Two novels were published by the Kenyan writer Miriam Khamadi Were: *The High School Gent* and *The Boy in Between* (described by Austin Bukenya, in the *Journal of Commonwealth Literature*, as 'excellent reading for schools'[62]).

In addition, there were two novels by Ugandans: *Son of Kabira* by Davis Sebkimaa (in Bukenya's view, 'a cynically humourous study of the dilemma of underdevelopment'[63]) and Laban Erupu's *Restless Feet* ('a prose epic of the experiences of a Uganda tribe in search of an identity just before the advent of European colonisation'[64]). Further novels included *The Bull's Horn* by Tumusiime-Rushdegé and Marjorie Macgoye's *Murder in Majengo*, published in 1972, which was described in the back-cover copy as an 'unusual novel, set in a Western Kenya town ... at once a whodunnit, a political thriller, and a social document'.[65] The novel *Defiance* by Abbie Gubegna was published in 1975 in Addis Ababa.

Publishing Charles Mungoshi's *Coming of the Dry Season*

The most significant book in the series was Charles Mungoshi's *Coming of the Dry Season*, which was published from Nairobi in 1972. These short stories recount episodes in the lives of poor black Rhodesians from early childhood to death. The first, 'Shadows on the Wall', relates the breakdown of the relationship between a boy and his violent father in which the boy is left mute: 'I don't know how I should talk to him. He has denied me the gift of language.'[66] The subsequent stories are connected by this sense of persistent psychological isolation in the face of abuse, poverty and powerlessness. The title story concerns a young man, Moab Gwati, who delays visiting his dying mother and instead spends the money for the journey on getting 'hopelessly drunk with a girl he had picked up in Mutanga's earlier in the evening',[67] and is then infuriated by the girl's expectation of a relationship: 'Why must they receive something else from what he intended to give – and then come back later to ask him for more of what he did not know how to give? He despised her. She had come back to complicate his world.'[68] The final story, 'The Accident', relates a car accident, in which a nameless African man, carrying a box of tomatoes, is killed instantly on impact by a car driven by a white man. The story reports the outraged response of the African passers-by towards the 'Boer' driver, for 'in his face they could not read anything. They felt he was indifferent'[69] and they predict, correctly, that the police will not prosecute him:

> 'They have got away with much worse before'
> 'But this time they won't'
> 'They will. Until you rule them'[70]

It was this last story that caused the book to be banned in Rhodesia in 1974. Evidently Kariara did not shy away from politics in marketing the book, for E. W. Krog, former director of the Rhodesia Literature Bureau, judged that, 'it would seem that the politically inspired back-cover blurb compiled by the publishers had as much to do with this as anything'.[71] As Patricia

Alden relates, the book was banned by the Censor Board in Rhodesia on the grounds that it was 'designed to cause hatred and ill-feeling in African minds against Europeans and that the circulation of this book [was] likely to harm relations between the white and black sections of the public'. The fact that this book was issued in a cheap 86-cent edition that 'must be aimed at the African market' was crucial to the decision to ban the book, for the African reader was deemed to be susceptible and undiscriminating:

> The Board is aware that the African is still tremendously influenced by the written word and many cannot distinguish between fact and fiction ... the Board is of the opinion that this book is likely to have a most unfortunate effect on the minds of a substantial number of African readers and to imbue them with anti-European ideas.[72]

The University of Zimbabwe launched an unsuccessful counter-attack arguing that Mungoshi's book was 'a serious work of literature' which 'seeks to educate the reader into a balanced and discriminating moral awareness of the issues raised'.[73] However, the ban remained until 1978. Following independence in Zimbabwe in 1980, the book was republished by the Zimbabwe Publishing House in 1982, where Mungoshi became the literary editor. For his later works, Mungoshi went on to win the Noma Award for African Writing in 1992 and the Commonwealth Writers Prize for fiction in 1998.

Retrenchment and withdrawal: branch literary publishing after 1970

As the branch profitability waned in the early 1970s, there were increasing tensions between Nairobi and London over the issue of literary publishing. John Bell was keen for all literary publishing to be centralised in London within the Three Crowns series. He wrote, 'The proliferation of individual creative writing series in branch areas makes increasingly difficult the building up of one international series of new writing from the developing countries.'[74] Bell suggested that if the Three Crowns editor deemed the literature unsuitable for Three Crowns, perhaps the branch should also refrain from publishing it: 'If the Three Crowns editor, after this consultation, decides that the work should not appear in the series in any form ... the Branch may decide that local publication outside the Three Crowns series should not be pursued at all in the present economic circumstances.'[75] The policy from London was to keep in check literary autonomy at the branch level. Bell was particularly concerned about Kariara's regular writing workshops that were held in Nairobi and was keen to limit his work in this area.[76] Increasingly, there were concerns at the Centre that Nairobi was spending too much time and money on this, particularly in view of its precarious financial position.

The only literary publishing that was encouraged by London for the Nairobi branch was literature for schools. Under Kariara, there was an effort to make supplementary readers culturally appropriate and to commission original publications specifically for the East African market, rather than using abridgements of old classics. Their Oxford Library for East Africa series was aimed at secondary schools in Kenya and Uganda. This was considered to be a welcome new development and was judged to be an 'attractively and economically designed series' by Austin Bukenya, in the *Journal of Commonwealth Literature*.[77] Titles from the Fiction in Africa series were republished as supplementary readers, including Miriam Khamadi Were, Davis Sebkimaa, Laban Erupu and Marjorie Macgoye. The series also included Barbara Kimenye's novels. Lewis wrote to London about this series in a rather apologetic tone: 'It is probably not sophisticated enough for international distribution in Three Crowns but it could well sell in schools outside Eastern Africa.'[78] Thus, supplementary readers were regarded as a means of satisfying both cultural and financial imperatives; they offered an opportunity of publication for local writers – including a number of women writers – whilst being cheap to produce and promising secure educational sales. However, efforts by African editors to expand beyond this low-status publishing genre tended to be curbed by London. Already restrained by London managers and editors, literary publishing by the branch was finally stalled completely as a result of economic factors. After 1973, the publication of all literary texts, except those with an assured educational market, was prohibited. This effectively signalled the end of the short period of branch experimentation in African literary publishing.

During the 1980s, many Kenyan-owned publishing houses went bankrupt, including the East African Publishing House in 1987, Equatorial Publishers and Transafrica. The small publishers Shungwaya, Mowa, Midi Keki, Bookwise and Njogu Gitene all stopped publishing.[79] Of the other British companies, Longman, Heinemann and Macmillan introduced local equity: Longman assigned 40 per cent equity to Kenyans and Heinemann assigned 60 per cent equity to Kenyans in 1985. By the 1990s, publishing was largely in the hands of local publishers or of multinationals, which had been largely localised. Small British publishers – Collins, Pitman, Cambridge University Press, Nelson and Evans – either closed their businesses or left them in the hands of local agents.[80] OUP was thus one of the few British publishers not to entirely shut down in this period or sell the branch to Kenyans. However, redundancies were declared and the publishing operation was cut right back.

This retrenchment of British publishers led to a rapid decline in literary publishing in the region. The *Journal of Commonwealth Literature* in 1978 reported 'a marked drop in the literary output of Tanzania and Uganda, and to a lesser extent Kenya itself, because of the marketing and distribution problems caused, and an increased reluctance by publishers to accept works of fiction, the sales of which have always been rather marginal'.[81] In addition, the collapse of the East African Community also led to the end of the East African Literature Bureau.[82] According to a survey by R. N. Ndegwa, in 1980 only nine works from the East Africa region were published, and only one of these by a British publisher.[83] He lamented that commercial publishers were tending to focus only on educational publishing, and were completely avoiding literary publishing.[84] The criticism was echoed by Valerie Kibera, a literature lecturer from Kenyatta University:

> Our creative writers have fallen silent. Publishers are partly to blame for the current situation. In the 1960s and early 1970s they actively encouraged new writers and serious literature, now in the harsher climate of the 1980s, they have retrenched and concentrated on the assured lucrative educational textbook market.[85]

As in West Africa, foreign publishers were blamed for withdrawing from the less lucrative literary publishing and concentrating on educational publishing alone.

Conclusion

This chapter draws attention to the contrast between the mission statements of the Eastern Africa branch managers and the negative critiques of OUP's work in East Africa by Kenyan publishers and publishing historians. Charles Richards set out with the high-minded ambition to contribute to 'all that is beautiful in printing and publishing' and to promote 'the provision of the printed word' in the region. Charles Lewis then picked up the mantle in his campaign to channel profits into local publishing and support local literary culture. The branch evidently achieved some of its goals to cross-invest profits into the establishment of academic, scholarly and literary lists, but this was carried out against a backdrop of commercial ascendency in East African publishing. OUP, together with Longman and Macmillan, dominated educational publishing in this period, and was criticised for enjoying a privileged position with regard to the governments and the educational boards in the region. OUP's programme in East Africa was carefully positioned in the 'field of wide-scale production' – the lucrative educational marketplace. Cross-investment in the 'field of restricted production' – the local scholarly, academic and literary marketplace – was carefully restrained by London. Dependent on the branch profitability, this programme was swiftly halted when the branch faced a financial crisis.

The variance between aspiration and practice was most clearly exhibited in the branch literary publishing programme. Kariara initiated the most ambitious and innovative literary publishing programme by OUP in Africa, but he was strictly bound by London in what he could achieve, and he was unable to retain new authors for his series. Even during the profitable 1960s, the literature published from Nairobi had to demonstrate a guaranteed school market and high print-runs. The branch was permitted to publish only for a local market; books considered suitable for a prestigious international marketplace were to be sent to London for Three Crowns, where they were frequently rejected for the series. Thus, in East Africa as in West Africa, the only book market that was significantly developed by OUP was the schoolbook marketplace; literary production was confined to this market with the effect that the literature served a utilitarian function within the examination system. As a leading publisher in the region, OUP exercised a significant impact on East African print culture where, despite the significant ambitions and efforts of local editorial staff, it served to perpetuate colonial structures of literary production and distribution.

4
Publishing under Apartheid: OUP in South Africa

> Historically discredited players who, only a few years ago, could talk the language of fundamental pedagogics (based on the National Party's ideology of Christian National Education) now present themselves as torch-bearers of liberation, democracy and progressive education.
>
> – Glenn Moss, 'Publishing in Post-Apartheid South Africa', p. 141

The intention in this chapter is to contribute towards writing the histories of publishers in apartheid South Africa. There are several histories in circulation of independent publishers in this period, of Ravan Press, Skotaville, Taurus, Ad Donker, Renoster Books, Bataleur and David Philip.[1] These publications emphasise the publishers' conflict with the state, their challenge of censorship legislation and their success in discovering new, marginalised authors. Educational publishers, by contrast, have been more circumspect about their histories in South Africa. For example, the officially commissioned *Oxford University Press: An Informal History* by Peter Sutcliffe, with its self-described 'episodic approach and its concentration on a few outstanding individuals', privileges the work of the Press in Oxford and London, but is virtually silent about the work of OUP in South Africa.[2]

The examination of the relationship between culture and commerce in the work of OUP turns here to the work of the Cape Town branch. I address the impact at the national level of OUP's interdependent system of generating economic and cultural capital, in particular by considering the impact in South Africa of the Delegates' directive in 1969 that 'the branches' obligation to be profitable remains'.[3] This is my main point of departure, as I examine the question of how OUP represented its cultural and commercial activities in that country.

This history of OUP in South Africa under apartheid is based on official and unofficial archival records, oral testimonies and written branch histories. It assesses, first, the development of the branch's general list alongside its educational list in the 1950s and 1960s, as well as the dilemmas and contradictions entailed in this dual policy. The chapter then goes on to review the change of management approach towards South Africa in 1970 and the ensuing crisis in the branch and conflicts in London and Oxford. It concludes with an overview of the impact of this strategy in the period 1971–94.

Academic and educational publishing, 1946–62

In 1946 OUP in Cape Town was converted from a sales office to a publishing branch. Fred Cannon continued as trade manager, and Leo Marquard was appointed as the new educational manager with a brief to bring out 'special books for Africa particularly in the educational sphere'.[4] However, Marquard's understanding of educational books was broad, and his main interest was in political publishing. Marquard was intensely involved in Liberal politics in South Africa. He was also a former founder of the student union NUSAS and a founder member (and later President) of the South Africa Institute of Race Relations. Although unsuccessful in his attempt to become nominated as a Liberal Association MP in the 1948 elections, he went on to become Vice President of the Liberal Party, founded in Cape Town on 9 May 1953, alongside Margaret Ballinger as President and Alan Paton as Co-Vice President.[5]

After the establishment of the Nationalist government in 1948, the new OUP branch was subject to an array of restrictions. The Suppression of Communism Act of 1950 prohibited the 'printing, publication and circulation of documents emanating from or reflecting the aims of communist organisations'. The Customs Act of 1955 strictly controlled the importation of material that was deemed to be objectionable in any way: the particular target of the customs officials was anti-apartheid work in cheap editions.[6]

David Philip was appointed as educational publishing assistant in the Cape Town branch in 1954, and in 1959 he was sent to open up an office in Salisbury, Rhodesia. His history of OUP in South Africa draws attention to the list that Marquard developed as editorial manager of the branch from 1947 to 1962, emphasising the high-profile authors published by the branch at this time and the prestigious publications concerned with the historical, sociological, anthropological and literary context in South Africa, which were published for the white, tertiary-level market. Philip's history portrays Marquard as a heroic individual, who established a tradition in the South Africa branch of anti-apartheid publishing:

> Leo Marquard, the liberalised Afrikaner, was the ideal person to set up the local publishing division of the Oxford University Press in Cape Town. This he did with distinction, publishing or initiating such books as Alan Paton's *Hofmeyr*, Edgar Brookes's *Civil Liberty in South Africa*,

> *Langa* by Monica Wilson, *The South African Economy* by Desmond Hobart Houghton, *The Afrikaner Bond* by T. R. H. Davenport, and *The Roots of Segregation* by David Welsh, and himself writing the often-reprinted *Peoples and Policies of South Africa*.[7]

Philip's history makes it clear that this liberal publishing programme had to be supported by educational publishing: 'Leo Marquard was required by the Oxford University Press also to develop primary textbooks for black schools, especially in English and Xhosa; these became the backbone of the Oxford University Press's list and helped to subsidise the historical, anthropological and political books.'[8] Thus, Philip does not censure the involvement of OUP in Bantu education *per se*, but regards it as a necessary adjunct to their cultural academic programme, and a means of cross-subsidising this list.

The Nationalist government set about reforming 'Native Education' in the early 1950s. The Bantu Education Act of 1953 established government-controlled, separate black schools. It centralised African education under the Department of Native Affairs and the Department of Bantu Education, outlawed the creation of schools for Africans without government permission, and provided for the state gradually to assume control over mission schools.[9] The architects of Bantu Education declared that 'native education should be based on the principles of trusteeship, non-equality, and segregation; its aim should be to inculcate the white man's view of life, especially that of the Boer nation, which is the senior trustee'.[10] Dr Verwoerd, then Minister of Native Affairs, introduced the Act as follows:

> When I am controller of Native Education I will reform it so that the natives will be taught from childhood to realize that equality with Europeans is not for them. ... The Bantu must be guided to serve his own community. There is no place for him in the European community above certain forms of labour. ... Education must train and teach people in accordance with their opportunities in life – according to the sphere in which they live.[11]

Kallaway has urged caution in taking this notorious speech as a reflection of the practice in schools in the 1950s.[12] He argues that Bantu Education 'made provision for mass African education and, in addition, it addressed issues of culture, tradition, and language, now considered to be of vital importance to good educational practice, even if it did so in ways that were frequently condemned for having dubious political motivation'.[13] Nonetheless, African schools received at the outset one-tenth of the funding of white schools per capita, and the disparity in government spending increased decade by decade. The net effect of this underfunding was overcrowded schools with inadequately trained teachers, and chronic shortages of books and equipment. In practice, there were not enough places for African students; 50 per cent of students entering the lowest primary grade were forced out before reaching the fourth year. Bantu Education, unlike white education, was neither compulsory nor free.[14] African parents and school boards or school committees were required to provide supplemental financing for their children's education, and while schoolbooks were free in white schools, in black schools parents had to pay for them.[15] According to David Johnson, 'secondary education was deliberately neglected because white labour was still able to meet the need for clerical, skilled and administrative workers'.[16]

In February 1955 Alan Paton asked Marquard to join an appeal he was involved with against Bantu Education, organised by the Africa Bureau in the UK. Marquard was invited to act as an advisor to the African Schools and Families Fund, which sought to support private schools for black students. Marquard replied to Paton refusing the invitation, and enclosing a copy of the letter he had written to the Africa Bureau, which explained his ambivalence about Bantu Education:

> I cannot agree that the Bantu Education Act 'virtually denies to African children the right to education as it is known in this country', or that it is 'a travesty of education', or 'a subtler form of slavery'. ... I cannot accept these statements or their implications. There are a great many things wrong with Bantu Education; but I believe that, having fought the Bill and lost, the best thing to do now is to accept the situation and to bend all energies to counteract its main danger – the growth of an embittered anti-white nationalism – to mitigate as far as possible its short-term inequalities, and to strengthen those parts of the Act that are, educationally, valuable. ... In saying this, I am not forgetting the published statements of the Minister for Native Affairs on the aims of Bantu Education, nor am I unaware of the grave dangers for South Africa of the views of which he is so eloquent an exponent. But I think that those dangers must be met on the political field and not in the school room. ... I regret having to differ from my friends; but there it is.[17]

Paton replied to Marquard on 17 March 1955:

> I am naturally sorry you could not advise the School Fund, but each must decide for himself. I admit the language of the statement is strong, yet bearing in mind the statements of Dr. Verwoerd, of the P. M., and Mr. de Klerk, I cannot but view the Bantu Education Act as an instrument of domination, and therefore I cannot tell myself that these strong statements are untrue. So long therefore as it is permitted to run private schools, I think they should be supported.[18]

In 1957, the Delegates and managers of OUP decided that educational publishing in South Africa was 'ripe for expansion', and that 'the expansion should be almost entirely in the area of education, rather than general, publishing'.[19] The white school market offered few opportunities for OUP to get its books prescribed because of the Nationalist government's preferential treatment of three Afrikaner publishers: Nasionale Pers (Naspers), whose board included D. F. Malan, formerly editor-in-chief of its newspaper *De Burger*; Perskor, which had on its board of directors B. J. Vorster, and H. F. Verwoerd (the first editor of its newspaper *Die Transvaler*); and HAUM De-Jager.[20] However, the Bantu Education Act presented new opportunities for OUP in entering the black schoolbook market. The Lovedale Press had previously been the major publisher of textbooks in African languages in South Africa. Jeffrey Peires notes that the *Stewart Xhosa Readers*, a graded series for primary schools edited by W. G. Bennie, were bestsellers for Lovedale, achieving sales of 56,000 copies every six months according to the accounts of 1942 and 1944.[21] The *Stewart Zulu Readers* also had some success in Southern Rhodesia and Swaziland.[22] However, Lovedale mission station was closed after the imposition of the Bantu Education Act, along with approximately the majority of other mission schools, as black schools were brought under the control of the Native Affairs Department.[23]

Bantu Education created a homogeneous market, with books prescribed centrally, and OUP actively sought to be a supplier of prescribed books. Following approval of the text from the Education Department, the publisher then set a cheap price on the texts, and aimed to sell the books directly to the students. It was the potential number of sales direct to students rather than the guarantee of sales to an educational department that provided profit for the publisher. The majority of the textbooks and educational magazines were prepared again by Perskor and Naspers, who were the lead publishers in this market, but OUP and Longmans, Green had a share.[24]

African languages were the prescribed medium of instruction in primary schools, which meant that there was instantly a need for literature in these languages. Marquard was quick to recognise this gap in the market and the branch became involved in the publication of literature in the vernacular in the hope of prescription by the Education Department for use in schools. As Gérard notes, 'Although the real purpose of this aspect of the Act was to achieve a definite lowering of overall educational standards by confining the black child to the limits of his tribal outlook, on the other hand, a fast-growing market was created, almost overnight, for vernacular literary productions.'[25] There are no references to these publications in the Oxford archive files, but 18 literary texts in Zulu, Sotho and Xhosa published by OUP Cape Town from 1957 to 1963 are deposited in the British Library. These were mainly poetry, drama and fiction in Xhosa, with two Zulu texts and one of Sotho poetry.

In addition to publishing literature for schools in African languages, the branch managed to gain a foothold in publishing language textbooks for Bantu Education, although schoolbook publishing was dominated by

Afrikaner publishing houses. A profitable line of publications for the branch were language courses in Xhosa and English. OUP published a large series of *Oxford Xhosa Readers* and *Oxford Xhosa Grammars* dating from 1956. In addition, *The Oxford English Course for Bantu Schools* was written by George A. Wright specifically for this market and published in 1959. David Johnson notes that 'the new syllabuses showed a dilution of the "standards" established for white schools. English teaching made adjustments to suit the demands of the different racially constituted education departments,' in particular with respect to 'state notions of black urbanization'.[26] Depicting rural African life, the text and illustrations in Standard 1 of *The Oxford English Course for Bantu Schools* were concerned with 'Things that live out on the veld', 'Herding cattle on the veld', 'Fetching a load of wood', 'A ride to the Town' and 'Hoeing the mealies'. The illustrations were of Africans in stores, on the farm and in the fields.

The process by which the branch obtained prescribed-book status for its texts is indicated in the correspondence between Marquard and Fred Hawksley, the administrator of the Bantu Education Board in Durban. Marquard sent him potential publications, and Hawksley in turn would make recommendations to the Central Book Committee. For example, in 1961 Hawksley notified Marquard that Frederick French's *English in Tables* might be prescribed if the editorial errors contained within it were corrected.[27] A month later, the book was approved by the Inspector for Bantu Education in their C List, which meant that it was to be bought by teachers and used in teacher training.[28]

There was a strong correlation between the aims of Bantu Education and the British Colonial Office's 'Native Education' strategy. Kallaway identifies the English roots of the Bantu Education Policy, in particular through the Phelps-Stokes Commissions of 1922–24, which attempted to provide an education that was adapted for African rural life, rooted in social and cultural values of African society.[29] That OUP was involved in publishing for 'Native Education' throughout British colonial Africa might explain the seamless transition in the South Africa branch to publishing for Bantu Education, which occurred without any documented opposition or debate within OUP.

Philip's history of the Cape Town branch depicts black educational publishing as a necessary means of funding the oppositional publishing; it does not examine the contradictions that this policy entailed. The anti-apartheid publishing of Marquard was, in fact, funded by direct involvement in Bantu Education, which the African National Congress identified as 'the most dangerous of any of the oppressive laws'.[30] There were public protests against the education system from the mid-1950s onwards. The ANC decided upon an indefinite boycott of primary schools, which began on the East Rand in April 1955, and then spread to townships nearer Johannesburg and to the Eastern Cape.[31] There were then riots and boycotts in 1961, in Eastern Cape and Transvaal boarding schools: St John's College in Umtata, at Emmarentia Bantu High School at Warmbaths, then at Healdtown, Lovedale and Kilnerton.[32] To illustrate the contradictions in branch policy, Bantu Education was directly attacked in a publication that Marquard and Philip themselves commissioned and edited, Mary Benson's 1963 biography of Albert Luthuli, which quoted the ANC leader's condemnation of the educational system as 'brain washing on a grand scale ... an attempt to enslave the minds and spirit of ten million people'.[33]

Constraints on Liberal publishing, 1962–70

In 1962 Marquard retired from the branch, and Philip was promoted to editorial manager, under the continued branch management of Cannon. Philip's own history describes himself as carrying on the political tradition established by Marquard during the remainder of the decade: 'When in 1962 I succeeded Leo as editorial manager of Oxford University Press, there was already a formidable list of oppositional books, which I needed only to nurture and encourage.'[34] However, during these nine years as editorial manager, Philip was constrained in an unprecedented way by censorship legislation. In reality, the branch was unable to publish many 'oppositional' books in this decade and was forced to resort to London publication for several of their more critical publications. In addition, Cannon was meanwhile developing the branch in a different direction, which led to conflicting strategies within the publishing programme.

Following Sharpeville in 1960, the government introduced a range of ever-more punitive measures. In 1963, the Publications and Entertainments Act created the framework for the censoring of publications, films and public entertainment on the grounds of moral, religious, sociological or political undesirability. This was later reinforced by the more stringent Publications Act of 1974. Under the terms of the Act, publication, printing and importing of undesirable publications could be prohibited and a blanket ban could be placed on a specific publisher. The system was administered by the government-appointed Directorate of Publications, headed by Judge Lammie Snyman, based in Cape Town. Publications could be submitted to one of the Publication Control Boards in the country, and the committee would reach a decision about the desirability of the publication without necessarily hearing any evidence, and without any legal argument. The production of publications that had been declared undesirable was a criminal offence, and distribution of the publication was also prohibited, and in cases of 'radical undesirability' the publications committee could declare that the mere possession of a publication was an offence.[35]

Overt censorship of publications was only one aspect of the legal arsenal adopted by the government. An effective means of silencing opposition was to issue a banning injunction. The Prisons Act of 1959 had already made it an offence to publish information about prisoners, and then in 1962 the definition of sabotage was extended to include all anti-apartheid activities, making it a serious offence to quote or publish the work of a prohibited person. Indeed, all the previous publications of a banned person were simultaneously excluded from publication.[36] After 1964 customs officials became more rigorous and began scrutinising all books, rather than just invoices.

The Liberal Party was to come under sustained attack from Verwoerd's government in the early 1960s. Two years after his retirement from OUP, while he was still acting as an editor and advisor to the branch, Marquard was subjected to two security raids at his home in Stellenbosch. By 1968, the Liberal Party had disbanded in the face of the Prohibition of Improper Interference Act, which made parties with multi-racial membership illegal. Thereafter, liberalism in South Africa became, according to Rich, simply 'a set of intellectual attitudes that had little political embodiment'.[37]

Throughout the 1960s, despite government censorship, Philip attempted to continue the anti-apartheid publishing tradition of Marquard. He published new books by Marquard's authors, and continued publication projects that Marquard had initiated.[38] Increasingly, however, the Cape Town branch had to rely on London to publish books that were in danger of being banned in South Africa. In 1960 there were concerns that Alan Paton might be detained, and plans were made for his biography of Jan Hofmeyr to be published in London. Anxiety intensified after 1962, when there were fears that Paton might be classed as a 'prohibited person' under the Sabotage Act, but in the event, Paton escaped a banning injunction and his *Hofmeyr* was published in Cape Town in 1964. However, the branch was barred from publishing Benson's *Chief Albert Lutuli of South Africa*, after he was classed as a banned person in 1958. On Philip's request, Rex Collings took it on for the Three Crowns series in 1964, but, as predicted, sales of the book were low, cut off as it was from its major market.[39] The biography set the tone for subsequent South African texts in the series. Benson condemned the apartheid legislation of the 'pro-Nazi' Afrikaner Nationalists, and wrote of the 'humiliating segregation and curfew laws'.[40] She also criticised the impact of the Pass Laws, the Bantu Authorities Act and the Promotion of Bantu Self-Government, which 'shackled the non-whites', and Luthuli's treason trial in 1956, which she describes as a 'prolonged, cruel farce'.[41] Of an original print-run of 6000 copies, by 1971 a total of only 1539 copies had been sold, at a loss of £169 to the Press.[42] The book was never permitted to be sold in South Africa and was taken out of print in 1973. However, this demonstates how the series was able to operate as a safety net; the Press was able to exercise its political independence as a multinational publisher to rescue a book that could not be published by the branch.

Monica Wilson and Leonard Thompson's *Oxford History of South Africa* was, according to Philip, the 'foster child' of Marquard, although it was published long after his retirement. Editorial work was carried out in Cape

Town but the two-volume *History* was published from the Clarendon Press in Oxford in 1969 and 1971. Leo Kuper's chapter 'African Nationalism in South Africa, 1910–1964' in the second volume contained quotations from banned people and unlawful organisations. Marquard, Philip and Cannon presumed that the volume would be banned on account of this one chapter, and argued that 'the availability of the work should not be jeopardised; ... that the chapter concerned was expendable in the interests of the availability of the rest of the work'.[43] The decision was made to publish the South African edition of the second volume with 52 blank pages where Kuper's chapter would have appeared, although the international edition was published intact. As a result the book was not banned, although the censor apparently argued that the missing pages were so annoying that he wished he could ban it. OUP has been criticised for being willingly silenced in this fashion, and for not even testing the system. Merrett writes that 'the publishers had achieved the state's purpose through a blatant act of self-censorship'.[44]

Censorship and collaboration, 1962–70

According to Philip, the OUP branch in Cape Town avoided any collusion with the government censors: 'To my knowledge when I was at the Press we never submitted anything to the censorship board, and we wouldn't have done.'[45] Marquard made a public speech at Rhodes University in 1962 against the impending Publications and Entertainments Act, which he argued would have a devastating effect on the book trade, in particular by encouraging publishers to submit their manuscripts to the censorship board before publication, to avoid losing money investing in books that would subsequently be banned: 'In that case, I cease to be a reputable publisher, and on my gravestone should be the inscription, Here lies a publisher by kind permission of the Government.'[46]

Yet, there is overwhelming evidence that Cannon, as trade manager of the Cape Town branch, submitted books before publication to the censorship board with alacrity. James Currey, who replaced David Philip as editor in the Cape Town branch in 1959, claimed that Cannon 'welcomed the establishment of a censorship board because he said it made life easier for a publisher than self-censorship'.[47] Cannon demonstrated a concern to keep the branch afloat under increasingly difficult political and economic constraints, and to avoid anything that might affect the educational sales of the branch. He attempted to intercept inappropriate books before publication, rather than risk importing books that might subsequently be banned, and face financial loss as a result.

This is demonstrated in Cannon's reaction to the proposed publication of Nkosi's *The Rhythm of Violence* as a Three Crowns book from London. The book was a controversial choice by Collings. He had to fight for this play in the face of a negative readers' report, but he supported publication due to the play's theme of violent race relations in South Africa:

> The play is set in this decade in Johannesburg and deals with the clash personally and ideologically between white and black and with some of the problems of non-racial co-operation. In some ways it seems to suggest that in the South African context of today racial harmony is impossible and that all attempts are really doomed to failure.[48]

Cannon was shown an advance copy and wrote back with his objections:

> Phew! I don't think that the play has a hope of being passed by the Publications Control Board – I must certainly submit the advance copy which reached me recently. Far be it for me to complain of the books which are to appear in this series but I must admit that I am more than surprised at this particular selection. Quite apart from the fact that it is not a particularly good play it is surely unwise to emphasise the clash of colour in this manner? What good does it do anyway? And who benefits?

Cannon added a handwritten postscript to his letter: 'It will be banned here, I'm sure (though I shan't agree with that!).'[49] In February 1964, Cannon submitted a proof copy of the play to the Publications Control Board, in advance of its 1965 publication in Three Crowns. Cannon was informed in March 1964 that the publication was, indeed, banned. It was deemed 'indecent, obscene or objectionable and that the importation and circulation thereof is prohibited'.[50]

By 1968, Cannon was anxious to obtain advance galley proofs for all OUP books relating to Southern Africa, 'not only for vetting from a banning point of view but also for editorial purposes'.[51] In March 1970, Cannon sent a letter to Jannie Kruger, the Chairman of the Publications Control Board, that clearly set out the process by which Cannon selected books from the UK for import:

> [we] invariably inspect proof copies of books to appear under the imprint of our Principals to decide if they will prove acceptable for sale in South Africa; and ... in turn, submit such proofs to you if we think that they are likely to be judged undesirable. ... I shall continue to act in this manner as I feel it is better for a book to be deemed undesirable before stocks arrive in this country than for it to be subsequently placed under embargo and, if then prohibited, for copies to be returned to England.[52]

As an agent for several other British publishers in South Africa, many of the books submitted to the board by OUP were from other publishers. For example, a proof copy of Richard Neville's *Play Power* was submitted to the board on 14 January 1970, shortly before publication in the UK by Jonathan Cape, and was subsequently banned on 6 February 1970. Further books that were submitted by the branch and subsequently banned included Lewis Nkosi's *Home and Exile* (published by Longman and banned in July 1967), J. J. Head's *How Human Life Begins* (published by Murray and banned in October 1970) and four books published by Cape: Robert S. de Ropp's *Sex Energy* (banned February 1970), Leonard Cohen's *Beautiful Losers* (banned March 1970), Regis Debray's *Strategy for Revolution* (banned May 1970) and Massima Teodori's *The New Left: A Documentary History* (banned July 1970).[53] McDonald notes that many British publishers, including Gollancz, Collins, Faber, Heinemann, Penguin and OUP, were aware that their local representatives submitted proof copies of their books prior to publication, and claims that they 'adopted a ... pragmatic stance' and 'worked with the system to try to secure the release of some of their titles'.[54]

Publishing for 'Bantu' schools continued apace in the 1960s. In 1963, the first African sales representative was appointed, Richard Mnyakama, who moved between his home in Cape Town and the Transkei and Ciskei. In 1968, Everett Moahloli was appointed as Transkei representative, with an assistant, Godfrey Ndugane.[55] Cannon reported the branch's success in publishing for the Bantu Education Department in his Annual Report of 1968/69. He described the close links he was establishing in the Transkei, the first Bantustan, including the Department of Education in Umtata, the capital, and reported his success in getting schoolbooks prescribed for 'Bantu' examinations:

> In South Africa several of our Xhosa publications were prescribed for examinations and sales of Oxford English Course for Bantu Schools and Oxford Xhosa Readers were good. Both these series should reflect much better returns at the end of the current year as we now have two African representatives in the Transkei, introducing these books to schools in that enormous territory and maintaining close contact with the Department of Education in Umtata. *Their Secret Ways*, prescribed for a Bantu examination, was extremely popular, some 26,000 copies being sold.[56]

In April 1970, Cannon retired after 40 years with OUP in Cape Town.[57] Finding a replacement proved difficult. Henry Blagden (manager of the branch suboffice in Johannesburg) turned it down: 'The number two whom we had all confidently expected to succeed refused, no-one suitable on the existing UK staff was prepared to take the job on.'[58] A South African living in the UK was appointed to the post, but he pulled out at the last minute. Jon Stallworthy, the poet, and London-based editor of the Three Crowns series, was seconded at very short notice to be caretaker manager at Cape Town for eight months from April to November 1970 while the company found a replacement.[59] Eventually, Neville Gracie, a retired lawyer and ex-mayor of Durban Westville, was appointed as general manager for Southern Africa in November 1970.[60]

During the 1960s, balancing the branch's interests in cultural and economic capital became increasingly difficult. In the context of punishing censorship legislation, the publication of oppositional texts for a restricted academic market involved constant confrontation with the state, or avoidance of confrontation through publication in London, which led to loss of sales for the branch. By the end of the decade, the branch was in a state of financial crisis: publishing for Bantu Education was successful, but was insufficient. Branch profits had declined from £21,624 in 1961 to a loss of £13,553 in 1968 (see Table 4.1).[61] The situation provoked a crisis in the Cape Town branch and major dilemmas in London and Oxford regarding OUP's future in South Africa.

Crisis and conflict, 1970–72

By 1970, OUP's involvement in Southern Africa was not only a financial liability but increasingly a public relations liability. The international anti-apartheid movement meant that trade with other branches became difficult. India refused to let its goods be exported to South Africa, and the only way to get books through was for payment to go through London.[62] The New York branch was cautious about importing books from South Africa; regarding a new series of paperbacks launched from Cape Town, the New York branch manager commented: 'I would have to say that the words "Southern Africa" at the present time would incline many people in the United States to have a negative feeling towards the books.'[63]

The OUP Secretary, Colin Roberts, and the London Publisher, John Brown, corresponded about the future of the branch, and met privately with the Delegates in Oxford to discuss the Press's position. Brown initially prepared a one-page statement defending OUP's involvement in South Africa, for fear of it being 'attacked within the University for having any connexion with South Africa'.[64] This statement reiterated OUP's cultural mission in Africa, its educational role in publishing local books, including in African languages, and its commitment to scholarship through the publication of academic books on South Africa by Paton, Brookes and Macaulay. On reading it, Roberts decided that it should not be released, as it simply raised a series of difficult questions:

> the more I read it and reflect on it, the more I hope we are not questioned – not that I think our policy is not defensible, but that it would be hard to persuade those who do not wish to be persuaded of the rightness of it. ... To illustrate the difficulties, you comment that Cannon is an Englishman, but say nothing about Gracie. Should we add that he is a South African

> of English descent and also a member of the Liberal Party? Similarly with Marquard. If we were to draw attention to his admirable political record, it may arouse questions about others. The books published by the Branch you list should certainly count to us for righteousness. On the other hand, the mere fact that our books are sold in Rhodesia will be apt to cause trouble.[65]

Brown was quick to concede that public scrutiny of OUP's policy would be best avoided:

> Like you, I hope very much that we are not questioned. This, of course, is an entirely emotional matter, not open to reason. ... Gracie is not a member of the Liberal Party because that, surely, is now banned, but he says he votes Progressive. Certainly he is very anti the National government, though I suspect that this may be based more on his English-speaking background than any truly liberal principles. Obviously we do take a risk with the appointment of a South African as manager and we shall certainly have to watch his publishing policy.[66]

Thus, avoidance of public debate about this 'emotional matter, not open to reason' became the official management strategy. However, there was to be a major – and very public – crisis in the South Africa branch the following year.

From 1970, the management in Oxford put pressure on the Cape Town branch to confine its work to profitable publishing for African primary schools. This was part of a series of directives from Oxford that reinforced the principle that the cultural and scholarly endeavours of the Clarendon Press should be funded by the profits from the overseas markets.[67] The parliamentary enquiry into the running of the OUP, resulting in the Waldock Report of 1970, recommended that branch publishing should be strictly on a 'profit-making basis' to generate the 'financial resources of the Press'.[68] According to this report, OUP was the largest publishing house in the United Kingdom, with a turnover of well over £10 million per annum and a heavy dependence on its overseas income.[69] It was evidently imperative that the Cape Town branch should be brought into line with OUP's general branch publishing strategy.

Anthony Toyne of Ely House in London was sent on an extended visit to South Africa in 1969 and drew up a five-year plan for the branch, proposing expansion into Bantu Education through the publication of language courses, dictionaries and mathematics courses, which involved translating and revising existing texts. Brown then wrote to Philip in April 1970, insisting on a change of policy:

> It is, as you know, the policy of the Press that Branch publishing should be profitable, that the main emphasis should be on educational books

> but that the smaller proportion should be in the general field. ... But the weakness of the Branch from a financial point of view has been its comparative lack of success in the specifically educational field, no doubt due to a lack of capital and staff, and this is what I hope will be corrected.[70]

Philip found the shift towards publishing for profit alone intolerable and resigned in protest, as he explained in his autobiographical history: 'One of the reasons for my decision to leave OUP was that it had been made clear to me by OUP, Oxford, that I would be expected to publish almost exclusively school textbooks and I preferred tertiary and general publishing.'[71] Philip's history is a lament for the slow decline of the OUP in South Africa from oppositional academic publishing to mass schoolbook publishing, from financially disinterested publishing to profit-centred publishing. He attributes this smothering of editorial independence to profit-seeking management in Oxford, but, in an interview, he also alludes to problems with the manager: 'I didn't want to continue publishing primary schoolbooks, especially as there was such a need for other books in South Africa. And Neville Gracie and I didn't get on.'[72] On resigning from OUP, Philip was involved in anti-apartheid publishing through his own imprint, David Philip Publishers (DPP), from 1971 to 2002, and took with him many OUP authors, most crucially Alan Paton.[73]

Following his sabbatical in the branch in Cape Town, Stallworthy returned to the UK concerned about the appointment of Gracie, and with major reservations about OUP's continuation in South Africa. As editor of Three Crowns, he tried to continue a liberal, anti-apartheid tradition of publishing within the series. He acquired international rights to publish Mtshali's *Sounds of a Cowhide Drum*, which was the third South African text published in Three Crowns. Published in 1972, Mtshali's poetry was described by Stallworthy as 'simple graphic poems by an African about life for an African in South Africa'. The poetry was regarded as a shocking exposé and indictment of conditions for black South Africans, as indicated in the *Evening Standard* review in 1973:

> What is remarkable about Mtshali's poems is their true depiction of the misery and oppression of South Africans. ... Few, if any, poets in South Africa have said the same things and escaped persecution. His harrowing poems have admitted white South Africans to a world most of them were unaware of. ... It is in this nightmare situation of violence and poverty that Mtshali has written his poetry. How long the South African Government will allow him to go on writing is anyone's guess.[74]

Stallworthy also secured Fugard for the series, publishing *Hello and Goodbye* and *Boesman and Lena* in 1973. Although few in number, the Three Crowns series supported South African writers who were vulnerable to banning constraints in their own country, and gave them an international platform. Through these publications, the series became associated with anti-apartheid and black South African literature; there was a marked contrast between the publishing policy of Three Crowns and the South Africa branch, as OUP in Cape Town altered its course in the late 1960s.

Stallworthy agitated for a further series of management meetings about the future of OUP in South Africa. John Bell, manager of the Overseas Education department, describes this in a letter to Philip in July 1971, following news of his resignation:

> All of us are distressed at your leaving the Press and at the general wave of departures that have followed on Neville's taking over. As you must know, there have been anxious debates over the problem ever since Jon came back: debates from which he was I think rightly excluded, the Management Committee having to take the responsibility for decisions without involving Jon in any of the consequences. But of course his views have been known and taken into consideration.
>
> Clearly things have got much worse than had been anticipated by the Management Committee (though not to you and Jon). It may be that something cataclysmic was needed before Neville could build. But you must not think that we are not *all* in considerable distress that you have felt obliged to go: and that at present things are so unhappy.
>
> Having appointed Neville, we must let him run things his way for a fair time. He won't find it very easy here at the end of the month: there will be a lot of hard questioning. I doubt if Jon will feel disposed to talk to him at all. But this won't restore *you*, and this is the most miserable break of all. I am extremely sorry about it, and wait anxiously to hear of your future. You have had a rotten year, may the next be a happier one.[75]

The change of official policy with respect to South Africa is clearly conveyed in correspondence between Alan Paton and John Brown, the London Publisher, in November 1973. Paton asked for a cancellation of his contract with OUP Southern Africa for the biography of Roy Campbell in the light of Philip's resignation: 'I must also be honest with you and say that I have no confidence in the present management of the OUP in South Africa, and am of the opinion that it would be antipathetic or merely indifferent to any work of mine.'[76] Brown agreed to cancel the contract and defended the transition of the branch towards Bantu Education publishing:

> Perhaps I can say that I think that you are wrong in your assessment of our present management in Cape Town because I suspect you have had only partial evidence. We did, however, in order to exist in South Africa and to satisfy the Delegates of the Oxford University Press, have to make some changes in policy of a kind which in easier circumstances we would

> not have had to make. Our publishing policy has changed and we are concentrating at the moment very much more on educational books for the Bantu schools at the expense of general publications.[77]

Stallworthy was appointed to All Souls College, Oxford, but evidently continued to campaign in the university over the situation in South Africa. In June 1972, he wrote to Colin Roberts to warn him that Herbert Hart, the legal philosopher and former Professor of Jurisprudence at Oxford, was planning to question OUP's operations in South Africa.[78] Hart wrote to Roberts asking about the conditions for black staff in the Cape Town office, urging that a policy of equal pay for black and white should be adopted, along with educational facilities for black employees: 'I think we could be exposed to very adverse comment if we do less than we could for our black employees. I am sure that the matter should be given attention quite seriously soon and I would hate it if comments appeared in the newspapers showing that we had less concern than other companies operating in South Africa (this is not a veiled threat!).'[79]

Roberts replied to Hart that he agreed that 'there is no time to be lost' in considering the question: 'It seems to me there are three separate but interlocked issues: the justification for our presence in South Africa ... our policy as an employer, and thirdly (something on which Jon Stallworthy has views and on which I have no direct information), the management of the branch.'[80] A meeting took place to discuss this, attended by Roberts, Brown, J. H. C. Thompson, Hart and Stallworthy, whose presence Roberts felt was necessary although 'Bruno [Brown] suggested that we meet without Jon Stallworthy on the ground that he is too emotionally involved.'[81] The outcome of this meeting in Oxford in 1972 has not been recorded in the archive, but evidently the decision was made that OUP should remain in South Africa. At this time certain other multinational publishers disinvested in the country in protest against its racial policies: Heinemann moved out in the 1960s, and McGraw Hill in the early 1970s.[82]

Publishing for Bantu Education, 1970s and 1980s

The main informant about the history of the Cape Town branch after 1970 is Gracie. He was the author of the annual branch reports, and he was interviewed for, and quoted extensively in, Riette Hart's unpublished 'Cape Town Branch: The Story of Oxford University Press Southern Africa', which was written for internal branch circulation in 1992, based on archival evidence and oral testimonies of branch staff.[83] Gracie forthrightly described the task facing him when he took over branch management:

> OUP is a 'foreign' company, and exchange regulations eventually didn't allow us to run an overdraft at all as this would amount to sending money

> out of the country. At the same time, there was no way that the Press could or would subsidize us when there was more and more pressure from some other branches to totally close down operations here. If we continued losing money this might be just the excuse they were looking for. It was therefore imperative that we build a 'cash cushion' to see us through.[84]

Gracie's Annual Reports for the years 1970 to 1974 testify to the importance of the Bantu Education market for the branch, and in particular the market in the Transkei. In the financial year 1970–71, 33,699 copies of Wright's *Oxford English Course* sold in the Transkei alone, and total sales of this title reached 64,806. Of 81,622 copies of Pahl's *Oxford Xhosa Readers* sold countrywide, 55,973 were sold in the Transkei. By 1972, Gracie was reporting that 'the major source of profit' came from these titles and affirmed the necessity for the branch to retain sales in this area.[85] In 1974 again, most of the profit from local publishing was from the sale of primary schoolbooks in the Transkei and Ciskei.[86]

In addition to publishing books locally, imported titles from Oxford were also prescribed for the Bantu Education Department. A memo from Gracie to Paul Binding in the Oxford Children's Book department demonstrates the size of the Bantu Education market by 1977. Gracie anticipated that the London-published *Jason and the Golden Fleece* would be prescribed for the Standard 3 English examination of 1980. He estimated that 87,000 pupils would need the book, expecting sales of 50,000–60,000 copies, sold at a price of 95 cents per copy.[87] This would far outstrip the sales for books prescribed for white schools in the Cape Education Department, which Gracie estimated at about 7000 pupils taking Standard 8.[88]

In 1974, the Publications Act amended the censorship legislation to provide for banning of all the output of a publisher and removed the right of appeal to the Supreme Court. The branch's response was to be even more cautious. Hart's history recognises the close relationship between the censors and OUP at this time:

> The Branch for most of these difficult years fortunately had a better relationship ... with those officials who'd been appointed to protect the nation's morals against possible corruption. Alison Neish, who in the 1970s was responsible for handling the List of Objectionable Literature, says the Branch had a 'gentleman's agreement' with the customs officials that it would submit anything they were unsure of, with a covering letter, in case there were any queries at a later date. If necessary, as in the case of Prof. Dugard's prescribed book *Principles and Policy of South Africa*, quotes on the back cover were blanked out or cut out by hand.[89]

There was a sharp decline in historical, political and sociological texts, and those that were published had reduced print-runs. The branch list became more commercial and the texts more anodyne. The few new titles that were acquired for the branch are indicative of its new direction. Gracie acknowledged in his report of 1972/73 that '[t]he tempo of editorial production of the Branch is still extremely slow and only four new works were published during the year'.[90] The only new publications were three economics texts and one school poetry collection. In 1973–74, Gracie wrote that 'Publishing activity was concentrated mainly on the production of new editions and impressions of existing books',[91] including Clarke's *Map Reading,* Kidd's *Wild Flowers of the Cape Peninsula* and Victor Pohl's *Farewell the Little People,* a collection of the author's versions of Bushman tales, in which the 'almost extinct little people of Southern Africa' were compared to 'Lilliputians, fairies, gnomes and elflike creatures'.[92]

Gracie systematically rejected all political or controversial titles, and sent proposals instead to London or the Clarendon Press. Between 1975 and 1978 Gracie rejected several texts: Robert Shoen's *The Demography of an Apartheid Society,* which he described as a 'monograph dealing with the processes of economic development and population change in South Africa ... we shall not publish it in South Africa';[93] Pierre Hugo's *Working Within the System: A Study of Contemporary Coloured Politics in South Africa;*[94] and a sociology title, *Prejudice under Pressure* (a 'rather detailed report and analysis of the racial attitudes and thinking of white South African artisans') by Randall Stokes and Edward Feit.[95] In each of these cases, the editors in London and Oxford similarly rejected the proposals on the basis of the limited market the titles would have, and there is no evidence that they were published by other British or South African publishers.

The branch's publishing strategy was symptomatic of the general approach of multinational publishers in this era, according to Philip, who maintained that educational publishers in the UK – including OUP – ceased to publish texts from the UK that were critical of apartheid in South Africa. They were, he claimed, concerned about their relationship with the government over school textbook prescriptions: 'there was no more critical material coming from London. There was a concern amongst transnationals about their education publishing prescriptions, and not wanting to do anything that might damage this.'[96] The OUP archival evidence supports this argument. OUP in London and Oxford turned down the oppositional titles that had been rejected by the Southern African branch, although as a multinational publisher they had freedom to publish them. They gave market-based reasons for their decisions, but it appears likely that OUP's local involvement in Bantu Education led to a lack of commercial independence.

Gracie's strategy was a great economic success, but did not make him a popular manager. In interview with Hart, Gracie admitted that he kept a tight rein on the branch finances and 'he was often very disliked for this and other reasons'.[97] In 1970, when Gracie took over, the branch lost £13,704, but in the Annual Report of 1971–72 he could announce: 'A record profit has replaced the losses of the two previous years. This has been achieved by a ten per cent reduction in overhead expenses and by firmly turning down uneconomic publishing projects.' In this financial year the branch achieved a net profit of £18,702 (see Table 4.1).[98] The fortunes of the branch in Cape Town continued to improve. Gracie was congratulated by Colin Roberts, Secretary of OUP, in 1973 on his success: 'Dear Neville, I am delighted to learn in such a substantial form that the Branch has had another successful year. I have not yet seen the figure, but shall look forward to doing so; meanwhile I shall have much pleasure in drinking the Branch's health.'[99] In 1974, Gracie announced: 'Profits in the last three years have now largely eliminated the losses incurred in the late sixties.'[100] Hart's history describes this period of economic success in the late 1970s:

> The Branch finances continued to flourish 'despite rampant inflation, the catastrophic fall in the price of gold, and a government clamp on private spending to offset astronomical public expenditure', and when sales exceeded £¼ million for the first time in 1977 every member of staff was presented with a bottle of champagne! This milestone was reached in spite of an imposition of 15 per cent duty on imported goods in the same year.[101]

By 1982, turnover in the South Africa branch had reached £1.18 million, and net profits in the branch, which were repatriated to London, rose to £114,305 (see Table 4.1).[102] Branch profit was based on sales of branch publications alone, and excluded the more significant profit from OUP books published in Oxford and London and sold through the Cape Town branch.[103] According to the deputy publisher in London, Philip Chester, 'by far the greater part of the turnover' of the African branches was derived from sales of books published in London, but this accrued to the general UK accounts, and was not broken down by individual markets.[104]

The South Africa branch was particularly important to the Press in this period in view of the sudden loss of the most profitable branch markets in East and West Africa, which had been vital to OUP throughout the 1960s and until the late 1970s. The Nairobi branch turnover amounted to over £500,000 annually from 1969 to 1972, but declined sharply in 1973 with the economic crisis in the region.[105] The Nigeria branch turnover rose to a peak of £9 million in 1977, constituting over 19 per cent of the total OUP turnover of £46 million, but the market failed in 1978 when the Press was forced to indigenise the business, and this was followed by a general economic collapse.[106] In this context, the South Africa branch assumed particular significance. By 1984, Gracie wrote in *The Record*, 'The growth of SA Branch since 1970 has outstripped that of any other branch by more than twice.'[107] Around this time, Gracie made an offer of a management buy-out to Roger Boning, director of the Press's Branch Headquarters in Oxford, which was rejected:

> Roger Boning turned my offer down as he said that, frankly, we had become too lucrative. Many of the other branches weren't doing very well at the time, the Press itself wasn't in wonderful shape, and they couldn't afford to lose Southern Africa.[108]

In 1987, there was an investigation by a senior OUP management team sent to Cape Town to decide if OUP should remain in the country, reportedly due to pressure from Oxford University students to disinvest from South Africa.[109] The outcome was a decision to remain in South Africa, although Gracie's management of the branch was evidently criticised. Gracie was bitter about the investigation and its conclusions, and he reported in the same interview with Hart that he decided to resign as a result, as he did not want to continue working under 'unpleasant' circumstances: 'I had had enough.

Table 4.1 South Africa branch accounts, 1959–82 (income from branch publications in £ sterling, excluding sales of imported OUP books from Oxford and London)

Year ending	Total sales	Gross profit	Net profit
1959	59,779	27,912	24,891
1960	61,846	24,045	20,071
1961	61,993	26,548	21,624
1962	60,062	7,037	-3,007
1963	64,256	17,981	9,966
1964	50,471	10,219	4,374
1965	52,920	18,648	7,652
1966	52,549	20,111	2,925
1967	57,682	19,547	4,289
1968	71,697	19,306	−13,553
1969	73,711	36,114	2,674
1970	76,945	17,233	−13,704
1971	95,690	36,184	−8,900
1972	96,759	45,288	18,702
1973	97,949	46,318	16,738
1974	110,067	52,012	9,844
1975	133,105	58,994	20,739
1976	168,560	78,002	42,134
1977	322,686	135,574	65,927
1978	433,483	188,194	15,940
1979	633,417	276,775	120,641
1980	NA	NA	NA
1981	910,662	297,080	120,889
1982	1,186,731	340,536	114,305

Source: South Africa branch accounts.

OUP was here to stay. I felt that there were no real challenges left, and didn't need to work, so I resigned some 18 months before my contract was due to expire.'[110]

Gracie's retirement took place in September 1987. He was temporarily replaced by Adam Butcher as manager of the African Region on 3 October, and James Clarke was then appointed as general manager of the branch, with Kate McCallum as educational publisher from 1988. Clarke remained in post until 1990, and was replaced by Smuts Beyers, who had formerly worked for Maskew Miller Longman. In 1990 there was a further visit by press managers Sir Roger Eliot, Secretary to the Delegates and Chief Executive of OUP, and the historian and Delegate, Sir Keith Thomas. In Hart's words: 'On the conclusion of this visit, the message was clear: Oxford University Press, which had been in this country for three quarters of a century, had no intention of withdrawing from South Africa.'[111]

In 1993 the Commissioner for Inland Revenue revoked the tax-exemption status of OUP in South Africa, arguing that 'OUP was a commercial undertaking conducting the business of a dealer in books and as a publisher thereof', and was therefore deemed liable for taxation.[112] OUP contested the decision twice. The first appeal was in the Cape Provincial Division of the Supreme Court on 31 March and 1 June 1994; OUP's argument was that it should be exempt from tax because it promoted 'high standards of learning and of scholarship by the universal distribution of educational, scholarly and academic works' and 'carrie[d] on other activities in Southern Africa through the OUP, namely the training of black teachers, curriculum development work, lobbying the local Education Department for the provision by the OUP of dictionaries and atlases to black schoolchildren and the teaching of dictionary skills, and involvement in public interest committees concerned with education'.[113] This appeal was unsuccessful, but following the further appeal to the Appellate Division on 24 and 30 November 1995, Chief Justice Michael Corbett ruled in favour of Oxford University. His judgement emphasised OUP's historical commitment to 'promote scholarship, education and culture' and its support of black education.[114]

Conclusion

This history of OUP in South Africa demonstrates a transformation in the relation between cultural and economic capital in the branch. Initially the branch functioned as a microcosm of the Press as a whole, whereby scholarly publications for the 'restricted' academic market were subsidised by the 'large-scale' educational marketplace.[115] Stratification was on racial lines: cultural capital was accumulated through OUP's publications for the white academic and tertiary market, and economic capital through the profitable black educational market. However, by 1970, the Cape Town branch was under pressure to conform to the international publishing policy of OUP, by which it became not only self-supporting but a source of income for the Press as a whole. The branch was required to concentrate exclusively on the acquisition of economic capital; there was evidently a realisation that serving the liberal academic market in South Africa jeopardised its position in the country. As demonstrated, the result was, in effect, closure of the general and scholarly list and focus on Bantu Education publishing.

As was the case for OUP in East and West Africa during the 1960s and 1970s, this global strategy was highly successful for OUP. Economic capital generated at the periphery supported the cultural endeavours in the metropole whilst symbolic capital accrued by the academic, Oxford-based Clarendon Press helped sell educational textbooks in South Africa. OUP's expansion into Bantu Education in South Africa paid dividends: from a reported loss of £13,700 in 1970, branch turnover in 1982 reached an unprecedented £1.18 million.[116] Undoubtedly this model of cultural production did entail a number of 'contradictions' and 'incompatibilities': after 1970, OUP South Africa was increasingly at variance with the liberal public profile promoted by OUP globally and, indeed, through the Three Crowns series.[117] However, OUP were successful in veiling their commercial interests in South Africa under apartheid – in 'abstaining from fully revealing their self-interested goals'.[118] This was achieved partly through OUP Oxford's geographical separation from this profit-centre, but also through careful attention to its self-representation in South Africa.

Correspondence between the London Publisher and the Secretary to the Delegates indicates their concern to prevent public scrutiny of OUP's programme in the country. However, Gracie was permitted to 'run things his way for a fair time', despite protests and resignations, and it was 16 years before there was a management investigation of OUP's operation in the country. Since the end of apartheid, OUP in South Africa has sought to rebrand itself as an investor in black education and culture, as demonstrated in its arguments in the Supreme Court. The narrative constructed by OUP that ultimately protected its tax status in South Africa emphasised its cultural and educational mission while being more reticent about the economic imperative – and significant profits – underwriting this project. OUP is evidently keen to draw a line under its past in South Africa; this chapter aims to shed light on this occluded publishing history.

Conclusion to Part I

This study of OUP's history in Africa from 1927 to 1980 suggests that its postcolonial publishing maintained significant continuities with its colonial past. OUP managed after the end of formal colonisation in Africa to consolidate successfully its dominant economic position in the African book trade by substituting relationships with the British colonial authorities with new relationships with the African political elite and with the examination boards in East and West Africa. In South Africa the strategy of publishing for Bantu Education closely paralleled the strategy of publishing for Native Education in the African colonies.

Throughout the period the relationship between OUP's metropolitan centre and African branches involved a system of cultural production that involved the cross-subsidisation of cultural, symbolic and economic capital. The Press's financial dependence on the African market was established under British colonial rule but increased exponentially in the decades after independence, as the overseas branches successfully achieved their principal objective to generate profits for the Clarendon Press and the London business.[1] By 1967, 55 per cent of the Press's income came from exports, and including New York and branch publications sales overseas amounted to 75 per cent of OUP's turnover. The overseas market, and particularly the African market, was vital for OUP in the postwar period and was a major factor in OUP becoming the largest publishing house in the United Kingdom by 1970.[2] By then it had a turnover of well over £10 million per annum, of which nearly £1 million was from sales in the East and West Africa branches alone.[3] This turnover rose to over £46 million in 1977, yielding a trading surplus of £6.6 million.[4] Nigeria became the most profitable branch not only in Africa in the 1970s, but worldwide, and at its peak, in 1977, branch sales constituted over 19 per cent of OUP's total income.[5]

In South Africa, the model of cultural production established by OUP initially followed a different trajectory from that of the African colonies. The publishing strategy established by Marquard and Philip in the 1950s and 1960s involved local cultural and academic publishing being funded by commercial educational publishing. However, this model was radically revised in the 1970s as the branch was brought into line with the economic system established for the rest of Africa. The list for the white, liberal academic market was virtually closed as the branch was required to focus on the educational market – particularly the Bantu Education market. OUP evidently realised that serving the white liberal academic market in South Africa threatened to jeopardise its commercial position in the country. At the point that the markets in East and West Africa became more precarious, OUP's expansion into Bantu Education in South Africa paid dividends: by 1979, turnover in the South Africa branch reached £1.2 million.[6]

There were certain modifications in OUP's publishing programme after the end of British colonial rule. OUP's early mission in Africa – epitomised by Parnwell's vision to spread Oxford primers throughout the continent – gave way to a new mission to give Africans a voice and to support local education, scholarship and literature. In the East and West Africa branches after independence, local publishing programmes were instituted to serve the local academic and scholarly communities. Yet, such initiatives were only permitted under the strict proviso that the branches still served to provide profits to London; local publishing was strictly contingent on the profitability of local educational publishing. Indeed, I have suggested that academic and scholarly publishing was also used as a public relations device by OUP managers, to protect their position in the face of allegations of neo-colonialism. The profitability of the African publishing programme was thus achieved without significantly damaging OUP's prestige or, importantly, its charitable status. The adoption of a system of cultural production that was both intellectually and geographically polarised meant that the non-commercial Clarendon Press was isolated and insulated from the African commercial enterprises that helped fund its publishing programme.

The case-study of OUP suggests that British literary publishing in Africa continued to follow colonial models of production and distribution in the postcolonial period. Literary publishing was subsumed within more profitable educational publishing, as established under colonial rule, and was intrinsically affected by the vagaries of this market. The only African literature fostered by OUP in Africa was for the schoolbook market: after independence, although African authors were sought to write literature for schools, this was published in the form of supplementary readers. Indeed, strict hierarchies of literary production were enforced, whereby the branches were permitted to publish literature for a local school market, but 'quality' literature was to be directed to London for Three Crowns.

Part II of this book turns to an examination of the Three Crowns series and, in particular, aims to address a number of questions raised by these preliminary conclusions. For example, the position of the Three Crowns series is explored in relation to the models of cultural production established by OUP. In particular, it studies how the hierarchies of literary production instituted by OUP affected the development of the series and examines what happened when radical literature was subsumed in traditional, colonial-style systems of literary production and consumption. It also considers the contradictions and ambiguities that resulted from publishing anti-apartheid literature in Three Crowns alongside a programme of Bantu Education publishing in South Africa. Part II questions, in essence, what role Three Crowns played within OUP's UK-based 'cultural' enterprise and its African 'commercial' enterprise, and assesses how these conflicting imperatives were reconciled in the series.

PART II
The Three Crowns Series, 1962–76

5
The History of Three Crowns

Introduction

Rex Collings, an editor in OUP's London business, discovered the plays of Wole Soyinka in July 1962. He set about trying to publish them, and attempted to persuade his manager that *The Lion and the Jewel* and *A Dance of the Forests* should be included in the Three Crowns series, an eclectic series of books about Africa that had recently been established by OUP. He described *The Lion and the Jewel*:

> As good English it should provide a prescribable text for examinations above school certificate. This does not really matter and is but an excuse for the play is good – so good that we ought to publish it. Not least of its merits being that it is so beautifully simple in speech as in plot, in setting as in execution. Produced over here – with an all African cast – it would be a wow.[1]

His manager in the Overseas Editorial department, David Neale, was against the idea, and suggested that this kind of publishing might be best left to the African branches.[2] Collings wrote an exasperated response: 'To put it quite bluntly – I want to publish the two Soyinka plays and the Easmon play. If I had a budget and a reasonable amount of independent choice I should certainly publish these.' He argued that Soyinka would certainly be suited for sixth-form school prescription, for a university and a general market in Africa, and emphasised the potential political benefits of this new venture:

> I am convinced also that there is still a place for us in African publishing if we can plainly show that we are not in fact only interested in selling enormous quantities of primary schoolbooks by expatriate authors. This is quite commonly felt and believed although it is not altogether true in fact. Politically therefore it is also important that we should publish. If we don't, I think we will have missed the bus.[3]

His arguments were evidently persuasive, as Neale gave him permission to begin acquiring African writing for the Three Crowns series. He started with the publication of the two Soyinka plays in 1963, and these were followed by further plays by Soyinka: *The Road* in 1965, *Kongi's Harvest* in 1967 and *Three Short Plays* in 1969. Three Crowns came to be dominated by African literature in English, and although the majority of works were drama, there were also poetry collections and short stories. For OUP, this was a significant departure from its general pattern of commissioning and writing texts in the UK for the African educational market.

This history of the Three Crowns series focuses on two issues that first emerged in this correspondence between Collings and Neale, and which were to remain contentious throughout the series history. Firstly, I explore how Three Crowns balanced cultural and economic capital. One of the questions raised in this initial correspondence was whether OUP should make a financial investment in African literature or whether it needed to be immediately profitable for publication to proceed. Forswearing the profit motive, Collings argued that OUP should publish Soyinka simply because the plays constituted good literature. However, Neale insisted that the literature should be profitable, and required solid evidence that Soyinka's plays would be 'prescribable' as set texts in African schools. The correspondence also indicates Collings's disquiet about OUP's profitable publishing in Africa, and his belief that cultural investment should serve to counterbalance this commercial gain. This argument was often repeated over the next 14 years, and proved to be vital in securing the survival of the series.

Secondly, I aim in this chapter to analyse what the history of Three Crowns reveals about the institutional structure of postcolonial African literary publishing. Neale's proposal that African literature should be published in Africa in the branches instead of London was a foretaste of a long debate about not only where African literature should be published, but also on how such literature should be perceived. Bourdieu describes the cultural field as 'the site of the struggles for the monopoly of the power to consecrate, in which the value of works of art and belief in that value are continuously generated'.[4] This chapter aims to trace the sequence of disputes that took place between London and the African branches over the editorial control of the series, which indicates how OUP negotiated and resolved struggles over the 'power to consecrate' African literature.

New departure: list building under Rex Collings, 1962–65

Three Crowns was initially a series specialising in African history, politics and development, and its authors were mainly British expatriates based in Africa. Its name was derived from the three crowns on Oxford University's coat of arms, which had appeared on OUP publications since the seventeeth century. The series was first established in 1961 by David Neale, and remained under his overall management until 1966. Rex Collings was the series editor from 1962 to 1965, and was responsible for developing the list, although Neale had to approve all new acquisitions.

Collings considered that the acquisition of Soyinka signified a change of direction for OUP, as he explained in a letter to Tani Solaru, the branch manager in Ibadan, in July 1962:

> In many respects this is a new departure ... and I think it is an extremely worthwhile departure too. But it is a new departure for this side of the Press, and it is so satisfactory that the quality of these plays is so exceptionally high – the difficulty is to find plays of an equally high standard to go with them.[5]

Collings was then given a degree of freedom and autonomy to build the list and try to find plays to accompany Soyinka's. Before working on Three Crowns, he had worked in the Nairobi office of OUP, with Charles Richards, and his interest in publishing African literature stemmed from this experience. Originally a Penguin editor, Collings was more familiar with trade publishing and paperback publishing than many of his OUP colleagues, a point picked up by James Currey:

> Rex Collings was the publisher at Oxford University Press who drove the concept of this new paperback series through against doubting colleagues. It was significant that he had his publishing apprenticeship at Penguin. He conceived of Three Crowns as a 'Penguin' series of African and third-world writing which would include 'Pelican'-type titles, such as *Seven African Writers* by Gerald Moore.[6]

Rex Collings's original vision was that Three Crowns should embrace all categories of African literature, including fiction, but this ran counter to OUP's publishing policy, which stated that the Press should not become the publisher of 'imaginative literature', and which issued an embargo on fiction publishing for the London branch. Collings wrote to Neale in July 1962, citing examples where the OUP had published novels, poetry and drama (including the World's Classics and The Oxford Library of Italian Classics), and claiming that there was pressure from the African branches to move into the publication of fiction. However, Three Crowns was given approval only to publish drama and poetry, and occasionally short stories, but not novels.[7]

The period 1962 to 1965 witnessed the main development and consolidation of the list, in which Collings and Neale published a total of 19 Africa-related titles for the series, including African literary criticism and anthologies (such as Gerald Moore's *Seven African Writers*, 1962 and Clive Wake's *Anthology of African and Malagasy Verse*, 1965), travel writing about

Africa (for example, Derek Hollingworth's *They Came to Mauritius* and Richard Pankhurst's *Travellers in Ethiopia*, both published in 1965), as well as general non-fiction titles about political issues in the continent (such as Benson's *Chief Albert Lutuli* published in 1963, G. B. Masefield's *Famine: Its Prevention and Relief* in 1963, and Denis Payne's *African Independence and Christian Freedom* in 1965). The main focus of the list was African drama, poetry and short stories, which constituted 12 of the 19 titles published in this period. The majority of these texts were by West African writers: Soyinka's *The Lion and the Jewel* and *A Dance of the Forests* (1963) and *Five Plays* (1964), de Graft's *Sons and Daughters* (1964), Easmon's *Dear Parent and Ogre* (1964), Clark's *Three Plays* (1964), Senghor's *Prose and Poetry* (1965), Egbuna's *The Anthill* (1965), Nicol's *The Truly Married Woman and Other Stories* (1965). From South Africa there was Nkosi's *The Rhythm of Violence* (1964), from Uganda, Kimenye's *Kalasanda* (1965) and from Ethiopia Tsegeye Gabre-Medhin's *Oda-Oak Oracle* (1965).

The marketplace for Three Crowns

Collings described the market for Three Crowns books as the consumer, or trade, market, predominantly based in Africa but also in the UK and the USA. At the outset, the series was sold through bookshops in the UK and marketed internationally, through the other OUP branches. A letter was sent promoting the series to the managers of the OUP branches in Toronto, New York and Melbourne: 'Even though the series is planned primarily for Africa, some original works in it are likely to be of interest elsewhere, with the growing world-wide interest in all African matters.'[8] On the title information sheets, Collings classified Three Crowns books as adult books, rather than as educational books, and he attempted to reach an international literary market by seeking reviews in UK journals and newspapers. Gail Low argues that Three Crowns was initially a metropolitan literary series, and only after 1965 changes of policy led it to become an African educational series, but sales records in the archive provide no evidence of success in this area.[9] Despite Collings's undoubted ambitions and efforts for the literature to reach a trade market, the UK market remained a minor market for Three Crowns books. From 1965 to 1969 on average only 15 per cent of Soyinka's total sales were to the UK, with similar percentage UK sales for its other African authors (21 per cent of Nkosi's play; 15 per cent of Easmon's; 11 per cent of de Graft, and 21 per cent of Egbuna's *The Anthill*).[10] The US market was even slower to develop, but by 1971, OUP New York bought over 28 per cent of Three Crowns titles.[11] There are parallels here with the African Writers Series, which had a similar ratio of sales to Africa and to Europe and America. Robert Fraser and Nourdin Bejjit note that at least 80 per cent of the total sales of books in the series were to Africa, whereas only approximately 10 per cent of the total sales were to Britain and 10 per cent to the United States.[12]

With regard to the African market, Collings originally expected Three Crowns books to be targeted at the general adult sector, describing the series as a 'loosely organised general series that would provide reading material on all kinds of subjects for the educated African adult'.[13] In his first memo about the Three Crowns series, he defined the African adult literary market he envisaged for the literature: 'there seems to be an interest in plays and drama in literate African circles, and there is certainly an interest in local writing'. He doubted that the plays would 'become prescribed reading in the schools or colleges', due to the fact that 'some schools might feel (wrongly I think) that the subject matter in general and some incidents in particular might not be suitable for young minds'. He concluded that: 'We should then be showing that we are providing a series of cheap paper backs for the African market that contains original imaginative work by Africans themselves.'[14] The 1964 promotional leaflet for Three Crowns explained that: 'This series arose out of the demand from Africa for inexpensive books other than the purely educational ones: books that could be read for leisure and enjoyment as well as for instruction and information; for general knowledge as well as particular knowledge.'[15] Collings did not expect high sales for the books: he originally anticipated a limited print-run for books in the series of between 3000 and 5000 copies. However, the intention to target the books to the African literary marketplace was soon abandoned, as commercial pressures on the series increased.[16]

The editors soon realised that the major market for Three Crowns books was not adult readers but the African school market, which constituted between 80 to 90 per cent of the total book market in East and West Africa in this period.[17] The selection of texts became increasingly dependent on their assignment for examinations in African schools. Currey considered that the examination boards in Africa were 'immensely important and fundamentally constructive' in their support of African literature: although there were many expatriates on the boards, he noted their interest in acquiring African literature for set texts.[18] Early on in the history of the series, a major factor affecting acquisition decisions was whether or not the examination boards planned to prescribe a book. A letter of 13 March 1963 from the West African Exams Council in Ghana to Neal Burton in the Ghana branch advised that if OUP published it in time, Joe de Graft's *Sons and Daughters* would be prescribed for the school certificate exam.[19] OUP replied one week later that they would go ahead with the publication in Three Crowns.

Thus, a dual-publishing system was soon in operation for Three Crowns, in which the editors sought to accrue symbolic capital for the authors and the series through publication for an international literary market, whilst simultaneously accruing economic capital through publication for the established African educational market.[20] The remainder of this chapter considers how Three Crowns struggled to satisfy these two conflicting imperatives.[21]

Series in crisis: Three Crowns under James Currey, 1965–67

Rex Collings suddenly left the Press to go to Methuen in July 1965, taking Soyinka with him.[22] According to Currey, Collings felt constrained by OUP: he was restricted in terms of the amount of his time he could devote to Three Crowns, his main job being the popularisation of academic texts for trade outlets in the UK. He was also frustrated by his inability to get the Press's embargo on fiction publishing lifted, as none of his colleagues wished to challenge the Delegates.[23] After working for Methuen for a short period, Collings established his own publishing company, Rex Collings Ltd, in 1969, which specialised in publishing for the African market.

With the departure of Collings, the series suffered its first major crisis. It fell into the hands of Anthony Toyne, manager of the Tutorial Books department, who insisted that the series was an educational series and stipulated, 'We are reluctant to include further creative writing unless it seems capable of adoption by teachers and examiners.'[24] Under his management, Three Crowns was brought into line with the rest of the African educational publishing programme.[25] All new acquisitions had to demonstrate a guaranteed schoolbook market; and he stipulated that creative writing should only be included if 'it seems capable of adoption by teachers and examiners'.[26] Two years later, the assistant publisher, Philip Chester, wrote of Three Crowns books, 'The few which have sold have done so because they have been "prescribed" as textbooks.'[27]

Currey was appointed series editor when Collings left in 1965. He had previously worked in the Cape Town branch, and in his spare time assisted Randolph Vigne with the South African literary journal *The New African*. He describes how Collings arranged for him to take over Three Crowns on his departure:

> Rex Collings was a crucial influence in my own publishing apprenticeship. He arranged that I should, while travelling back through Africa in 1962 on leave from Oxford University Press in Cape Town, meet the writers in heady Lagos and Ibadan. When he went to Methuen he managed to make sure that I could take over Three Crowns and all his other pioneering general academic publishing on Africa.[28]

Currey's editorship of the literary list lasted for 18 months and during this unsettled period only four literary titles were published, all of which had been previously acquired by Collings: Clark's *Ozidi* (1966), Kimenye's *Kalasanda Revisited* (1966), Soyinka's *Kongi's Harvest* (1967) and *The Tree Climber* by the Egyptian writer Tewfik Al Hakim (1966). These were joined by two works of criticism by Anthony Brench in 1967: *The Novelists' Inheritance* and *Writing in French from Senegal to Cameroon*. Currey claimed that there was little managerial support for Three Crowns at this time, and that the series was being stalled by the Press. The series was only a small proportion of his total editorial responsibilities, and he felt that he had to be surreptitious about his interest in African literature. Currey then left for Heinemann Educational in April 1967, where he became editor-in-charge of the African Writers Series. He was immediately struck by the contrasting enthusiasm there for African literature, particularly on the part of Alan Hill, Van Milne and Keith Sambrook.[29]

In 1968, the decision was made to split the Three Crowns series in two. It was resolved that Toyne should retain the education section (that is, literary criticism, biographies, travel writing and anthologies) in the Tutorial Books department, and the creative literature (that is, drama, poetry and short stories) was handed over to Jon Stallworthy,[30] editor of the Oxford Poetry list, under the management of John Bell in the House Books department (the area of OUP dealing with general publishing). Toyne, in fact, failed to develop the non-fiction section and no new acquisitions were made.

The survival of Three Crowns during this uncertain period was mainly due to pressure from the African branches. Charles Lewis in particular campaigned for the continuation of Three Crowns, as branch manager in Nairobi, urging that it should be continued.[31] At branch level there was an awareness of the valuable public relations served by the series, as expressed in the 1966 strategy document: 'The Three Crowns books in particular do give an impression that the OUP is not just publishing in the branch areas for what it can get out of them in the way of large sales of schoolbooks.'[32] The same report refers to the publicity value of African literary publishing gained by their competitors: 'Longmans, for one, have decided that this has been valuable publicity for us and are going into paperback publication of African authors in competition with us and with Heinemann.'[33] Looking back, Currey also acknowledges the kudos and competitive advantages secured for Heinemann through the African Writers Series, suggesting that it became 'an exploitative part of Heinemann's strategy in Africa. ... It was a key factor in enabling Heinemann to seize educational contracts from under the noses of established companies with a far longer presence than upstart Heinemann.'[34] African literary publishing thus served an important public relations function at the branch level, by promoting OUP in Africa as an investor in culture.

Caution and constraints: Three Crowns under Stallworthy, 1967–71

Jon Stallworthy took over responsibility for Three Crowns for the four years from 1967 to 1971. A poet himself, from New Zealand, he made efforts to revive Three Crowns and to transform it from a specifically African list to a 'Commonwealth literature' list, representing literature from various OUP branches. 'Commonwealth literature' at this time was developing institutionally as a sub-discipline within English literature, as demonstrated by the establishment of the *Journal of Commonwealth Studies* in 1965. In terms of Indian writing, Gurcharan Das's *Larins Sahib* and Raja Rao's *The Cow of the Barricade* were included in Three Crowns on the request of the Bombay branch, but the Indian market was acknowledged to be problematic. In the case of *Larins Sahib*, Stallworthy had to work hard to get the text accepted for the series. It was felt that the sales in the India branches would not warrant the large print-run typical of the Three Crowns titles and, as a result, the print-run was reduced from the usual 10,000 down to 2500.[35] Only a handful of Three Crowns titles were published during Stallworthy's three years as editor, including one work of Caribbean literary criticism, *The Island in Between* by Louis James, *The Gods are Not to Blame* by the Nigerian Ola Rotimi, and a few works by existing Three Crowns authors: *Three Short Plays* by Soyinka (1969 but acquired earlier), *Through a Film Darkly* by de Graft (1970) and *Daughters of the Sun* by Egbuna (1970). An important development for the series was Stallworthy's interest in South African writing. He was acting branch manager in Cape Town from 1969 to 1970, and was keen for the list to include more South African, anti-apartheid literature.[36] He acquired Mtshali's poetry volume *Sounds of a Cowhide Drum* (1972), as well as Fugard's plays: *People Are Living There, The Blood Knot, Hello and Goodbye* and *Boesman and Lena*.

However, Three Crowns was particularly constrained by directives from the Delegates in this period. In particular, the standing instruction from the OUP Delegates in 1969 repeated the embargo on fiction publishing: 'no new fiction for adults is to be published, unless it has an educational market'.[37] In 1970 the Waldock Report made recommendations for establishing the division of responsibility between the London office and the overseas branches. The report recommended that the Clarendon Press should be supported by the commercial enterprise of London and the overseas branches, and that stringent controls were to be placed on these publishing programmes. It advised that the branches should 'publish books within certain defined fields and markets on a profit-making basis' and should 'engage in publishing within wide limits', but the report reiterated that 'current fiction' should be excluded as a genre.[38] These recommendations informed future OUP policy, but the new constraints were particularly resented in the African branches. Bill Mitchell in Ibadan and Charles Lewis in Nairobi challenged this policy of the Press and urged a reconsideration of the Delegates' standing instruction and argued for the publication of novels by African writers.[39] Lewis, for example, argued that 'Longmans and Heinemann have far too long monopolised this area.'[40]

Stallworthy registered his frustration at the lack of investment in the series by OUP: 'We are not achieving our aims and will never get a satisfactory return in terms of money or prestige unless we are prepared to invest a good deal more money in the series than we are at present.'[41] He advocated as a result that the series should be either discontinued or invested in to a greater degree. John Brown, the London Publisher, expressed his own concerns about Three Crowns: 'I am anxious about this series. I don't think we have the right formula.'[42] He instructed that no more commitments should be made until a further review was carried out.

Calculating profit: Three Crowns review, 1971

The review of Three Crowns was conducted during the Branch Managers' Conference held in London in March 1971. The subsequent policy adopted for Three Crowns brought many issues to a head, and indicated the financial expectations that were imposed on the series. In the review document it was calculated that the series was running at a loss, and was recorded as £3092 in debit.[43] Sales figures to 1 January 1971 indicated that Soyinka's books were the most successful on the list, generating an overall profit to London of £1945, with average total sales of nearly 15,000 copies of each title. However, the remaining titles in Three Crowns during this period precipitated an overall loss of £5035, with average total sales of only 3259 copies per title. Three Crowns was branded a financial liability.

The accounting methods in place made it extremely difficult for titles in Three Crowns to demonstrate a profit.[44] Each book was sold to the African branches at the educational discount of nearly 42 per cent of the net price, and a 33.3 per cent discount to other branches and the home trade. The African branches were the main purchasers of the texts,[45] and they obtained a profit from the books in their own market, but this was not factored into the calculations. As such, it appeared that the series was running at a loss, despite generating profits to OUP as a whole. Even titles that had sold well failed to make a profit for London General Books. Thus, by 1971, Soyinka's *The Road* had sold 11,972 copies but generated a loss to London of £224, and his *Three Short Plays* sold 13,939 copies and generated a loss of £272. Similarly, Clark's *Three Plays* sold 7821 copies and generated a loss of £94, while Egbuna's *The Anthill* sold 4279 copies of its 5000 total print-run but still managed to achieve a loss of £45. The fact that London appeared to be subsidising the branches for Three Crowns was resented by those involved with the series. Preparing for the series review in 1971, Stallworthy wrote to his manager, John Bell: 'We in London are publishing for the Branches, and ... the prestige the series brings OUP is of greater value to the Branches than the Centre.'[46]

When the accumulated credit and debit figures were circulated, Philip Chester, the assistant publisher, noted that the series was being unfairly judged by different criteria in relation to other 'prestige' series, such as the World's Classics: 'Surely, it is *always* the few honourable best-selling titles in a list which pay for the rest.' He commented on the relatively high sales for the majority of Three Crowns titles compared with this series. The annual sale of the 20 most recently published World's Classics texts in 1971 was only 500, against Three Crowns average annual sales of 2200 per book.[47] These 20 books included reprints of European canonical works, by Charlotte Brontë, Molière, Tolstoy, Trollope, Voltaire and Conrad. It is also interesting to compare Three Crowns sales with the Oxford Paperback series, which was published by OUP in London for the UK general and tertiary educational market. Canonical English literature reprinted in the Oxford Paperback series achieved average annual sales that were much lower than the sales of Soyinka. For example, according to the trading account figures of 1970, the Oxford Paperback Milton achieved annual sales of 3009 copies, the Blake edition achieved 3221 sales and Wordsworth's *Poetical Works* achieved 3687 copies.[48] However, in the same year, 18,421 copies of Soyinka's *The Lion and the Jewel* were sold.[49] Original drama from African authors was evidently expected by OUP to yield a similar or higher volume of sales to that of reprinted literature by major European authors.

Despite concerns about its profitability, Three Crowns survived once again because of pressure from the African branches. The decision made at the conference was that 'efforts should be made to continue the series'.[50] John Bell issued proposals to revive and revamp Three Crowns, outlined in a letter to the branches in 1971. The restrictions on fiction publishing were finally lifted and the imprint's remit was broadened to encompass all literature. A new cover and typographic design by Ruari McLean were commissioned for the series. However, these new proposals for a relaunched series provoked a major attack on the editorial policy of the series from the African branches.

Metropolitan control

From the outset, Three Crowns was based in London under the management of British editors. A metropolitan editorial policy was regarded by the series managers as essential for this process of legitimising African literature. Manuscripts were selected exclusively by British editors, academics, educators and education specialists. The Three Crowns policy was first explained in the review document of 1966 entitled 'Towards a Definition of Policy':

> London may well be the best place for central control. ... The basic problem is that London is still the best publishing centre for the whole of Africa ... attitudes being what they are, books published in London will probably sell better overall than ones published in a branch.[51]

In 1969, there were rumblings of discontent about the British-based gatekeeping policy in Three Crowns. Charles Lewis, in particular, urged that Jonathan Kariara, the Kenyan literary editor in the Eastern Africa branch, should have a greater role in the acquisition of texts for Three Crowns. His suggestion was promptly rejected by John Bell.[52]

Bell's letter of October 1971 set out a centralised editorial policy for Three Crowns. He proposed that 'all work in the field of creative writing that a Branch thinks worthy of publication should first be sent to Ely House for the Three Crowns editor to read. In consultation with the Branch he will decide whether or not the work should appear in Three Crowns.'[53] This letter unleashed a swift and hostile response. Roger Houghton, the new manager of the Eastern Africa branch, retorted: 'Are we now to admit to our local authors in this very sensitive field that the final judgement of their scripts rests with London?'[54]

Bell proposed the appointment of an advisory editor in the person of Arthur Ravenscroft, the South African founder editor of the *Journal of Commonwealth Literature*, who was based in the School of English at Leeds University.[55] The editorial manager in Ibadan, Bill Mitchell, argued that Nigerians would not be impressed by this appointment:

> We are a little puzzled by the suggestion to appoint an outside editor. It is difficult to imagine the function he will fulfil. We surely don't need an outside arbiter to take editorial decisions about inclusion or non-inclusion of script in the series? We cannot be thinking that his Anglo-Saxon name appearing on the books will add marketing appeal – such a device would be wholly counter-productive in the West African market.

Mitchell also raised concerns about the 'Commonwealth literature' concept: 'We have some reservations about the Three Crowns concept ... in not many years time it may be as bizarre to lump "Commonwealth" authors together into special series as it would today be to publish Irish and Australian writing within special series.'[56] Despite the dissent from the branches, the policy was reiterated by Bell. He conceded that branches would continue to exercise autonomy over their own literary publishing programmes, but confirmed the London-centred editorial policy.[57]

Thus, the model of postcolonial literary production that was designed in OUP was highly stratified. While the African branches were permitted autonomy over their own literary publishing for the local market, they were refused any decision-making role in the construction of this new canon of African writing. It is interesting to compare this policy with that of the African Writers Series, which secured Achebe as chief editorial advisor from the start of the series in 1962. In an interview, Currey described how Achebe would visit the Nairobi branch about twice a year in this capacity. However, Achebe was not paid a fixed salary by Heinemann, but was instead paid a fee for his work. Editors would evidently present new manuscripts on a Wednesday morning, and present outside opinion about them, and at the meetings, Currey noted, 'Hill always asked "and what does Achebe think of this?", and if he was not there, then the manuscript needed other strong support.' The manuscripts arrived from a variety of sources – they were not all filtered through Achebe – but he vetted the first 40 titles of the series. However, communication with him was more difficult during the Nigerian civil war, when he was actively fundraising for Biafra.[58] Thus, Heinemann relied on their foremost African writer as a high-profile advisor of their series, yet, fundamentally, Heinemann's policy paralleled that of OUP: the final editorial decision was made in London by British editors.

Decentralisation and closure: Three Crowns under Ron Heapy, 1971–76

Ron Heapy became editor of Three Crowns in 1971 following Stallworthy's departure from OUP and remained in that position until 1976. Despite Bell's rhetoric about increased commitment to the series, many of the same problems continued. Heapy was, again, only released to work on the series for one day a week and the acquisition policy for the series continued to be guarded. Heapy drew up ambitious plans for the series with Arthur Ravenscroft, now editorial advisor for Three Crowns. A memo of 1972 listed 19 new projects, which aimed to create a broad Commonwealth literature list. However, of these proposed titles only four came to fruition, and the contract with Ravenscroft was terminated in June 1973.[59] *Hello and Goodbye* and *Boesman and Lena* by Fugard were published in 1973, as well as Arnold Apple's autobiography, *Son of Guyana*. Also, at the recommendation of the Delhi office, Heapy took on the publication of *The Policeman and the Rose* by Raja Rao, but he proved to be a difficult author, leading Heapy to write to the Delhi office: 'the author is hunting me quite ruthlessly and I am beginning to feel oppressed'.[60] In the end the manuscript was passed back to the Delhi office, where it was published in 1978. Ravenscroft and Heapy's plans to publish the others lay dormant: Nkosi's 'Martin Luther King', Walije Gondwe's 'Will the African Flowers Bloom', Nwosu's 'Stories of Lagos' and Welcome Msomi's 'Umabatha', along with various critical works, were all abandoned, remaining unpublished to this day. Ravenscroft complained bitterly about the cautious editorial policy in 1972. He lamented the fact that Wilson Harris had withdrawn his poetry 'Eternity to Season' from OUP: '[The] system of controls and counter checks ... must deprive Three Crowns of the keen edge of direction that the series needs, with consequent delays in decision making and a tendency towards "metropolitisation"(!) and uniformity in the flavour of what is ultimately published.'[61]

There was some slackening of the centralised control of the series during this period, in practice if not in theory. Heapy exercised a policy he refers to as 'guerrilla publishing' by encouraging the branches to use the Three Crowns imprint for texts that they published themselves. These texts were published as part of the Three Crowns series only for the branch market, although this was never an officially endorsed policy.[62] Thus, in Ibadan new titles were acquired specifically for the Nigerian market under the Three

Crowns imprint, initially under the editorial control of David Attwooll. These included three plays by Rotimi: *Kurumni* (1971), *Ovonramwen Nogbaisi* (1974) and *Our Husband Has Gone Mad Again* (1977). Soyinka's *Madmen and Specialists* (1971) was also licensed from Methuen exclusively for the Nigerian market and was published in Three Crowns.[63] Permission was also given for titles to be reprinted in the branches, but this made the series increasingly unviable, as Ron Heapy registered in his letter to Ibadan:

> I am getting worried that we are going to be left with the non-saleable rump of Three Crowns here. I seem to have arrived with a collection of stuff that is out of church jumble sales, and I am giving away the more profitable items like Oxfam. ... Meanwhile Three Crowns here is going to generate no money and suspicious glances are being cast at me.[64]

The uncertainty about the series was exacerbated by the decision to close the London offices of OUP and to move personnel to Walton Street in Oxford. Three Crowns moved with Ron Heapy into the Education department in Oxford.[65] Yet, Heapy was even more constrained than ever in the aftermath of this move, and wrote in a memo to the Addis Ababa office: 'As you may have heard, the place is in a state of financial crisis, that is, there is now [sic] money. I am asked to cut back on forthcoming books, and in particular I am asked to cut back on Three Crowns.'[66]

The decision was finally made in April 1976 to close Three Crowns as a British-based list. The reasons given were that it was considered to be insufficiently profitable for the educational division and too much of a 'vehicle for creative writing in Branch areas' for Division 2.[67] The branches were allowed to continue using the Three Crowns name and logo if required for their literary publishing, and some exercised that option. The brand name was used for Ibadan's drama publications in 1976, and after the forced divestment of OUP in Nigeria in 1977 Three Crowns lived on, for a short time, in the newly formed University Press. The Delhi branch published 17 titles in the New Poetry in India series from 1976 to 1986.[68] This was the most successful new manifestation of the Three Crowns series. While this handover of Three Crowns to the branches was interpreted by Heapy as a rightful end to UK control of the series, and as an example of greater federalism in the OUP empire, essentially this signified the end of any commitment to publishing African literature for an international market. The list was dissipated and the series identity lost.

The retreat from African literature

In closing its African literary publishing list in 1976 OUP was a forerunner of other British publishers. As the schoolbook markets collapsed firstly in East Africa, and thereafter in West Africa, British publishers rapidly withdrew.

In 1982, the *Journal of Commonwealth Literature* noted of East Africa, 'Since 1978 this region's literary output has been diminishing at a considerable rate, particularly in the production of works in English. Each year, less and less gets produced, especially in poetry, drama and criticism. This state of affairs could be attributed to economic and financial constraints ... this is especially true of commercial publishers.'[69] Longman published its last two titles in the Drumbeat series in 1985, and Heinemann's African Writers Series' rate of acquisitions contracted dramatically after 1981, after which it functioned mainly by its backlist.[70] Bernth Lindfors criticised British publishers as fair-weather investors in West African literature:

> One is tempted to conclude ... that the publication of West African literature in English in the 1980s has been conditioned greatly by economic factors. Western publishers, having engaged in a 'scramble for Africa' at a time when opening up new literary territories was quite profitable, now are bent on a 'scam from Africa' that will leave the remaining unexploited resources ... to native companies. Writers are thus at the mercy of unfavourable economic forces, one pushing a foreign industry into decline, the other hindering an indigenous industry from taking off.[71]

Chakava described a situation in Kenya in the late 1980s in which there was no real interest amongst publishers in venturing into the fiction and general publishing market. The locally incorporated Heinemann Kenya was, he wrote, the only publisher in the country to launch a broad publishing programme in the mid-1970s, including the publication of popular fiction in the Spear Books series, and fiction in other African languages. He claimed that no single work of literature came out of Kenya in the 1980s.[72] With the closure of the Nigerian Foreign Exchange market in April 1982 and the collapse of most other African economies in that decade, the British withdrawal from literary publishing was complete. From the 1990s, publishing in Africa was mainly in the hands of local publishers or multinationals that had been largely localised.

Conclusion

Rex Collings had high hopes that Three Crowns would offer a departure from OUP's publishing strategy in Africa. He aimed to promote the books to an international market – thus reversing the usual flow of OUP books from Europe to Africa – and to cross-invest profits from educational publishing into the publication of literature for an adult literary market in Africa. However, Three Crowns was rapidly absorbed into the colonial publishing system that Collings had sought to challenge. Editorial control was centralised in London and a hierarchical literary policy was devised, whereby 'high-brow' African literature was selected and published from the centre, but popular, educational or local-language literature was published by the branches. British control over the elite African literature was contested by editors and managers in the regional branches, but the efforts of the Eastern Africa branch to secure African writers' involvement and local editorial participation in Three Crowns were firmly resisted by OUP managers. Yet, the series history also demonstrates how crucial the African branches were to the survival of the series. The argument that Collings first used to persuade his manager to embark upon African literary publishing was used repeatedly by branch managers and editors to secure the future of the series. By publishing African literature for an international market, Three Crowns provided a conspicuous exception to the normal pattern of producing profitable schoolbooks for a mass market in Africa. This high-profile literary investment was employed by the branches as important publicity – it was a means of allaying charges of 'neo-colonialism' – and Three Crowns was widely regarded as an emblem of OUP's liberal publishing policy in the continent.[73]

However, there were serious limitations to this publicised cultural investment. Books in the series were subjected to constant financial scrutiny, although the accounting methods in place made financial success virtually impossible to achieve. There were markedly different commercial expectations applied to Three Crowns than to the comparable London-based literary series, the World's Classics Series. Investment in the World's Classics Series was evidently acceptable to OUP; the symbolic capital accrued by European canonical literature, for a UK market, was valued more highly by OUP than that accrued by African literature for an African educational market. As a result, the majority of books on the Three Crowns list failed to generate the profits that were demanded, and the series was branded a liability.

The history of Three Crowns directly challenges the liberal arguments that literary publishing served as compensation for Western monopolisation of the African book trade.[74] Although Three Crowns was employed by OUP for public relations purposes, this series history demonstrates that investment in African literature remained marginal; African literature was expected to yield profits in line with the rest of OUP's Africa publishing programme.

6
Judging African Literature

> The power to narrate, or to block other narratives from forming and emerging, is very important to culture and imperialism, and constitutes one of the main connections between them.
>
> – Edward W. Said, *Culture and Imperialism*, p. xiii

Introduction

Shortly after being appointed Three Crowns editor, Collings wrote a letter to Ivor Wilkes at the University of Ghana, expressing his uncertainty about his new role:

> Our difficulty is that here in London we can only judge the plays from within the western tradition. The plays may be written in English, good English, and may follow the conventional western pattern of acts and scenes but the content, the ethos seems to be quite different. Who then can we turn to for help? Firstly to tell us what the tradition is within which they are written and secondly to advise us whether these plays are 'good' or 'bad' within that tradition. We obviously have to take the decision whether or not to publish but we need help and guidance to do so. ... The problem I find is fascinating, but at the moment I am floundering about like a non-swimmer in the deep end.[1]

This chapter examines how Collings and his successors grappled with the creation of a new African literary list. It charts the editorial deliberations over the selection criteria for the series, and examines how the aesthetic and commercial value of the texts was judged. OUP was one of the earliest publishers involved in the formation of African literature as a publishing category. This study identifies the institutional framework around the production of literature in this series, in order to gain an understanding of the publisher's interventions in African postcolonial writing.

The discussion here focuses on the selection of African literature, and begins with the list-building process, by which the editors established the identity of the series and its future direction. The acquisition process is broken down into two parts: firstly, the means by which authors were accepted into the series, and, secondly, the aesthetic and commercial judgement of the manuscript. At each of these stages, exemplary case-studies have been used to gain insights into the contested terrain of African literature at this time, and reveal how African literature was being defined by British publishers. For the list-building stage, a case-study of Léopold Sédar Senghor is considered; and for the acquisition process, a case-study of Raymond Sarif Easmon is used. Finally, the judging of literary and commercial value is explored with reference to the case-study of John Pepper Clark.

List-building

Recent scholarship has focused attention on how British publishers influenced the production of a canon of African literature. For example, Bernth Lindfors has demonstrated the dominance of literature published by multinational publishers – and particularly the African Writers Series – in African university literary department reading lists.[2] According to Phaswane Mpe, this dominance of the African Writers Series as *the* canon of African literature furthered the illusion of homogeneity in African literature and led to a privileging of West African literature over the literature of other regions.[3] In addition, Loretta Stec notes, in her analysis of the constitution of Heinemann's canon, there was a strong bias towards literature written in English and by male writers.[4] Although the African Writers Series dominated the process of African literary canon formation, OUP was simultaneously involved in this process, and it is enlightening to explore how this process was carried out.

The series served to group disparate African writers under a single umbrella category, and to promote a concept of African literature as a homogeneous entity. Chidi Amuta criticises such categorisation: 'In this totalising fixation with Africa as a vast homeland of the exotic, the linguistic, ethnic and class heterogeneity of Africa is conveniently forgotten.'[5] However, in publishing terms, the creation of a genre is an important marketing strategy. In this case, it served as a means of gathering together writers who had little in common except their continent of origin.[6] The definition of 'genre' in publishing terminology is subtly different from its definition in literary studies, in which it describes broad categories of literary composition. Genres of literature are created by publishers as a means of categorising and ordering the book market; as Claire Squires writes, 'the prolific and diverse nature of the marketplace demands it; the sheer number of individual product lines calls out for some sort of taxonomy'.[7] How, then, did OUP contribute to the definition of 'African literature' as a new publishing genre?

Three Crowns editors sought from the beginning to publish the critical texts that provided the apparatus for classifying and theorising African literature. The first book in Three Crowns was Gerald Moore's *Seven African Writers*, published in 1962. Collings developed this section of the list by acquiring Clive Wake's *An Anthology of African and Malagasy Poetry in French* (1965), Anthony Brench's *The Novelists' Inheritance in French Africa* (1967) and his parallel anthology published in the same year, *Writing in French from Senegal to Cameroon*.

Three Crowns had a strong bias towards West African literature, with seven of the 14 series authors coming from this region. One explanation might be that Soyinka's reputation in Nigeria attracted several other playwrights from the region to the series. In addition, the most prolific literary activity was taking place in West Africa in the 1960s, whereas East Africa was described as suffering a 'literary drought' in the late 1960s, with several publishers competing for a limited number of new manuscripts.[8] Collings attempted to develop a more regionally balanced list, and was prepared to make compromises to achieve it. For example, regarding Gabre-Medhin's playscript 'Oda-Oak Oracle', Collings wrote to Charles Lewis in Nairobi: 'The play is not outstandingly brilliant, but an adviser thinks that it is worth publishing. It will, at least, give us an Ethiopian author and an Eastern African play.'[9] He then also tried to balance the list with additional acquisitions of authors from Uganda, Egypt and South Africa. However, after Collings's departure from OUP, there is evidence of several manuscripts and proposals from East Africa being put forward by Charles Lewis and Jonathan Kariara, but being specifically rejected for Three Crowns and considered 'not quite good enough'.[10]

The manuscripts for Three Crowns were expected to be written in 'good English'. Only two texts in the series were English translations: Senghor's *Prose and Poetry*, which was translated from French, and Tewfik Al-Hakim's *The Tree Climber*, which was translated from Arabic. Collings's editorial report of 1963 quotes the *Times Literary Supplement* article of 10 August 1962, which praised Clark and Soyinka's appropriation of English as the language of literature: 'Writers like Clark, Soyinka and Christopher Okigbo are widely influenced by modern English poetry. But they have gained complete mastery of the language. To them English is just the perfect tool.'[11] Soyinka became the linguistic standard-bearer for the series, and editors tended to lament the inferior grasp of English by other writers.

There was a distinct gender-bias in Three Crowns: only two of the 23 authors published in the series were women: Benson and Kimenye, both of whom were regarded as rather second-rate within the series. Benson was the second-choice author to write *Chief Albert Lutuli*, and the book was only published in the series after being banned in South Africa. Kimenye was the only woman creative writer in the series, but *Kalasanda* and *Kalasanda Revisited* were regarded in a schoolbook vein: Charles Richards in the Nairobi branch first suggested to Neale that *Kalasanda* be published either in a 'series of Modern African Writers or a high grade Supplementary Reader'.[12] As previously related, Lewis and Kariara in Nairobi tried to secure women writers for Three Crowns, including Rebeka Njau and Ama Ata Aidoo, and, indeed, they wanted Aidoo to become a literary scout for Three Crowns in Ghana, but they were thwarted in their efforts.[13] The list they constructed in the Eastern Africa branch included a large number of women novelists and poets, but this literature was deemed within the organisation to be substandard, regional writing rather than world-class international literature.

Three Crowns was actively involved in creating the emerging canon of African literature. In a period in which literary culture was still structured in terms of high and mass culture, Three Crowns operated in the field of high culture. It was confined to the more 'autonomous' literary genres of drama, poetry and short stories as a result of the prohibition on fiction publishing, which might have contributed to the editors' sense of responsibility for the creation of a new canon of literature. Arguably, publication by OUP assisted in the process of 'consecrating' the writers, for many of them went on to achieve recognition by the UK and US literary establishments.[14] For example, seven of the Three Crowns writers have been deemed influential enough to be listed in the *Dictionary of Literary Biography*: Clark, de Graft, Fugard, Mtshali, Nkosi, Rotimi and Soyinka. Indeed, Harold Bloom's *The Western Canon* lists only 12 African writers, and four of them are Three Crowns authors: Soyinka, Clark, Fugard and Senghor.[15]

This overview of the list-building strategy of Three Crowns illustrates how OUP contributed to the creation of 'African literature' as a publishing genre. The books in the series were predominantly by male West African anglophone writers. Thus, Three Crowns exhibited the same regional, gender and linguistic bias as Mpe and Stec identified in the African Writers Series.[16] The discussion turns now to a debate held early in the history of Three Crowns about the publication of Senghor, which illustrates well the extensive negotiations that took place over the selection criteria for this new list of African writing.

Case-study 1: list-building and Léopold Sédar Senghor's *Prose and Poetry*

Senghor's poetry was first published in French by Les Editions du Seuil in 1948. A selection of his poetry and prose was translated into English by John Reed and Clive Wake, British lecturers at the University of Rhodesia and Nyasaland. At Collings's suggestion, they sent him the manuscript in March 1962, with an introductory letter explaining that 'We have undertaken this translation because we feel that Senghor's poetry may be of interest and even a stimulus to English-speaking Africa, where the standard of poetry writing is so poor.'[17]

The only external reader for the collection was Maurice Bowra, classics scholar, former Vice Chancellor of Oxford University and one of the

Delegates of OUP.[18] He compared Senghor's poems with those of the French poet St John Perse, and was particularly interested in their representation of Africa: 'I find them interesting and impressive, even in English, and they throw a flood of light on what is to most of us an entirely unknown world.'[19]

Neal Burton, OUP representative in Ghana, wrote a less complimentary report on the poetry, in which he complained about the Walt Whitman influence, and feared that the message of negritude might be unhelpful in Ghana:

> Senghor, no doubt, is gifted with a thorough, very simple vision: black blood and pastoral heart and careless laughter versus the machine consciousness, the heartless dry ruthlessness of Europe. The trouble is that there are too many poems here. In quantity his poems cloy, seem repetitive, slide into and eclipse one another. And his frenchified, oratorical, Gideon-Whitmanesque tone, I must admit is particularly suited to bore me easily. I suppose that we should support this. But unlike the translations in Rhodesia, I do not think Senghor's style, or even vision, will be particularly helpful to a rising writer in 'British' territory. On the contrary: the flow of oratory, with a Laurentian message of black blood, could actually be harmful.[20]

A third report by Mr Usborne from within OUP ponders whether Senghor should be regarded as French or African. He recommended that the book be regarded not as a work of literature but as a sociological example of French colonial practice: 'Senghor's interest, for us, surely lies in his Frenchness, and general with-it-ness, rather than his Africanness or négritude. ... Wouldn't it be best to consult someone now who knows about French Africa, négritude, etc., rather than about poetry?'[21]

The decision was eventually made to publish two editions of Senghor's works, in hardback and paperback, each translated, edited and introduced by Reed and Wake. The hardback, *Léopold Sédar Senghor: Selected Poems*, was edited by Jon Stallworthy for the Oxford Poets series. It had to be approved by the Delegates of the Press, and received their approval at the end of October 1962. Collings was keen to add Senghor to Three Crowns as a paperback, and wrote to his manager in support of the acquisition, reiterating (in more positive terms) the comparison with Whitman: 'The nearest equivalent in the English language to the idiom which Senghor uses is the idiom of Whitman and his followers.'[22] Collings's concept for this edition was that it would be a 'selection of Senghor's prose and verse in a paper edition especially for the sixth-form school and university market in Africa'.[23]

Lengthy negotiations were carried out with Les Editions du Seuil, and an author royalty of 2.5 per cent was agreed for the paperback rights.[24] The hardback edition was eventually published in 1964 with an introduction of 5000 words, and was issued at the higher price of 15s. *Prose and Poetry* was published in Three Crowns in 1965 at a price of 6s 6d, but sales were modest: only 3042 copies had sold by 1971. The 10,000 print-run proved to be too high, and the book ran at a loss of £398 after four years.[25]

Many of the poems selected for *Prose and Poetry* reflect on the impact of Europe on Africa. For example, 'Chaka' commemorates the Zulu hero in the face of the violent European invasion:

> They are landing with rulers
> Set squares, compasses, sextants,
> White skin, clear eyes, bare speech and thin mouths
> And thunder on their lips.[26]

Likewise, 'Prayer for Peace' concerns the inerasable impact of the slave trade and European colonisation:

> Lord God, forgive white Europe
> ...
> For Thou must forget those who exported ten millions of
> my sons in the leper-houses of their ships
> Who killed two hundred millions of them.[27]

The prose in the volume consists of short extracts from his published essays, which collectively set out the manifesto of negritude: 'It is time to define this word which so lends itself to polemical and to contradictory interpretations. Quite simply, *négritude* is the *sum total of the values of the civilization of the African world*. It is not racialism, it is culture.'[28] The excerpts sought to define the essential qualities of African civilisation and assert the primary significance of 'cultural liberation' over political liberation: 'Our renaissance will be more the work of African writers and artists than of politicians. We have seen from experience that there can be no political liberation without cultural liberation.'[29]

The acquisition of Senghor illustrates the quandary faced by OUP editors and readers in determining the selection criteria for African literature. Senghor's status as President of Senegal ultimately ensured that he would be published ('I suppose that we should support this' in Burton's words), but the judging process is still very revealing. OUP's mission in Africa was one area of debate: the translators regarded it as imperative that poetry was disseminated 'as a stimulus to English-speaking Africa', but Burton, on the other hand, paternalistically questioned whether it was fitting for OUP to publish in anglophone Africa the work of a prophet of negritude with its 'message of black blood'. The other area of debate was how to judge it aesthetically. Bowra favoured its publication because it represented an exotic 'entirely unknown world', whereas to Usborne the poetry was of interest because of Senghor's 'Frenchness', regarding him as an archetypal product of assimilatory colonial practice. It seems that Collings was most persuaded by the fact that the poetry fitted into pre-existing literary models by being 'Whitmanesque'. This case-study illustrates the protracted deliberation over the acquisition strategy: the level of contention aroused at OUP over a single manuscript did not augur well for Collings's ambition to build a new list of African literature.

The process of acquisition

Bourdieu writes that: 'Entering the field of literature is not so much like going into religion as getting into a select club: the publisher is one of those prestigious sponsors ... who effusively recommend their candidate.'[30] This present study of the editorial process begins at the crucial stage of manuscript acquisition in OUP (as 'sponsor'), and it examines the process by which authors (as 'candidates') gained entrance to the series (the 'select club').

Two hypotheses about the postcolonial author's access to international publication will be explored. For Casanova, the cultural hierarchies that disadvantage the postcolonial author are largely based on national lines. She writes of the struggles facing authors attempting to achieve recognition in the metropolitan literary world, and describes the problems facing 'writers on the periphery, who, having to struggle in very tangible ways ... to gain admission into its central precincts, are more clear sighted than others about the nature and the form of the literary balance of power'.[31] By contrast, according to Amuta, the international literary establishment is segmented primarily by class. He writes, 'The writer, in the African instance and up to the present time, is a member of a minority elite whose preparation for the social practice of writing is furnished by a relatively high level of formal Western education.'[32] How, then, did African authors attain publication in Three Crowns, and what were the necessary preconditions for their acceptance into the series?

As few African writers had literary agents in the early 1960s, most literary manuscripts for Three Crowns were obtained through various brokers. There is evidence of an informal network of Europeans who had connections with African writers, and who intervened with OUP on the authors' behalf. For example, Joan Littlewood of the Royal Court Theatre Workshop initially recommended Soyinka to Collings. Likewise, the manuscript of Tewfik Al-Hakim's *The Tree Climber* was sent to Collings by his translator, Denys Johnson-Davies, in 1964. Several of the African-based OUP branch managers and editors were also involved in the acquisition of authors' manuscripts. Charles Richards in the Nairobi office sent Collings the short stories of Kimenye about rural life in Buganda, which would eventually see publication in the collection *Kalasanda*, while Neal Burton, based in the Ghana branch, negotiated the acquisition of de Graft's *Sons and Daughters* and Clark's *Three Plays* for Collings. Fugard's *Hello and Goodbye* was first recommended to Stallworthy in 1968 by Charles Lewis and Jonathan Kariara of the Nairobi branch.

Many of the Three Crowns titles had previously been published within Africa, and were acquired for Three Crowns through liaison with the original publisher. For example, Clark's *Song of a Goat* (1961) and Soyinka's *Three Plays* (1963) were first published by Mbari, which was founded in 1961 in Ibadan by a group including Ulli Beier, Clark and Soyinka.[33] This was described by Collings as 'the Ibadan organisation roughly equivalent to the Arts Council, partly funded by the Congress for Cultural Freedom'.[34] In addition, Mtshali and Fugard were first published in South Africa, and negotiations took place with their South African publishers. Robert Fraser argues that the international publishers should not be credited with the discovery of new literature in Africa, as in reality they published literature that had already been published locally by mission presses and government literary bureaux: 'What is absolutely clear, *pace* the self-congratulatory claims of certain international publishers, is that African literature and its dissemination began, and was initially fostered, on the spot. It was never "introduced" or principally nurtured, from outside.'[35] The evidence of Three Crowns supports this argument that OUP, as an international publisher, did not so much unearth new talent as disseminate literature internationally that had already achieved national acclaim. For example, de Graft and Gabre-Medhin were already established directors of drama studios, Davidson (Abioseh) Nichol was the Vice Chancellor of University College, Freetown, and Senghor was, at the time of acquisition, the first President of Senegal. These unwritten rules of entrance into the series would have particularly disadvantaged women authors, with their more limited opportunities for colonial education, international university scholarships and public roles; the acquisition strategy goes some way to explaining the striking under-representation of women in Three Crowns.

Once manuscripts had been sent to the series editor, the process of literary judgement began. Commissioning and acquisition for Three Crowns were conducted from London. Three Crowns manuscripts were required to undergo a process of editorial quality control before a so-called 'pronouncement' was made on the text. Each manuscript was first read by the series editor, who, if they considered the text worth publishing, would then pass it onto one or two readers of their choice for review. OUP readers tended to be academics in British universities, British academics in African universities or internal editorial staff at OUP in London. There is no evidence in the history of Three Crowns of Africans ever being asked to read or judge a manuscript. External readers were given a small honorarium in return for their report. Editors were evidently free to accept or ignore the advice of the reader, but if the editor wished to publish the manuscript, they had to support their proposal with positive readers' or reviewers' comments. The editor then completed a 'new title proposal' form, quoting excerpts from the positive readers' reports. This proposal was sent to the manager of the Overseas Editorial department (Neale during Collings's editorship), who made the final decision. Later in the series history, new titles had to be approved by the Delegates.

This overview of the acquisition strategy for Three Crowns draws attention to the process of entry into this 'select club'. Writers evidently faced obstacles in terms of nationality, class and gender. The decision-making process was conducted from London, and each manuscript was subjected to stringent evaluation by a range of British agents of 'consecration' and 'legitimisation': for example, brokers, editors and publisher's readers.[36] The writers were also members of a 'minority elite' – they were highly educated, widely acclaimed, their plays had been performed, and in several cases the texts had already been previously published. In addition, many of the authors held prominent social or political positions in their own countries.

The following case-study of the acquisition of Easmon illustrates the process by which he managed to attain publication in Three Crowns, and assesses the role of the different agents in this process.

Case-study 2: the acquisition of Raymond Sarif Easmon's *Dear Parent and Ogre*

Easmon's *Dear Parent and Ogre* was recommended to OUP by Marion Bieber of Congrès pour la Liberté de la Culture after the play had won second prize in a play-writing competition sponsored by the Congrès on the occasion of Sierra Leone independence in 1961.[37] His play had also been performed in Lagos by Soyinka's theatre company, 1960 Masks, in 1961.

A drawing-room three-act play, *Dear Parent and Ogre* satirises the old and new African elites, as they jostled for position at the point of independence. The protagonist, Dauda Touray, is a lawyer who belongs 'to a family that has, since time immemorial, ruled and shaped the destiny of its people', who expects to return to his former power in the wake of decolonisation: 'we Africans are now winkling the white men out of Africa ... with the white men gone, we who ruled before have every hope and intention of ruling again'.[38] Sekou, by contrast, is a young man from the Sierra Leone underclass who has established himself in Europe as a successful recording star. A conflict ensues when Sekou returns to Sierra Leone equipped with fluent French and a Rolls-Royce, intent on marrying Dauda's daughter.

The first reader of the play, an OUP editor, recommended publication. He described it as 'about conflict ... between the old and the young, and between the old tribal class systems and the new more democratic outlook ... this is all rather well brought out, both through the plot, and more so through the characters, who are well drawn and realistic'. He concluded that 'on the whole I like it'.[39] The second reader was Richard Brain, editor in the Overseas Educational division, and a future editor of Fugard. He was categorical that the play should be rejected because he felt it was of poor literary quality: 'This play might be suitable for performance by the repertory company of an obscure Midlands town. Certainly the last half contains enough assaults, hysterics, silvery laughter, etc.' He also felt that the play's negative portrayal of African politics made it unsuitable for publication: 'I think that the picture of the champagne-swilling privilege of the rulers, the rough but subservient police and the remarks about politicians, would make it unsuitable for any Afro-Asian Country.'[40]

Collings, who was himself keen to publish Easmon's play, had to put the plan on hold in the face of this negative report. He was only able to persuade Neale to accept the publication of the play when it became clear that Easmon would otherwise be published in the African Writers Series.[41] Acknowledging that its literary quality was questionable, Collings wrote to Neale, '"Dear Parent and Ogre" is certainly not up to the Soyinka/Pepper Clark level but holds its own well with Sutherland and de Graft.'[42] An offer to publish was issued, and Easmon was pleased to accept the terms offered: a 10 per cent royalty and an advance of £100.[43] The book was published in 1964, but the print-run of 10,000 copies proved very optimistic. By 1971, only 4000 copies had sold, and the book reported a loss of £291.[44] Easmon later sent Collings another play, *The New Patriots*, a play dealing with corruption in the civil service, but he rejected this outright, judging it to be too political. Collings wrote to his manager, 'The New Patriots is definitely out, it is too political in the personal way, the character of leading Sierra Leonean families are but thinly disguised.'[45]

The acquisition of Easmon involved a tripartite process of quality control, constituting the recommendation by a broker (here Marion Barber), the sanction of readers (the OUP editors), and the approval of the series editors (Collings and Neale). *Dear Parent and Ogre* was only just deemed acceptable, and *The New Patriots* was rejected outright on grounds of its political unsuitability. This case-study provides a good illustration of the significant problems facing African authors in getting a text past all these 'gatekeepers'.[46]

Acquisition: assessing literary and commercial value

A major lacuna in studies of colonial and postcolonial publishing is the consideration of the role of the Western publisher in the selection and rejection of postcolonial literature. This study now turns to the criteria by which the new African writing was judged by the publisher, analysing which type of postcolonial discourse was adopted and promoted and which was blocked. Collings and his successors sought to establish a series of the highest quality African literature for a literary marketplace (in Africa as well as the UK and USA), but the series came under increasing pressure to be profitable by achieving sales in African schools. It explores how these dual imperatives for the series to yield both symbolic and economic capital simultaneously influenced the acquisition process.

With respect to contemporary British literary publishing, Claire Squires maintains that the publishing decision is always informed by a careful balance of commercial and literary judgements: 'A publisher ... would, arguably, base his or her decision to publish neither on bald economics nor on cultural value alone, but rather calculate the appropriateness of the text to the market that will receive it, which is, so to speak, playing the field.'[47] In the case of Three Crowns, there is a noticeable transition in the editorial files from a preoccupation at the outset with literary quality alone, to an overriding concern after 1966 with the market for the literature.

At the outset, editors and readers evidently considered that 'pure aesthetical judgements' of literature should not be contaminated by commercial considerations; they were resistant to judging manuscripts according to their market potential.[48] For example, the acquisition of Senghor reveals significant procrastination over the literary qualities of the manuscripts but no evidence of any attention to the commercial value of the books. There were, instead, protracted negotiations over the literary value of the manuscripts. Manuscripts were evidently judged against a set of Kantian aesthetic values, in particular seeking literature of 'universal communicability',[49] as well as literature that was 'disinterested'.[50] As a result, there was wide support for manuscripts that supported a mythical and primitive, or rural and unsophisticated Africa. Texts that were perceived as overtly political were negatively reviewed, as was literature that was considered ephemeral. The editors sought to map Western influence onto the literature they reviewed, whilst at the same time eschewing literature that they considered to be derivative.[51] In this respect, OUP editors were evidently reflecting a more general response of the European literary establishment to the emerging African literature. Chinweizu, Onwuchekwa and Ihechukwu argued that Western critics and academics expected African literature to conform to European literary canons.[52] Similarly, Amuta wrote of 'a certain nebulous universalism which saw African literature as part of the "human" literary heritage which did not necessitate the adoption of fresh evaluative criteria'.[53] While sharing many of his colleagues' aesthetic values, Collings adopted a more inclusive policy. In his desire to build a list, he increasingly ignored readers' negative comments and recommended the acquisition of texts regardless. This is apparent in both the Senghor and Easmon case-studies cited above. Likewise, he also adopted Nicol's *The Truly Married Woman* and Nkosi's *The Rhythm of Violence* in spite of negative readers' reports.

After Collings's departure in 1965, list development was paralysed over the search for books that were good enough for the series, with the frequent lament of OUP editors over the lack of quality literature. The 1966 document entitled 'Towards a Definition of Policy' alludes to this: 'in English-speaking Africa there are few poets of much quality'.[54] Regarding plays, the report concluded, 'we get sent the manuscripts of many diffuse plays which ramble through numerous acts; the authors tend to think of a play rather than a novel as the vehicle of expression of their story but do not have experience of the limitations of the medium'. Yet, there was also an admission that the standards might be too rigid: 'With works of imagination the problem is trickier. Theoretically quality is an important criterion. In actual fact it is subjective. London probably needs to listen to the branches rather than judge the quality of plays, for instance, by West End standards.'[55] The same complaint about the poor quality of the manuscripts was still being repeated in 1974 by Heapy. He wrote to Arthur Ravenscroft, editor of the *Journal of Commonwealth Literature* and former editorial advisor for the series: 'Three Crowns goes in fits and starts. We have two plays coming from India and five books coming from Nigeria. Manuscripts come and go in and out of the office. Most of them are not very good and I don't like to trouble you with them.'[56] The exacting notion of literary quality adopted by the editors and readers of Three Crowns manuscripts seriously inhibited the series development.

A further reason for the diminishing rate of acquisitions was that after 1966 series editors were permitted to adopt only manuscripts that could demonstrate a guaranteed market in Africa; there is thereafter plenty of evidence of manuscripts being rejected on commercial grounds. In March 1966, James Currey rejected the proposal to publish Salih's 'The Wedding of Zein and Other Stories' on account of its limited marketability to the African school market rather than its intrinsic literary quality: 'Our problem is that since we publish stories for a somewhat specialised market we shall have to consider them in relation to that market and not in relation to the conventional English literary scene.'[57] A year later, Philip Chester rejected outright a number of Ethiopian manuscripts submitted to Three Crowns: two novels ('Tobbaye' by Afawerk Gabre Yesus and 'Fitawari Belay' by H. H. Rai) and three plays ('Tweodros' and 'Azmari' by Tsegaye Medhin, and 'Snatch and Run' by Mengestru Lemma). The reason he gave was that '"Three Crowns" is now an educational series, i.e. entrants must have educational possibilities. It does not seem to me that any of these ideas qualify on this basis.'[58] In 1967, S. S. J. T. Samkange's manuscript 'African Fireside Tales' was rejected 'since there seemed to be no significant market'.[59] In 1968, Anthony Toyne rejected A. C. Brench's proposal to develop African literature in French because 'we are not greatly encouraged to suppose that such a scheme would flourish ... I am afraid that our few adventures in the publication of French material in Three Crowns do not lead us to believe that we can successfully publish such material for English-speaking Africa.'[60] By 1973, Heapy was weighing up whether or not to publish the novel 'Defiance' by the Ethiopian writer Abbie Gubegna. Somewhat lugubriously, he admitted, 'I am more concerned about the lack of a market than about the lack of quality to be honest.'[61] In the end, the book was rejected from Three Crowns, as the Ethiopian office could not guarantee sales of 9000 copies to its local market, as well as sale of subsidiary rights to American publishers.[62]

The process of the acquisition of John Pepper Clark, which is examined next, illustrates how the literary and commercial value of African literature was assessed at the earlier stage of Three Crowns history, under the editorship of Collings. The case-study sheds light on how OUP's aesthetic judgements resulted in the promotion of a specific type of postcolonial writing.

Case-study 3: assessing the literary and commercial value of John Pepper Clark's *Three Plays*

In March 1963, Collings attempted to secure for the Three Crowns series the plays of Clark.[63] Although *Song of a Goat* had already been published by Mbari in Ibadan, the other two plays, *Masquerade* and *The Raft*, had not yet been published.

All three plays are set in the Delta region of Nigeria and are written in verse. *Song of a Goat* is a tragedy self-consciously following the Greek classical tradition, but set in rural West African society. Zifa, the protagonist, is impotent, and his wife Ebiere, fearful at the prospect of childlessness, embarks on a sexual relationship with his younger brother, Toyne. The affair leads to tragic results. Finding them together, Zifa swears that he will kill them; Tonye then hangs himself, and Zifa, in grief, walks out towards the sea and drowns himself. The sequel to this tragic tale is *The Masquerade*, which concerns Tufa, the son of Ebiere and Toyne. He is on the verge of marriage to a young woman, Titi, when his parentage is disclosed. According to local custom, he is thus considered to be a very unlucky choice for Titi, but she resolves to marry him regardless. Her father seeks her out in a rage, and shoots her by accident. In revenge, Tufa kills Titi's father, and then turns the gun on himself. Both plays follow the form of a Greek tragedy, with the neighbours playing the part of the chorus. *The Raft* is an equally calamitous play about four lumbermen, whose log raft is cut adrift on the Niger. The play takes the form of a series of soliloquies by each character in which they recount their life stories in turn, as they face imminent death.

Collings wrote to his manager at length, to justify the acquisition. He first quoted from a review in the *Times Literary Supplement* in 1962: 'Only an African could have written Mr Clark's tragedy *Song of a Goat*, even though European influences in the play are numerous.'[64] He then quoted from Gerald Moore's review of the same play: 'Clark's brilliant play *Song of a Goat* is not in the least derivative, soaked as it is in an intensely local sense of life, yet its formal structure is almost exactly that of Greek tragedy.'[65] Associating his plays not only with Aeschylus but also with Sophocles and Shakespeare, Collings evidently regarded Clark's plays as ideal for Three Crowns: they demonstrated stylistic continuity with European canonical literature whilst encapsulating an 'authentic' Africa.

Collings then ruminated at some length about the potential problems for the school market of publishing plays full of sexual allusions. Collings insisted that the book should not be judged by its suitability for the African school market: acknowledging that *The Raft* was unsuitable for school use, he argued that this should not be grounds for its exclusion from the series:

> Of the literary merits I have no doubts but the bawdiness of *The Raft* is something to which some educational authorities might object ... there are certainly some people who would feel that this kind of book ought not to be published at all, and if published, certainly not by OUP. ... The book is of course not meant nor written for schools (any more than *Macbeth* was).[66]

In the event the plays were accepted by Neale. Clark was offered the exceptionally high royalty rate of 15 per cent on both UK and overseas sales, together with an advance of £125, which he accepted. This contrasted with the 7.5 per cent royalty rate that was standard for the African Writers Series at the time.[67] *Three Plays* was classed as an adult book, and no adjustments were made to the text to make it suitable for an educational market. Despite Collings's insistence that market factors should not be taken into account in selecting Clark's plays, this publication was one of the most successful titles in Three Crowns and the sales figures indicate that it was adopted in schools. Of the initial print-run of 10,000 copies, 7821 had sold by 1971, and a reprint of 5000 was authorised.[68] By 1972, Clark had received a total of £175.09 royalties over his advance.[69]

Clark's second Three Crowns publication, *Ozidi*, was published in 1966. The play recorded the Ozidi legend, an epic tale of the Ijo-speaking people in the Niger delta, which originally took seven days to perform. Ozidi, the young warrior, sets out to avenge the murder of his father, and the play concerns the series of bizarre and violent events that ensued. It was described as a play that is 'based on the great Ijaw saga and takes place in that country where the Niger River and the sea interlock in the Delta. In this play dance, music, mime and poetry interlock with the supernatural.'[70] The book achieved record sales for Three Crowns, and by 1971 of the 10,000 copies initially printed, 4675 copies had been sold.[71] It was then selected by the West African Education Committee in 1976–77, after which Heapy instructed the printing of an unprecedented further 21,000 copies of the book.[72]

The acquisition of John Pepper Clark's *Three Plays* demonstrates Collings's determination that the book should be judged by aesthetic values rather than commercial values, indicating Collings's 'disavowal of the "economic"'.[73] Collings tried to direct the series towards the literary and general marketplace in Africa, and this case-study is evidence of his ambition to provide books for 'adult and university work ... and for general educational reading', and his resistance to commerce being a deciding factor in the selection of literature for Three Crowns.[74] In the event, Clark was one of Three Crowns' major success stories; he was one of the very few authors who simultaneously managed to achieve symbolic and economic capital for the series. Ironically, although not originally intended for the African schools market, Clark's plays became some of the bestsellers of the series, and achieved educational sales that were matched only by Soyinka's.

Conclusion

The case-studies in this chapter provide an insight into the way in which British publishers exercised influence over the emergence of African literature in this period. Through the manuscript selection process, OUP editors and readers assumed the role of judges of African literature, and attempted to create a series of 'high literature': a new literary canon for the continent. They measured literary achievement according to established literary traditions and canons and decided which postcolonial literary discourse would be promoted, often favouring texts that presented a primitive, exotic Africa. The next chapter examines how this strategy was extended to the processes of literary production, by which books were codified as 'authentic' and archetypal African products.

This chapter has highlighted the particular difficulties faced by African authors in being accepted for the series. The expectation of OUP that the series should deliver symbolic capital and economic capital simultaneously led to irresolvable tensions in the series: the editorial quest for universal, disinterested literature was at odds with the publisher's requirement for profit. This array of literary and commercial demands meant that very few manuscripts were deemed to be of publication standard, and there was a discernible reduction in new titles on a year-by-year basis.[75] Although the publisher and editor held the power to decide which narratives would be published, this study argues that of equal significance was their 'power to block other narratives from emerging and forming': the acquisitions record of Three Crowns attests to a gradual silencing of African authors throughout the series history.[76]

7
Editing Three Crowns

How have postcolonial theorists and critics explained the relation between European publishers and editors and the African literature that they published? Several formulations have been attempted, but the subject has generated little sustained empirical research. One line of argument, expounded mainly by African Marxists, and articulated here by Ngũgĩ wa Thiong'o, describes European publishing of African literature as 'a reflection of the neo-colonial situation':

> We take from our languages, and the material is processed in European language and resold in Africa as African literature. ... It borrows from African life and orature, the material of imagination is processed through European languages, and the packaged material in between hard covers becomes African literature. ... Once again Africa produces, the West disposes.[1]

In *Decolonising the Mind*, Ngũgĩ expands a little on the ways in which the publisher served to 'process' African literature through publishing for a global market. He expresses an anxiety that his 'defiance' towards colonial structures that is embedded in his novels is rendered 'impoverished on the stage of commercial publishers',[2] and again reiterates that European publishers' insistence on works written in the language of the colonisers both undermines and distorts the intrinsic meaning of African literature.

A contrasting line of argument, which has been propagated mainly by publishers themselves, depicts the publisher as a vital patron and sponsor of African literature. For example, Becky Clarke, former commissioning editor of the African Writers Series, describes the publisher as a champion of African writers, who gave 'freedom and voice' to the African author. She describes the series as a means by which 'African literature became known to the world and to other Africans':

> The African Writers Series ... has become the standard bearer – the canon. ... The idea is that these books display certain universal and timeless

> qualities, thereby setting up standards that will endure. ... The series gives agency to the African because the novels, short stories, plays, poetry, and autobiographies are written by Africans about Africans, telling their own stories in their own voices for both Africans and non-Africans. Publications in the late 1950s and early 1960s publicised the nationalist struggles for liberation against colonialists and in a contemporary context continue this championing role in giving freedom and voice to the artist in exposing dictatorships, intolerance and inequality within African societies.[3]

Between these positions expressed by Clarke and Ngũgĩ, a number of critics have attempted to develop more complex models of the relation between British publishers and African writers. Recent research into the publishing of African literature has examined the ways that the publisher modified the authors' texts in the creation of literary products that supported dominant discourses on Africa. According to André Lefevere the interaction between African authors and British publishers resulted in the formation of a 'hybrid poetics'.[4] His overview of the development of a literary system in Africa after the Second World War proposes that texts which travelled from Africa to Britain were 'filtered through the dominant system', and this process demanded writing that 'tended to respect English poetics in all but one element: theme, which is frankly African, and gives these writings a kind of exotic novelty value'.[5] Gail Low's examination of the editing of Tutuola's *Palm-Wine Drinkard* by Faber & Faber, which builds on an earlier study by Bernth Lindfors, concludes that the editorial strategy led to the publication of 'exotic' and 'authentic' African literature. She argues, however, that although the resulting book – an example of 'naive art' – was well received by critics in the UK, it was received with embarrassment and dismay in the Nigerian home market.[6]

Graham Huggan provides an important analysis of publishing as a process of literary representation through his theorisation of the 'postcolonial exotic'. Following Said, he defines exoticism as 'an aestheticising process through which the cultural other is translated, relayed back through the familiar'[7] and he argues that the African exotic was adopted by the publisher – Heinemann's African Writers Series – as a marketing device. Thus, the publication of African literature was a process of cultural translation between Africa and the West. According to Huggan, the editor exercised this role largely through creating paratext for the printed books that emphasised the anthropological dimensions of the series, and that promoted the texts as representations of 'African society, culture and history'.[8] Nourdin Bejjit dismisses this thesis on account of Huggan's misassumption that the literature was produced predominantly for the Western consumer. He argues, 'It might be argued that these African artists and writers supported the circulation of their works as "exotic" and "primitive" artefacts. But in the absence of archival documentation this statement can only be dealt with as a free-floating hypothesis.'[9] In this chapter,

Huggan's 'free-floating hypothesis' is related to the evidence of Three Crowns, questioning whether the editors of Three Crowns sought to publish exotic and primitive African literature and, if so, asking why this was the case, given that the main market was the African school market.

This chapter assesses whether the publisher's impact on postcolonial literature was one of support and patronage, literary 'hybridity' or literary domination. Many studies of this subject have tended to rely on the final published texts for evidence rather than examining any of the editorial or production processes involved. However, this study contends that focused archival study of these processes of literary production is required in order to understand the exact nature of the publisher's editorial interventions in the literature.

This chapter includes four author case-studies, which reveal the responses of authors to the publisher's definitions of African literature, and give an insight into the relationships that were established between British editors and African authors. For the copy-editing process, the case-study of Tsegaye Gabre-Medhin is considered; for the design and production processes, the focus is on the case-studies of Barbara Kimenye and Obi Egbuna, and finally, for the promotion process, the case-study of Oswald Mtshali is examined.

Copy-editing Three Crowns

The copy-editing process for Three Crowns literature followed a standard editorial sequence. First, the editor would negotiate with the author over any suggested substantial changes. The author's manuscript was then copy-edited by the Three Crowns editor, and returned to the author for their approval of the corrections. The corrected manuscript was then sent by the editor to the Production department for typesetting. After being proofread by the editor, the text was sent to the author for final checking before being passed to Production for printing.

In contrast to the protracted and cautious selection process, the copy-editing process tended to be hastily conducted by Collings, and editorial mistakes frequently slipped through. However, he was conscious of the need to make the texts accessible to an international market, and on occasion he requested from the authors introductions, epilogues and glossaries to explain their texts. Jon Stallworthy was more interventionist as an editor than Collings, as were Carol Buckroyd and Richard Brain, who covered for him in his absence. Stallworthy and Buckroyd copy-edited the manuscripts with greater precision than Collings, and also tended to request more explanatory material from the authors. For example, in editing Mtshali's *Sounds of a Cowhide Drum*, Mtshali was asked by Stallworthy to supply a glossary and was given an extensive list of suggestions for changes to the poetry by Buckroyd.[10]

The practice of explaining African life, mythology and customs in the paratext of a book is described by Huggan as part of the 'exoticising' process.[11] This study now turns to an examination of the editorial processes surrounding the work of Gabre-Medhin to determine if there were attempts to create either 'exotic' or 'authentic' African literature.[12]

Case-study 1: copy-editing Tsegaye Gabre-Medhin's *Oda-Oak Oracle*

Tsegaye Gabre-Medhin was acting director of the Haile Selassie I Theatre in Addis Ababa, and the author of several published plays in Amharic. However, six of his Amharic plays were, in effect, censored in Ethiopia, as they failed to receive the necessary written permission that would allow them to be staged. *Oda-Oak Oracle*, submitted to Collings for review in 1964, was his first English play and was described by the author as a 'ritualistic myth'. He emphasised the ancient mythology at the heart of the play:

> The 'Oda' is a large tree which the primitive South-West Ethiopians used to worship. In fact, worshipping trees, mountains, rivers or rocks was and still is (in certain cases) an age-old practice of the whole of Africa, or of the major part of the continent. This play is based on a sort of Black people's legend told of gods and God, of love, fears and sacrifices.[13]

The play is based on a traditional Ethiopian legend: the protagonist, Shanka, is under a curse that his first-born son should be sacrificed to the ancestral spirits, as interpreted by the oracle of the sacred Oda-Oak tree. He defies the oracle by refusing to consummate the marriage, for fear of causing his child's death ('If I yield / Nine moons is not so distant'[14]). His best friend, Goaa, betrays him by sleeping with his wife, Uketee, who becomes pregnant. The oracle then pronounces that Shanka and Goaa should be matched in 'a combat to the death'[15] in which Goaa dies. Uketee later dies in childbirth, and although the baby survives, the village elders decree that both Shanka and the baby should be sacrificed to the violent, approaching mob, as a punishment for disobeying the oracle.

John Reed, the translator of Senghor's poetry, expressed satisfaction with the subject matter in his reader's report, stating that 'this short mythological play has a certain power', but not quite knowing if this was due to the subject matter or the skill of the writer. He recommended that the play be published with a longer introduction explaining the myth:

> the introduction explaining the myth ... might be made larger and more explicit for the benefit of foreign readers. ... As it stands the whole work will, I think, leave a European reader rather baffled. ... How valuable a work like this is cannot be judged directly. Primitive simplicity is easy to fake.[16]

Following Reed's suggestions, Collings requested extensive changes to the text before publication in order to explain the mythology of the play. He asked Gabre-Medhin to lengthen the introduction as Reed advised, and to eliminate 'some of the rather archaic and over literary English, for example, phrases such as "Ay, but" and "sinned you have"'.[17] The author agreed to the alterations, and suggested that he would write a 'sort of epic at the end of the play which I hope would clarify the theme for foreign readers'.[18] However, in the event, Gabre-Medhin decided against the epic, and concentrated instead on a lengthened introduction.[19]

Collings's relationship with Gabre-Medhin demonstrates his support and concern for his authors. Collings made efforts to get the author a placement at a British university; he sent a copy of Gabre-Medhin's book to a history professor at Edinburgh University, hoping to encourage him to offer the author a year's work. He also wrote to the British Council on his behalf, writing: 'At the moment Tsegaye is suffering from acute frustration and from being cut off from new African literary and artistic developments.'[20] Through this editing process, the author developed a close and dependent relationship with his editor, and Gabre-Medhin was evidently bereft when Collings left OUP. After hearing the news of his imminent departure, he wrote:

> Although you did not write me about it, I have heard the sad news both from Pankhurst and Rogers; they said that by the end of this month you shall have left OUP. Just when we are planning to do a lot together, why did this have to happen![21]

The copy-editing of Gabre-Medhin's work illustrates the editorial concern over highlighting the mythological elements of the text to make the text more accessible for a wider marketplace: to universalise it for an international market. Gabre-Medhin was self-consciously complicit in this process, and was more than willing to cooperate with the editor's suggestions. Indeed, the full title of the play was taken from the author's early letter to Collings: *Oda-Oak Oracle: A Legend of Black Peoples, Told of Gods, of Hope and Love and of Fears and Sacrifice*. This case-study confirms Huggan's arguments about the publisher and the African author working together in the creation of exotic literature for the foreign reader.[22] However, although designed to appeal to the Western reader through its primitive and tribal connotations, in the event this book was one of Collings's least commercially successful acquisitions (Figure 7.1). There is no evidence of the book being adopted by examination boards, and the local Ethiopian market was small.[23] Of the 10,000 copies printed in 1965, only 2155 had sold by 1971, and the book reported a loss of £349.[24]

Design and production in Three Crowns

This study now turns to the design and production of Three Crowns books, and in particular focuses on the physical form of these published books.

Figure 7.1 Tsegaye Gabre-Medhin, *Oda-Oak Oracle* (1965), front cover. By permission of Oxford University Press

Gérard Genette's theory of paratext provides a framework for the analysis of the interventions of the publisher in the book as a material product and for an interpretation of the cultural meaning ascribed to them. He dissects the book to explore the publisher's and author's 'thresholds of interpretation', and argues that paratext ensures 'the text's presence in the world, its "reception" and consumption in the form ... of a book'.[25] Although Genette's main interest is the author's paratext, the concern here is with the 'publisher's peritext': specifically the cover design, the genre and series identifications, the format of the book and the typography.[26]

Three Crowns editors retained a strong influence over the book's design and production, having responsibilities that would now be carried out by a book's designer. The editor was responsible for selecting a cover illustration or photograph for the book – sometimes with the involvement of the author – as well as for writing the copy for the back cover and for stipulating the format and typeface to be used. This section charts the ways in which the editor's interpretation of the literature was manifested in the physical form of the book: in other words, how 'a paratextual element ... can make known an intention, or an interpretation by the author and/or the publisher'.[27] Yet, the paratext also bears testimony to the significant commercial constraints on the books in the series.

The jacket designs for the early books in the series were intended to attract the attention of the Western consumer. Collings proposed that Three Crowns should follow the format of Penguin Plays, which were targeted specifically to the UK trade market.[28] The books were published in crown octavo format (7½ x 5 in.), the size of a modern mass-market paperback. In addition, the books were encoded as distinctively African by the use of primitive illustrations or distinctively African photographs. Several books had illustrations of African village scenes, masks, animals or intertwined figures (for example, Tewfik Al-Hakim's *The Tree Climber* and Clark's *Three Plays*). In addition, two have photographs of an African landscape (Egbuna's *The Anthill* and Soyinka's *The Road*, see Figure 8.4), and others bear photographs of Africans (de Graft's *Sons and Daughters*, 1969 edition, and Soyinka's *The Lion and the Jewel*, 1993 edition). By attempting to represent through the paratext archetypal representations of 'African society, culture and history', Collings attempted to exoticise the books for a Western trade market.[29] However, this was in stark contrast to other aspects of the books' paratext, which served to underline that the books were destined for the African educational market. For example, the production quality of the books was poor: they were thin, the covers were cheaply produced, and as a result the books had the appearance of schoolbooks rather than of trade paperbacks.

The series branding – a vital aspect of a publisher's branding strategy for the trade market – was inconsistent. As noted by Genette, codifying a book as part of a series is a major strategy for classifying a book for the reader: 'the series emblem ... amplifies the publisher's emblem, immediately indicating to the potential reader the type of work, if not the genre, he is dealing with'.[30] The series identity for Three Crowns was represented by a black band along the base of the front cover of the book, with the words 'A Three Crowns Book', together with a colophon of three crowns. However, the colophon varied in size, style and position on the cover throughout the series. Indeed, it did not appear at all on Egbuna's *Daughters of the Sun* (see Figure 7.2). The spines of the books also varied: although all had the three crowns colophon placed vertically at the base of the spine, there was great variety in other aspects of the design. Typographically, the majority of the books had serif typefaces on the front and back covers, but Clark's *Three Plays*, Benson's *Chief Albert Lutuli* and Egbuna's *The Anthill* all used a sans-serif typeface. So, while there was an attempt to present the books as a unified series, the series identity was confused. In the absence of a book designer, Collings himself advised the Production department on the book design, and this led to inconsistencies and omissions. The lack of a series brand and identity was in marked contrast to the African Writers Series, with its Penguin-like colour-coded covers, logo and grid system layout.

In 1971 the decision was made to relaunch the series with a new design, appropriate for both the UK market and the branch markets. The renowned typographic designer Ruari McLean was employed to create a template for the series and was also given the brief to design covers for Fugard's *Hello and Goodbye* and *Boesman and Lena* (see Figures 9.2 and 9.3), together with Mtshali's *Sounds of a Cowhide Drum*. The exotic identity was completely abandoned in favour of a bold, streamlined, grid system, which used a sans-serif typeface and a bright primary-coloured background with black and white text. The format of the book was altered from the imperial crown octavo to the metric B format (13 x 19.8 cm). This format corresponded with that of books for the middle- to highbrow UK trade market, for example that of the Oxford Paperback series, and this format was also considered to be more appropriate for the American market.[31] Thus, the change to a 'trade paperback' format signalled a renewed attempt to target the UK and US trade markets as well as the branch markets. The new book design attempted to classify the genre of the book for the consumer and the bookseller, following the tradition established by Penguin in the 1930s and later adopted by the African Writers Series. According to these paperback publishing conventions 'genre specifications' were 'symbolised by the choice of colour'.[32] This was explained by Heapy to the African branch managers: 'We propose to put all plays in red, poems in green, novels and short stories in a primary blue, and autobiography in a deep yellow.'[33]

Heapy had ambitions for Three Crowns to become a federalised series, owned by the branches as well as London, and he hoped that the new design would be adapted by each of the branches for their own literature. However, although the design brief had evidently been to create a reusable design template, it failed in one crucial respect.[34] It generated instant and fervent dislike from the branches, the very markets for which the series had principally been redesigned. The new page design met with unanimously negative reviews from the branches.[35] In the absence of any more positive suggestions, Heapy went ahead with Ruari McLean's design, despite privately agreeing with his colleagues that it was ugly.[36]

The implementation of McLean's new design was also not entirely satisfactory. There were problems regarding the printing quality of Mtshali's and Fugard's books. On receiving the newly printed *Boesman and Lena*, Heapy wrote to the Production department complaining about uneven typesetting of the book: 'Who is printing these by the way? I hope it is not the same lot that did *Sounds of a Cowhide Drum*, which was a good example of Pakistani bazaar printing – with respect.'[37] As Genette observes, 'typographical choices may provide indirect commentary on the texts they affect';[38] certainly the cheap production methods adopted for the new Three Crowns books betrayed the books' cheap mass production for the African marketplace. In addition, it was not long before McLean's design template was tampered with. There was the question of what to do with old Three Crowns books, and rather than incur any expense in redesigning them, it was decided to resize them to fit the new format, and superimpose the new logo on the cover. This was the case for the reprint of *Sons and Daughters* (reprinted in 1979) and Soyinka's *The Lion and the Jewel* (reprinted in 1993).

Thus, the paratext of the Three Crowns books reveals the conflicting expectations and demands placed on the series. The publisher's struggle to target the Western literary market in tandem with the African market is particularly evident in the following case-studies of the publication of Barbara Kimenye and Obi Egbuna.

Case-study 2: the design and production of Barbara Kimenye's *Kalasanda*

Kimenye sent her manuscript of eight short stories of Buganda village life to the OUP Eastern Africa branch, whereupon Charles Richards, the manager, passed them on to Rex Collings for possible inclusion in Three Crowns. The author was a journalist from Uganda, a short-story writer, and one of East Africa's most prolific children's writers. Several of her children's book had been published by the branch: those for secondary school children were published in the Oxford Library for Eastern Africa; the majority of these concerned the adventures of the schoolboy Moses and his friends at the Mukibi Educational Institute for the Sons of African Gentlemen. Her other adventure stories were published in the Oxford Readers for Eastern Africa series, for primary school children, and also in Nelson's Rapid Reading Series.[39]

The interlinked short stories in the collection depict contemporary rural Bugandan life. Kimenye consciously sets out to focus on the lives of 'ordinary people who seldom hit the headlines, and never catch the eye of tourists'.[40] The village is described as an unprepossessing 'straggling collection of small, mud homesteads set in shambas of varying sizes'.[41] Kimenye depicts a timeless and authentic rural existence: 'a more conservative and complacent community would be difficult to find in the whole of Buganda', and the stories tend to be structured in terms of the opposition between the stable social hierarchy of the village and the insidious threat of infiltration from beyond.[42] The tales are replete with stock comic characters: Nantondo the widow, who is the village gossip, the young Ggombolola Chief who had 'completed an extensive course in Local Government at Oxford', the owner of the Happy Bar, Maria Ssentamu, with her 'sumptuous curves', and Daudi, the village intellectual with an 'abnormally large forehead' and a 'burning ambition' to get an overseas scholarship.

Richards recommended Kimenye to Rex Collings on the advice of Edgar Wright, a lecturer in English Literature at Nairobi University. His judgement was that 'it is a Buganda "Miss Mitford"'.[43] On the basis of this rather slight recommendation, and Richards's estimate of a good potential market for the book in East Africa, Collings and Neale accepted it for Three Crowns.[44] Kimenye was offered a 10 per cent royalty and a £50 advance.[45]

During the editorial and production processes, there were points of conflict between author and editor over the way that her Buganda village was represented in the book. She registered her dislike of the archetypal book title 'The Village', that had been decided upon by the Nairobi branch of OUP. She wanted instead the more specific title 'Kalasanda', explaining, 'I don't care at all for "The Village", which in any case is the title of the first explanatory chapter.'[46] Collings agreed to this. She then wrote objecting to the cover illustration for the book, which she regarded as inaccurate for the region she describes:

> Thank you for sending me the photo-copies of Mr Kiwanuka's drawings, but, clearly, they will not do. They are totally lacking in humour and fail completely to project the warm personality of a Kigand village. Even the houses are wrong, having the characteristics of tribal homes in the Eastern and Northern provinces of Uganda, rather than those of Buganda.[47]

She offered to find an appropriate artist and send samples of work to Collings. At some expense, Collings paid off the original artist, Mr Kiwanuka, giving him 70 per cent of his agreed fees, and he commissioned instead her preferred artist, Norbet Kagwa, demonstrating his willingness to concede to the author's requests over the editing and design of her book.

Evidently Collings neglected to copy-edit the text carefully. Publication of the book coincided with Collings's departure from OUP, and it was Anthony Toyne who sent Kimenye the advance copy of the book. Instead of the customary editorial congratulations on the publication of the new book, Toyne took the opportunity to berate her for textual ambiguities and stylistic clumsiness on a page of the book, which would, in fact, have been Collings's editorial responsibility:

> A re-reading of not only this sentence but the whole page makes us feel that there are a number of avoidable obscurities. ... You may wish also to tighten up the style of the intervening sentences.[48]

The production process for Kimenye's book is evidence of the publisher's desire to represent her work as archetypal and representative of all Africa, in an attempt to broaden the market for her works and to appeal to the foreign reader. However, the author resisted these universalising efforts, rejecting the title 'The Village' as well as the generic illustrations of African rural life. Evidently more concerned about the local readership, she insisted on a more specific title and illustrations that reflected her own region more accurately.

This editorial debate over the intended readership of *Kalasanda* can also be traced in the subsequent critical response to the publication. Peter Nazareth, in *Literature and Society in Modern Africa*, suggested that the stories were chiefly of anthropological interest, offering foreign readers an insight into the lives of the marginalised: 'The good uncommitted writer makes us see and feel how such apparently dull lives existing in little backwaters of society and ignored by the world are actually full of interest.'[49] Edgar Wright's review, likewise, in the *Journal of Commonwealth Literature* pronounced that the book's main strength was its authentic representation of an archetypal African village: 'It is a contemporary village with its local pride, local personages, local contradictions of traditional and modern ways of life and thought.'[50] However, a review in the Kampala-based literary journal *Transition* by Hebe Welbourn, a British medical writer in Uganda, questioned the book's appropriateness for local East African readers. She judged the book to be 'an entertaining diversion for anyone who enjoys village gossip', but the remainder of her review ponders the vexed question: 'For whom is the book written?' In her view, the language and style 'sometimes cumbersome, sometimes slangy' made it inappropriate for schools, but she also deemed it unsuitable for Buganda villagers themselves as 'it has been conceived in English and would not really translate into Luganda'.[51]

Despite being intended initially for an adult readership, *Kalasanda* was, in the event, widely adopted as a set text in East African schools. It sold relatively well: of the 10,000 copies printed in 1965, at a price of 5s 6d per copy, 6715 had been sold by 1971. The sequel, *Kalasanda Revisited*, was less successful, however. With the same print-run, only 2236 copies sold in the five-year period from 1966 to 1971.[52]

Case-study 3: the design and production of Obi Egbuna's *Daughters of the Sun*

In 1968, while 'languishing in Bristol jail', Obi Egbuna submitted to the Press four short stories for their consideration.[53] He had been imprisoned for his 'Black Power' activism, specifically for delivering a speech at Speaker's Corner which was regarded as incitement to murder police officers. His play *The Anthill* had been published by the Press in 1965, but two other plays were rejected, and these he had reworked into short stories.

The theme that runs through the stories is the collision in African society between traditional beliefs and practice and European culture and religion. 'Divinity' is a tale of violent religious conflict in an African village between a Catholic catechist and his son, a signed-up member of a secret Juju association. 'The Scarecrow of Nairobi' recounts an acrimonious encounter between a settler family in Kenya and an African member of the Black Power movement. 'The Medics' centres on the conflict between an American Peace Corps medical student, a Nigerian writer and a village 'witch doctor'. 'Daughters of the Sun' is ostensibly a traditional folk tale recounted by an old woman to 'a traveller by profession, a collector of legends'.[54] However, at the story's conclusion, the narrator anticipates 'converting her lively imagination into practical currency', thus signalling the author's self-conscious awareness of the market value attached to African exotica.[55]

The two OUP editors who acted as readers for these stories were positive, and recommended publication. Liz Stanley praised the 'haunting, romantic theme and style' of the 'Daughters of the Sun', and the 'disturbing and convincing element of mystery and horror, tension and anticipation ... the primitive fear of the unknown' of 'Divinity',[56] whereas Gareth Reeves also praised the 'haunting quality' of the stories.[57] Jon Stallworthy was Three Crowns editor at the time, and he accepted the short stories on the basis of these reports. He set about promoting the books by drawing attention to their religious and mythological themes. Stallworthy's back-cover blurb promoted the book in terms of Egbuna's 'mastery of the ancient art of story-telling' and his ability to evoke 'the Africa of legend'.[58]

However, there was a disparity between the themes that pleased the European critics and those that would be well received in Africa, which was acknowledged to be the main market. Evidently primitivism was deeply unpopular there, making the author susceptible to bleak comparison with Tutuola. Egbuna was sensitive to the reception of his works in Nigeria, and he requested two alterations to Stallworthy's proposed publicity:

> Many thanks for the blurb ... and of course for all the flattering attributes in it. I think it is superb and, as you'll find, I have suggested only two minor word substitutions. One is in line 6 where I have deleted 'juju' and inserted 'village Divinity' in replacement; and the second is in line 8 where I have scratched out 'witch-doctor' and introduced the phrase

> 'traditional healer, witch doctor to him', instead. It may seem ridiculous, I know, but, knowing my country-men as I do, I rather suspect that the words 'juju' and 'witch-doctor' on the cover blurb could easily alienate the African intellectual (the core of our African market) who has become ridiculously sensitive to such words since Tutuola's 'Palm-wine Drinkard'.[59]

Negotiations during the design and production process demonstrate similar misunderstandings in Britain of the local Nigerian market. The original cover design, illustrated by Bill Botten, depicted the daughters of the sun as two identical naked African women, side by side against the sun, but this illustration was rejected by the Nigeria branch. The editor at Ibadan wrote to Stallworthy: 'We feel that while the two figures should remain, they should be draped through to the neck in a long tunic and yet show that they are feminine. In its present form the design is unacceptable, and will have very strong reactions in Africa.' Stallworthy made a note on the memo, 'I'm afraid we must redo, as Nigeria is the major market,'[60] and in the finished cover illustration, the figures are accordingly clothed in white tunics (see Figure 7.2). *Daughters of the Sun* was published in 1970 at a cover price of 10 shillings. The print-run for the first edition was 7500 copies, but there are no records of the total sales: the only indication is that 951 copies of the book were sold in the first year. This was a high level of initial sales and suggests that the title went on to become commercially successful.[61]

This case-study shows how OUP editors attempted to navigate the conflicting demands of the Anglo-American and the African literary marketplaces in the production of Egbuna's stories. The paratext of the book became the site of this conflict, and in response to the demands of the author and the local branch, changes were made in order to accommodate local Nigerian readers. However, even after compromises had been reached, Egbuna's complex stories of contemporary African society and racial identity were still represented by the publisher as 'haunting', 'romantic' and 'primitive' folk tales, and were packaged with exotic paratext promoting them as stories about the 'Africa of legend'.

Promoting Three Crowns

This section explores the strategies that were employed in the marketing and promotion of Three Crowns books. Claire Squires argues that in contemporary literary publishing, marketing is an 'act of representation' and a 'dynamic process by which desires for a book's transmission are both communicated and created'. Juliet Gardiner's study of contemporary authorship likewise argues that the publisher's 'epitext' (that is, the posters, advertisements, press releases and other promotional literature) are all intrinsic to the meaning of the book.[62] However, Three Crowns exemplifies

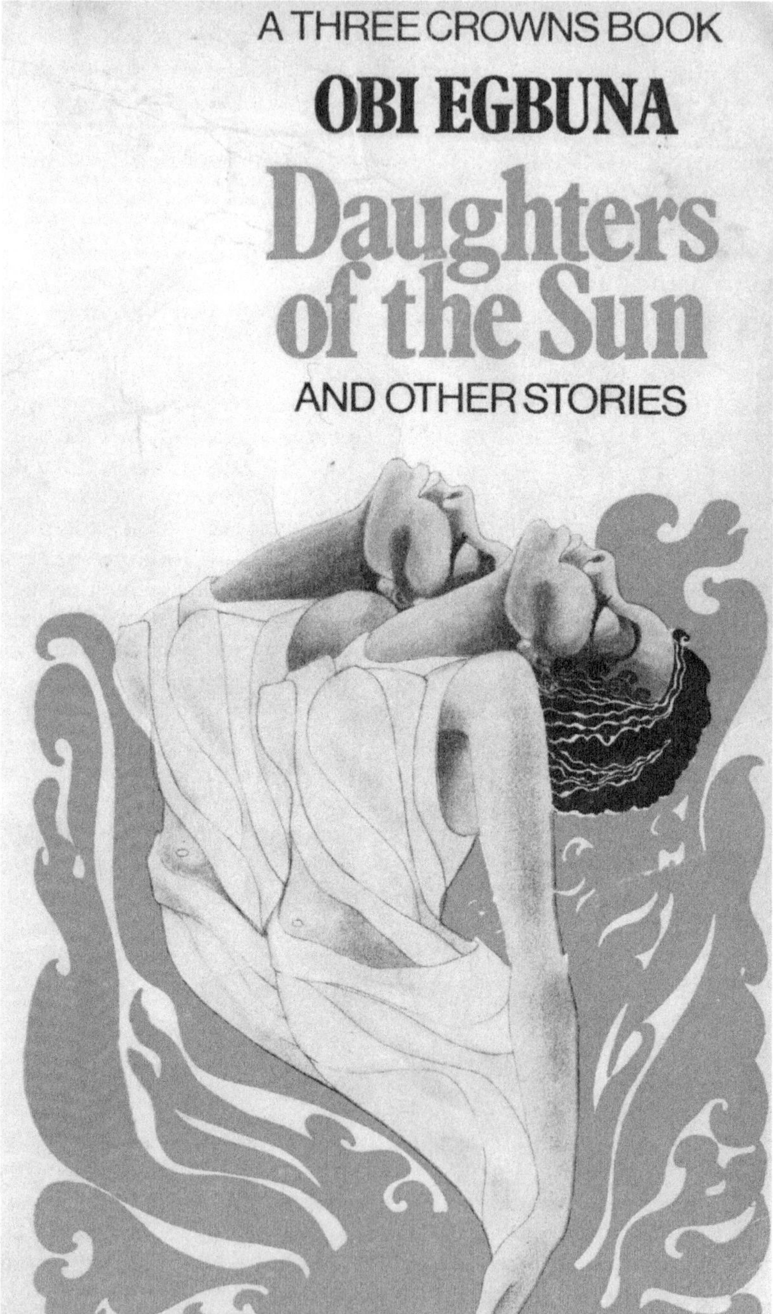

Figure 7.2 Obi Egbuna, Daughters of the Sun (1970), front cover. By permission of Oxford University Press

an earlier publishing tradition, in which there was no separate marketing department and no budget allocated to a marketing or promotional campaign. On occasion, simple black and white leaflets were produced to advertise the series, but promotion was mainly through sending review copies to the international press and to theatre companies. There was limited success in this area, however, as the press tended to review only hardback editions. Only in the exceptional case of Mtshali, described below, did the editor organise a promotional event for the author.

As a multinational publisher, OUP aimed to give authors an international forum as well as facilitating the adoption of their books in African schools. The books were promoted to OUP branch managers worldwide, in the hope that they would sell copies for their regional markets. Most crucially for Three Crowns sales, the books were publicised by the African branches to the local examination boards. This led to the adoption of several of the books in the series, for example plays by Soyinka, Clark, de Graft and Fugard, which was vital for sales and for public recognition of the authors within Africa. Evidently, the reason that Three Crowns could operate without widescale reviews and without expensive advertising was due to its privileged status in Africa: this rested on the almost monopolistic position that the educational British publishers occupied. OUP could rely on established and non-competitive supply routes, as well as on assured, guaranteed markets. In addition, the reputation of the imprint was evidently an important factor in the symbolic production of the authors' works. The process of publication by OUP, a prestigious and 'consecrated' publisher, was a way of legitimising authors by branding them as Oxford authors; this was evidently influential for their acceptance in both the metropolitan and the US market, but also in the African school market.[63]

Case-study 4: promoting Oswald Mtshali's *Sounds of a Cowhide Drum*

In 1970, the South African writer and literary editor Lionel Abrahams sought a publisher for Mtshali's poetry collection *Sounds of a Cowhide Drum*.

The poems in the volume concern the lives of black South Africans: a washerwoman, a labourer, prisoners ('men shorn / of all human honour / like sheep after shearing'[64]), a drunk in the street, a miner, and a young shepherd on the veld. Daily racial discrimination is the subject of 'Always a Suspect', in which a black man dressed 'like a gentleman' is asked to produce identity papers: 'I show him / The document of my existence / To be scrutinized and given the nod.'[65] 'An Abandoned Bundle' describes 'a mutilated corpse – / an infant dumped on a rubbish heap',[66] while 'Nightfall in Soweto' describes the violence of daily life in the township: 'I am the victim / I am slaughtered / Every night in the streets.'[67]

Abrahams sent the manuscript to Guy Butler, Head of English at Rhodes University, and editor of the New Coin poetry series. However, during this period of stringent censorship in South Africa, Butler was cautious, and suggested that it should be checked by a lawyer before publication:[68]

> I, for one, do not want this author to be persecuted on account of a legal technicality which may be got over by means of minor verbal adjustments which in no way affect the total impact, directness or integrity of the writer. The law is, proverbially, an ass, but a potentially dangerous one.[69]

Abrahams decided to withdraw the manuscript as a result, leading Butler to suggest that he might try Oxford University Press instead, perhaps considering that as a multinational publisher it was less vulnerable to banning constraints:

> I think you should approach the Oxford University Press, Cape Town. … I saw David Philip (editorial manager), and took the liberty of telling him of Mtshali's ms. I was assured that they would be very interested indeed to look at the poems. … Stallworthy was present, and thought it possible that the volume might be included in the 'Three Crown' series, I think. Anyway, I'm sure they will give it the most sympathetic reading, and I'll be very surprised if they don't take it. The firm has, of course, large African and overseas ramifications.[70]

Abrahams decided instead to establish his own imprint, Renoster Books, in Johannesburg and publish *Sounds of a Cowhide Drum* himself in 1971. It was published for the South African market, with a Foreword by Nadine Gordimer; the book escaped banning injunctions and was an immediate bestseller, exhausting five editions and over 10,000 copies by the end of the first year, and selling 17,000 copies by 1973.[71]

On his return to London from South Africa in 1971, Jon Stallworthy contacted Abrahams to seek international publishing rights for Mtshali beyond South Africa, writing, 'We like to think that we could give Mr. Mtshali the international audience his fine poems deserve.'[72] Both author and publisher agreed to the proposal, and Stallworthy wrote to ask the Secretary for permission to publish the book: 'These are at once the most powerful, the most exciting, and the most promising poems by an African that I have ever read.'[73] Approval was duly given, and the book was incorporated into the Three Crowns series.

The publishing agreement of 28 October 1971 stipulated that Mtshali should gain 10 per cent royalty on UK sales, 7.5 per cent on overseas sales and an advance of £38.00 on signing the agreement, followed by a further £38.00 on first publication.[74] Renoster retained the South African rights and US rights to the poetry, but Abrahams was clearly taken aback by the extent of the British territorial rights that he had inadvertently assigned to OUP. He was informed by OUP that the former British colonies 'are generally recognized to be part of the British Publisher's exclusive market and any attempt to make them a non-exclusive area must, and will, be strongly resisted by us'.[75] The British Commonwealth Market Agreement, in operation from 1946 to 1976, gave British publishers a significant advantage in reaching an international marketplace.[76]

Stallworthy's book announcement for *Sounds of a Cowhide Drum* compares his situation to that of the First World War poets: 'Mr Mtshali's poems – bitter, shocking, tender – all bear the unmistakeable mark of the Front Line that must win for him in the rest of the world the recognition he has already so overwhelmingly won in South Africa.'[77] He then promoted the edition by means of a back-cover blurb which compares his poetry with that of Wilfred Owen:

> Like Wilfred Owen he writes from 'the front line' about man's inhumanity to man and like Owen he appears to have been tempered and toughened by the forces of suffering and humiliation through which he has passed. Few English or American poets born in 1940 write with such authority, such controlled passion, and such compassion.[78]

Stallworthy then arranged an unprecedented promotional tour for Mtshali. He contacted Charles Osborne of the Poetry Book Society in London, sending him a copy of the book and asking 'whether we want to invite him'.[79] After long negotiations, Mtshali was invited to the UK on a lecture tour by the society. Neal Burton described the arrangements:

> He arrives in fact this weekend and will be in the country for a fortnight with a string of speaking engagements up and down the country, the Poetry International coming towards the end of his appearance. The Press are already interested.[80]

His tour of readings and recordings took him to Leeds, Brighton and London. It was funded jointly by the British Council and OUP, and Mtshali was also invited to the African Centre and to the Leeds University Department of English, organised by Ravenscroft. The tour was well publicised, and the *Evening Standard* reported the event at Queen Elizabeth Hall:

> Former Black dishwasher and floor-scrubber and now poet extraordinary Oswald Mtshali hit London's cultural highlights when his poetry reading got him big applause at the Queen Elizabeth Hall. Mtshali, one of South Africa's most remarkable and successful poets, appeared with W. H. Auden and Allen Ginsberg at Poetry International 73, the Poetry Book Society's annual poetry festival.[81]

This was the only example of an author-promotional event launched by Three Crowns, and it illustrates OUP's successful 'consecration' and 'legitimisation' of the 'Former Black dishwasher and floor-scrubber' poet.[82] Cinderella-like, he was transformed and given an assured place within the Anglo-American literary establishment.

It is significant that this publication and promotion of Mtshali took place at the same time as the major crisis unfolded in Cape Town over the branch's new policy of withdrawing from academic and oppositional publishing and its decision to concentrate on publishing schoolbooks for the Bantu Education Department. This acquisition can be seen as part of Stallworthy's protest against the Press's South Africa policy, and as evidence of his attempt to position and promote Three Crowns as an anti-apartheid series. Indeed, the publicity events might also have served to promote Oxford University Press as an anti-apartheid publisher, and to mask their controversial policies in South Africa.

Mtshali received criticism for courting liberal 'white patronage' in the publication of his book. A fellow South African poet, Keorapetse Kgositsile, said in an interview in February 1978:

> the white patronage nonsense one could even see by the fact that he would even allow a liberal like Nadine Gordimer to write an introduction to his book. Nadine Gordimer, like Vorster or like any other European in South Africa, does not have the capacity to understand what goes on in the black community, or to understand what goes on in Mtshali's mind or his feelings. How she could make a comment about his work escapes me.[83]

In a similar fashion, Ann McClintock regards Mtshali as 'lodged between the intellectual elite and the community',[84] and she writes that his poetry 'met with a hearty round of applause for his deployment of some of the familiar favorites of the Leavisite tradition', in particular by Gordimer's 'rapturous preface to the first edition' which 'invoked Auden and Blake'.[85] These two critics make the assumption that Mtshali actively courted such endorsements and patronage during the publication process. However, in the case of this edition, at least, Mtshali was cut off from the publishing process; there is no record of direct communication between OUP and the author. Decisions were carried out either by the editors in London or in consultation with his South African publisher. This publicity strategy, which compared Mtshali with Wilfred Owen and positioned him alongside W. H. Auden, and which republished Gordimer's endorsement of his book, was instigated and arranged for him by his British publisher.

Conclusion

How, then, do these publishing case-studies contribute towards an understanding of the production of African postcolonial literature? Evidently, the arguments about the British editor as a patron and champion of the African author have some validity. The editors invested time and determination in their support of the authors, and were committed to giving them an international platform for their writing. Collings fought to get authors published, often in the face of negative readers' reports; he insisted on their publication even when the market for their books was uncertain, and he accommodated the authors' ideas for the editing and production of their books. He negotiated relatively high royalty rates for his authors – an average of 10 per cent of the list price, compared to the average rate of 5 per cent to 7.5 per cent offered by other paperback publishers.[86] In addition, books that were subject to censorship in the authors' own countries were published and offered a world stage.[87] Stallworthy also showed persistence and commitment in his acquisition, publishing and promotion of his authors. For Collings and Currey, Three Crowns was the beginning of a lifelong commitment to African publishing: they both left OUP to pursue careers in African publishing in less constrained environments, eventually creating their own eponymous imprints.[88]

However, to describe the editors as simply 'champions' or 'supporters' of the author fails to take account of their impact on the literature. Indeed, Lefevere's metaphor of a 'hybrid literature' – implying the fusion and merging of two equal literary traditions – also fails to convey the unequal power relations existing between the African author and British editor. The arguments of Ngũgĩ and Amuta do not take into account the complexities of the interaction between authors and editors, but they perhaps come closer to capturing the essence of this asymmetrical relationship, by which British publishers exercised a determining impact on the emergence of African literature in this period.

These case-studies demonstrate that at each specific stage of literary production, the Three Crowns editors sought to assimilate the writers' work within Western literary marketing trends, either by incorporating the literature within Western literary traditions or by codifying it as archetypal, authentic and exotic. However, this editorial strategy, which endeavoured to 'universalise' the literature for an Anglo-American market, was at variance with the distribution strategy used for the books, which targeted them predominantly at the African market. The succession of debates and conflicts instigated by the editorial and production processes is testimony to the discomfort of several of the authors with this publishing strategy, and to the contradictory demands that were placed on books in the series.

8
Publishing Wole Soyinka

Presenting the Nobel Prize for Literature to Wole Soyinka in 1986, Lars Gyllensten praised his 'commitment as a dramatist and writer of poetry and prose to problems of general and deep significance for man, modern or ancient', and his ability to synthesise 'a very rich heritage from [his] own country, ancient myths and old traditions, with literary legacies and traditions of European culture'. Gyllensten went on to describe *A Dance of the Forests* as 'a kind of African "Midsummer Night's Dream", with dryads, ghosts, spirits, and gods or demi-gods'. Soyinka's responding Nobel lecture urged the rest of the world to sever all cords with 'the pariah society that is Apartheid South Africa', and called for 'the end of racism, the eradication of human inequality, and the dismantling of all their structures'.[1]

A number of recent works have examined the tensions between Soyinka's persona as a universal writer – a status confirmed here by the Swedish Academy – and his political activism, which was signified by Soyinka's acceptance speech.[2] Biodun Jeyifo, for example, writes: 'it is apparent that many aspects of his radical political activism sit rather uneasily with his general reputation as an "obscure" writer, an "elitist" artist',[3] while Mumia Abu-Jamal, the death-row journalist, writes:

> Wole Soyinka is far more than the appellation 'African Writer' would suggest. He is that, to be sure, but he is an aggressive cut above, marked by a political militance and critical incisiveness that places him in total opposition to the post-colonial and neo-colonial state.[4]

This chapter assesses the role of Soyinka's first international publisher, OUP, in the transition of his literary identity from writer-activist to 'universal genius'.[5]

OUP published a total of seven of Soyinka's early plays in the Three Crowns series: *The Lion and the Jewel* and *A Dance of the Forests* in 1963, followed by *The Road* in 1965, *Kongi's Harvest* in 1967 and then the collection *Three Short Plays* in 1969, which comprised *The Strong Breed, The Trials of Brother Jero* and *The Swamp Dwellers*. This is the first detailed study of Wole Soyinka's publishing history, which draws on records in the OUP Oxford archive and on records in the Leeds University Library Special Collections.[6] Adapting Darnton's model of the 'Communications Circuit', this chapter is structured around the life-cycle of these published plays,[7] reviewing first the performances of the plays, before moving on to consider their editing, production, marketing, sales and reading. In addition, the paratext of the published plays is examined to see how the physical form of the books and the accompanying publicity influenced the interpretation and reception of the early Soyinka works.[8]

Soyinka has long been regarded as the archetypal alienated postcolonial author. Chinweizu, Onwuchekwa and Ihechukwu famously branded Soyinka a 'Euromodernist' who has 'assiduously aped the practice of twentieth-century European modernist poetry' and exercised 'voluntary cultural servitude'.[9] Oyenlyi Okunoye later argued that Soyinka, along with other members of the Mbari Club, was 'part of an emergent elite incapable of authentic self-expression, and caught in a crisis of identity'.[10] The following section investigates the negotiations between Soyinka and OUP during the process of publication. It reappraises these arguments, and suggests how theories of postcolonial authorship might be re-evaluated in the context of publishing histories.

Soyinka in performance

In his biography *Ibadan*, Soyinka describes the first performance of *A Dance of the Forests* as 'subversive, cynical, iconoclastic ... it mocked the glories of the past and was pessimistic about the future'.[11] He also described, in an interview with James Gibbs, how he deliberately tailored the productions of his plays in order to highlight topical political analogies:

> for me a play on the page is really cold and dead and my real instinct has always been to see the play fleshed out. I don't feel that the play is completed until I've actually seen it live on the stage. I think I am as much a director as I am a playwright, and when I begin to direct a play I have no respect at all for my text.[12]

In directing a 1961 performance of *The Trials of Brother Jero* in Ibadan, Soyinka adapted the script to target the newly elected Nigerian politicians, provoking 'shocked comments and scandalized opinions' according to one reviewer.[13] Soyinka reported a similar audience response to his production of *Kongi's Harvest* at the University of Ibadan in the early 1970s. Having been recently released from 27 months' incarceration during the Nigerian civil war, Soyinka revised this satire on the tyranny and autocracy of African rulers to directly target General Gowon and the federal military government: 'I had reinterpreted *Kongi's Harvest* with a military image on top at a very direct reference point. ... After that there was flak, but it was too late.'[14] The key aim was evidently to provoke a strong audience reaction to his plays in performance, as he explained in a later interview with Gibbs: 'first you have to arouse in the people a certain, well, to put it crudely, a certain nausea towards a particular situation, to arouse them at all to accept a positive alternative when it is offered to them'.[15] These brief accounts of the writing and direction of his early plays suggest that Soyinka represented himself as a writer-activist, and as a critic of the new political elites operating in Africa. The study now turns to the publishing strategy for these plays, and considers how the publisher dealt with this political critique in Soyinka's writing.

Acquiring Soyinka

Rex Collings, as editor of the Three Crowns series, went on tour to West Africa in the early 1960s, on a quest for an African Shakespeare: 'I was travelling round Nigeria searching for budding Shakespeares and Byrons.'[16] He considered the search to be successful, for his letter continued: 'we now have the playwright; but the poet eludes us'. For, while in Nigeria, Collings heard rumours of Soyinka, and on his return to London, he continued his pursuit by writing to Joan Littlewood of the Theatre Workshop:

> Whilst I was in Nigeria I was told that you had discovered what was purported to be an extremely good play by a local dramatist. ... We are anxious to publish the works of local authors wherever possible and it did appear to me that if the play was suitable for acting then it would probably be suitable for us to publish.[17]

Littlewood passed on Soyinka's name and address and ended the letter: 'I think he is a brilliant writer, and I have passed your letter on to him.'[18] After an invitation from Collings, Soyinka took playscripts of *The Lion and the Jewel* and *A Dance of the Forests* into the Ibadan office. After being read by the branch manager, T. T. Solaru, the manuscripts were forwarded to Collings, who arranged for them to be reviewed by several OUP editors and British academics.

A Dance of the Forests is a more complex play, concerning the gods, humans and the dead, which satirises the tendency of African nationalism to romanticise its past, and which draws comparisons between modern-day corruption with tyranny in African precolonial history. A community comes together to celebrate a 'Gathering of the Tribes' festival, a giant tree is carved into a totem in a grove in a forest, and arrangements are made for members of the illustrious dead to attend. However, all does not go according to plan, for one of the carvers causes his assistant to fall to his death, and instead of glorious forefathers attending, the 'spirits of the restless dead' arrive.

In a play within the play, the humans are taken to the Court of Mata Kharibu, where they confront their crimes in a previous existence.[19]

The Lion and the Jewel is, by contrast, a bawdy comedy set in a Nigerian village in which the 72-year-old village chief, Bale Baroka, and the young schoolmaster, Lakunle, compete to marry a village girl, Sidi, resulting in her seduction by the old chief. The readers' reviews in the archive collection concern this play rather than *A Dance of the Forests*. John Bell, manager of the House Books department of OUP, London wrote of *The Lion and the Jewel*, 'I've read this with great enjoyment ... as an authentic African play it certainly deserves publication by somebody, and possibly by us.'[20] Gerald Moore, author of the Three Crowns volume *Seven African Writers*, eulogised its unique qualities in his reader's report, stating, 'To my mind it is the [most] outstanding play so far produced in Africa, alike in its boldness of conception, the range and power of its dramatic effects and the beauty of its language.'[21]

While there was consensus about the literary quality of *The Lion and the Jewel*, there was some disagreement about its suitability for the school market, which is further evidence of the editorial struggle to satisfy two conflicting imperatives for African literature. One editorial manager's report raised concerns about the 'basic theme of virility which would not normally figure in your school textbooks quite so undisguisedly', and also commented that 'the discomfiture of the butt figure, the schoolmaster, is perhaps a little alarming in its implications'.[22] Collings argued that *The Lion and the Jewel* was suitable for A-level prescription, making a further analogy between Soyinka and Shakespeare: 'This is not alas an altogether suitable play for schools – but nor is an unexpurgated Macbeth. But ... as good English it should provide a prescribable text for examinations above school certificate.'[23] The argument was persuasive, and he was permitted to go ahead with arranging contracts with Soyinka. These were drawn up on 14 September 1962 between Collings and Soyinka, covering publication of these plays both individually in paperback and as a combined hardback edition. This was the first time that the two had met, and it was, in Collings's words, 'a marathon session'.[24]

There was then further debate about whether the plays should be copy-edited to ensure their suitability for African schools. Tani Solaru, manager of the Ibadan branch, suggested that *The Lion and the Jewel* be altered: 'The one point which may make the play unsuited for young people is the undue emphasis on sex and the sensual. ... But I do not think it would be too difficult for the author to make the necessary changes to render these passages more decorous for youthful ears and minds.'[25] The Ghana-based editor, Neal Burton, disagreed: 'this is genuine creative writing, of great interest and vigour, and is not something which we could regard as for the normal junior school situation (in other words open to considerable "editing" at our suggestion)'.[26]

Collings shared this view, and editorial interventions in Soyinka's plays appear to have been light. Soyinka was praised for submitting clean manuscripts on time; for example, the marked-up typescripts of *A Dance of the Forests* and *The Road* contain only minor typographic corrections, such as those relating to punctuation, missing words and spellings. Thus, although the plays were identified as suitable for the African school market, the editors resisted any censorship of Soyinka for this market, and insisted that, as literary works, they should not be subject to the same editorial interference as educational titles.

The editorial response to Soyinka's next manuscripts demonstrates the acquisition policy that was applied. In 1963, Soyinka sent manuscripts of *The Road* and *Camwood on the Leaves* to Collings. *The Road* focuses on the lives of two outcasts: the Professor, a former lay-reader, and Kotonu, a driver who has been traumatised by an accident, both of whom live in a shack at the side of the road, making a living by selling forged licences and scavenging for plunder from the wreckage of car accidents. *Camwood on the Leaves* was first broadcast as part of the Nigerian independence celebrations on Radio Nigeria. Its main concern is the relationship between the Reverend Erinjobi and his son, Isola, and the conflict when the father discovers that his son has made a local girl pregnant. Isola refuses to take a beating for his actions, and the play ends with Isola accidentally killing his father.

In his reader's report, the African literature critic Edgar Wright concluded that while *The Road* was certainly worth publishing, the radio play *Camwood* was not. His verdict was that *Camwood* was 'heavy with dark and tragic meaning, and the result is portentous, symbolic melodrama that sags like a windy Yorkshire pudding'. Although it 'might possibly go down well with Nigerian audiences, I would suggest that it wouldn't do Soyinka's reputation in general much good'.[27] By contrast, Wright interpreted *The Road* as symbolic and universal, judging that it 'is not specific; it is anywhere and represents a way of life, modernity, violence, false values' and that 'the virtues of the play outweigh any obscurity'. Collings agreed to turn down the more accessible *Camwood* and publish the more obscure play *The Road*, reflecting a concern at OUP to present Soyinka as a complex, literary and universal writer. The decision disappointed Soyinka, as he regarded *Camwood* as one of his favourite plays.[28] He wrote to Collings: 'Is there any reason why Camwood isn't going into the collected edition? I thought we agreed it should.'[29]

Thereafter, Soyinka's commercial success and literary reputation were assured, and subsequent manuscripts were acquired without a review process. OUP obtained rights from Mbari, the Ibadan publishers of *Three Plays* (1962), for *The Strong Breed, Brother Jero* and *The Swamp Dwellers*, to be published as a hardback *Five Plays* (alongside *A Dance of the Forests* and *The Lion and the Jewel*) and as a paperback, entitled *Three Short Plays*.[30] The last of Soyinka's long plays to be acquired by OUP was *Kongi's Harvest*, but the only surviving archival information on the acquisition of this play is the publishing agreement signed by Soyinka and Collings on 5 February 1965, under its original title 'The Metamorphosis of Buffy'.

The acquisition of Soyinka sheds some light on the processes of entrance into and exclusion from the postcolonial literary field in this period. The process of canonising Soyinka was evidently underway and, in the tradition of liberal humanism, the editors read Soyinka's plays as allegorical and archetypal, presenting him as a complex, literary and universal writer, whose work, like an 'unexpurgated Macbeth', was suitable for advanced study in African schools.

Soyinka and the Three Crowns series

Soyinka rapidly became the main draw for the Three Crowns series in attracting new African playwrights, for example Lewis Nkosi, John Pepper Clark, Joe de Graft, Obi Egbuna and Athol Fugard. By 1968, Philip Chester, the assistant publisher in London, considered that Soyinka was crucial to the series identity: 'The title "Three Crowns" largely, no doubt, because of the subsequent fame of Soyinka, is thought to have a certain réclame amongst creative writers.'[31] Yet, Soyinka was critical of the Western conception of African literature as a homogeneous entity, and objected to the desire for African exotica. In an earlier article in *The Horn*, a magazine published by the University of Ibadan, Soyinka wrote: 'The struggle against "authenticity" is one which will have to be fought by future West African writers, against the demands of foreign appetite for that "unspoilt" stuff.'[32] In 1966, Soyinka wrote an angry letter to David Neale, after finding out that the New York publisher Hill and Wang planned to include *The Lion and the Jewel* in an anthology of African drama:

> this particular anthology appears to me to be a typical uninformed lumping-together of material which the new African enthusiasts indulge in, and I have no wish to see my work represented in it. Should I not, at least, be informed about these matters?[33]

OUP backtracked rapidly from these negotiations. However, Jon Stallworthy later claimed that Soyinka did not want to be in the Three Crowns series, but, instead, wanted to be published in his own right.[34] Thus, although Soyinka was considered crucial to the success and reputation of the Three Crowns series, he objected to the 'uninformed lumping-together' of literature from African writers within one publishing genre.

Author–editor relationships

The relationship that developed between Soyinka and Collings was a lifelong literary partnership, but it is one that has been entirely ignored in biographies and critical studies of Soyinka; Collings fails even to get a mention in Soyinka's autobiographies.[35] Contact between OUP and Soyinka was initially brokered through the Ibadan branch, but gradually a close working relationship developed between author and editor.

Collings secured exceptionally high royalties for Soyinka: they varied from publication to publication, but for UK sales he was generally granted 15 per cent, and for overseas sales anything between 7.5 per cent (for *Kongi's Harvest*) to 15 per cent (for *The Road* and *A Dance of the Forests*).[36] These contractual arrangements came to be much bemoaned by subsequent OUP editors in London and the branches, who felt that this pushed the price of the publications up too high.[37] Soyinka gained a considerable income from his royalties: for example, in the two years from 1967 to 1969 his royalties amounted to £1233.[38]

The arrangement between author and publisher was threatened, however, when Soyinka announced in 1965 that he had set up his own Ibadan-based publishing company, Orisun Editions, to publish 'cheap acting editions for schools'. This was a joint venture with Bola Ige, and on the letterhead it announced that Orisun Editions was a publisher of 'poetry, short stories, plays, acting editions, africana'. He proposed to begin with the publication of *Brother Jero* along with Clark's *Song of a Goat*, and had plans to later include *The Swamp Dwellers*, *Camwood on the Leaves* and *The Lion and the Jewel*, and he suggested 'some kind of working arrangement with Oxford University Press especially anything that will take the actual burden of publishing off our backs'.[39] David Neale and the Ibadan office expressed alarm that the new cheaper editions would kill off the OUP's paperback editions of Soyinka's plays and would damage the sale of *Five Plays*.[40] In the event, however, no further mention was made of this enterprise, and it seems that it never came about.

When Collings left OUP for Methuen in 1965, he negotiated that Soyinka would go with him.[41] Soyinka's first title to be published by Methuen was a poetry collection entitled *Idanre* (1967), and thereafter, Methuen published a number of Soyinka's plays and poetry, including *Madmen and Specialists* (1971), *A Shuttle in the Crypt* (1972, in association with Rex Collings), *Camwood on the Leaves* (1973), *The Jero Plays* (1973) and *Death and the King's Horsemen* (1975).

In August 1967 Soyinka was imprisoned in Nigeria for writing an article for the *Daily Times* in Lagos that appealed for a truce with Biafra, and for visiting Biafra in person to meet leaders, in Soyinka's words, 'to present a definite political alternative'.[42] For 27 months he was incarcerated in Kaduna prison, without charge, most of it spent in solitary confinement. Whilst in jail, Soyinka smuggled three handwritten poems, entitled 'Prisonettes', to Collings in London, together with a cryptic letter conveying his plight. Collings published the poems as a small pamphlet, *Poems from Prison*, published in 1969, which was the first title under the Rex Collings imprint. Throughout Soyinka's imprisonment during the civil war, Collings campaigned on his behalf, keeping the UK press aware of his situation.[43]

After his release, Collings continued to publish Soyinka's work under his own imprint, including *The Man Died* (1972), *Season of Anomy* (1973), *Ogun Abibiman* (1976), *Ake: The Years of Childhood* (1981), *Opera Wonyosi* (1981) and, finally, *Requiem for a Futurologist* (1985). Soyinka would use Collings's offices in Paddington as a base when he was in the UK. Collings continued to work primarily in African publishing, but suffered huge losses following the collapse of the Nigerian economy in the mid-1980s; he died in 1996, aged 71.[44]

Collings was evidently crucial to Soyinka's relationship with OUP, and after his departure, OUP's editorial communication with the author came to a near standstill, despite the fact that Soyinka's valuable copyrights continued to be the property of the Press.[45] While Soyinka was in prison, there is no evidence that OUP staff in Nigeria or in London campaigned on his behalf, and after his release Soyinka had very little contact with the publisher. Jon Stallworthy and Ron Heapy made several attempts to renew contact as series editors, but with little success. Faced with Soyinka's failure to answer correspondence, they were forced to make decisions about reprints and editions of his plays without his formal approval.[46] There was an increasing disassociation between Soyinka and his published texts at OUP, as his plays came to be regarded as simply the publisher's property, to be marketed for maximum sales.

Production of Soyinka

The paratext of Soyinka's early plays was designed to appeal to the UK trade market, in terms of format, jacket illustrations and series branding. Collings decided that the plays should follow Penguin Plays and be published in crown octavo format.[47] Representations of rural Africa featured on the jacket illustrations of the first two books, designed by the Sudanese artist Taj Ahmed. The cover for *The Lion and the Jewel* was of an African village, with a title in stencil lettering form (Figure 8.1).

On the front cover of *A Dance of the Forests* were trees, with faces and creatures – perhaps human, perhaps animal – intertwined in the branches. Stylised figures in African wrappers and cloths are positioned below (Figure 8.2). The jacket for *Kongi's Harvest* was designed by a new artist, Jimo Akelo, and the front cover carried an illustration of an African striped coat and shield, and on the back cover, a mask and carvings (Figure 8.3). Thus, *A Dance of the Forests* and *Kongi's Harvest* – plays that were deemed to be politically subversive in performance – were exoticised as publications. Soyinka was also positioned within the publishing genre of African literature, with the Three Crowns series name and colophon occupying central positions on the front covers. The peritext of Soyinka's books served to impose a

Figure 8.1 Wole Soyinka, *The Lion and the Jewel* (1963), front cover. By permission of Oxford University Press

Figure 8.2 Wole Soyinka, *A Dance of the Forests* (1963), front cover. By permission of Oxford University Press

Figure 8.3 Wole Soyinka, *Kongi's Harvest* (1967), front cover. By permission of Oxford University Press

stereotypical African image on the literature, but this intervention occurred without Soyinka's authorisation, and he was dissatisfied with these cover designs.[48]

When it came to the publication of *The Road* and *Five Plays*, Soyinka attempted to get a new artist to design the covers, writing, 'I notice that the cover is being designed by the former artist. But I told you I'd ask an artist here to do it and I've done so already.'[49] He was too late for *Five Plays*, and although Collings agreed to a new jacket design for *The Road*, the roughs were submitted too late to be used and the book was rushed through production with an indistinct photograph of a dirt road on the front cover (Figure 8.4).

By 1969, there was a major fracas over the design of Soyinka's books. After Collings's departure, a new illustrator, Lazlo Acs, was commissioned for *Three Short Plays*. His jacket illustration was of a tree, the trunk of which made up the capitalised author's name, with four African figures below (Figure 8.5). The design proved to be unpopular in both US and African markets. The New York branch refused to stock it, declaring, 'It is, unfortunately, completely wrong for our market. We cannot order any copies of your edition.'[50] The Nairobi branch then attempted to reduce its order of the book, complaining that the cover design was 'almost insulting' to Soyinka, considering that he was 'Africa's leading playwright'. It complained that 'the author's name, cascading down the page, does not do any credit to Soyinka, as it is almost impossible to read. Surely Soyinka's name is the most important thing, and the main selling point.' In addition, the primitive cover was regarded as patronising, giving 'the impression that the book is aimed at a primary level. ... In conclusion, we think Soyinka's plays deserve more serious treatment.'[51] Yet, the offending cover design of *Three Short Plays* was retained and reused in all the reprints of the book. As late as 1983, the design was still being used for the fourth impression of the book.

The peritext of Soyinka's books also signalled their destination for the African schools market: the production quality was poor and the covers were cheaply produced. There was disquiet over the way that Soyinka's books resembled the supplementary readers that accompanied the profitable *Oxford English Course*. John Brown, the OUP London Publisher, issued damning criticism of the series: 'we got hold of Soyinka and just added as and when someone submitted something, Rex Collings being the editor. We produced them to look like supplementary readers and not paperbacks.'[52]

Eventually a two-tier production strategy was devised for Soyinka's books. The decision was made that Soyinka had become 'too big for Three Crowns', and that he needed to be positioned in 'the Press's mainline publishing in London and New York'.[53] He was moved into the Oxford Paperback series for the UK and US markets, with his first volume being published in November 1973 and the second in 1974, both with simple typographic cover designs. The Oxford branding was more prominent on the covers and

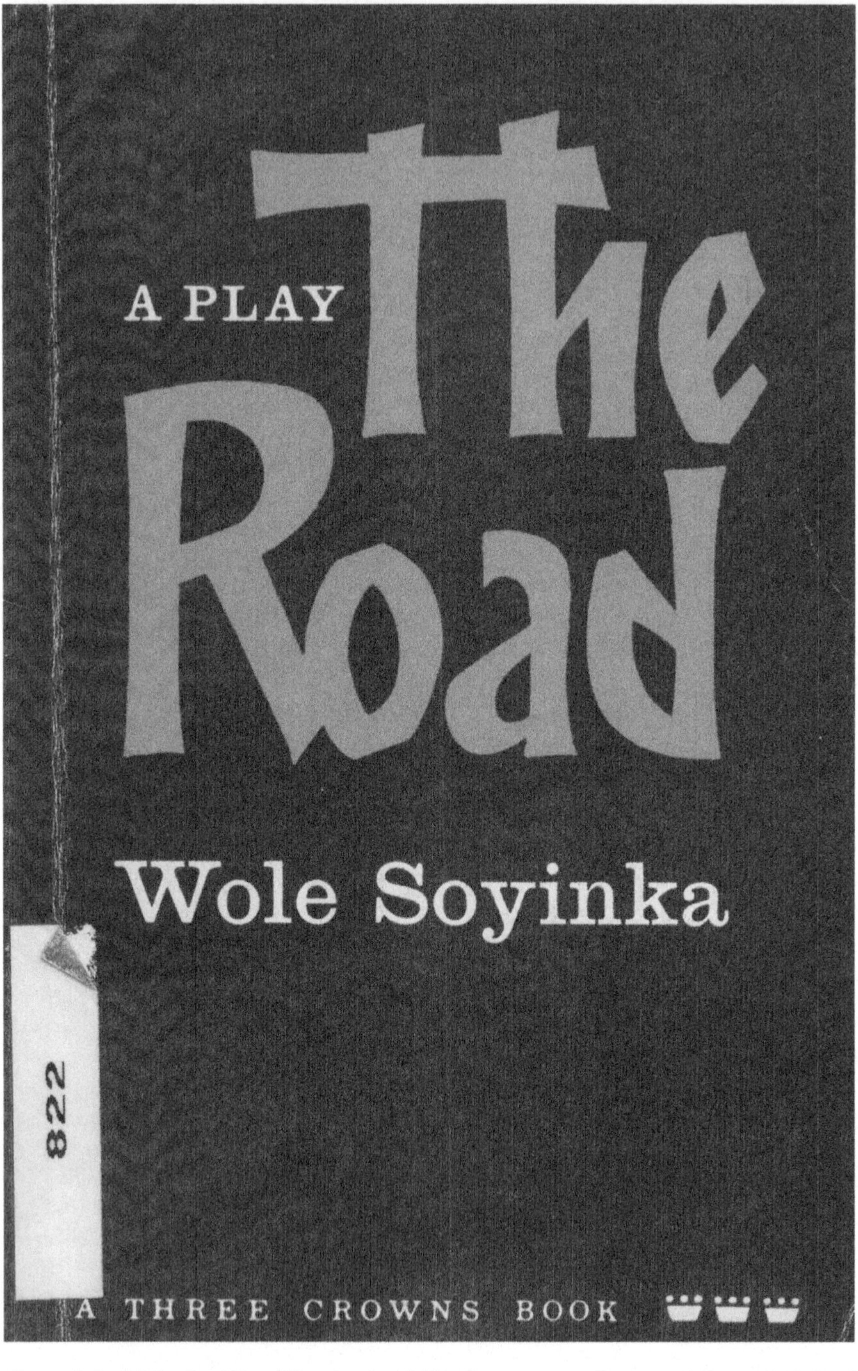

Figure 8.4 Wole Soyinka, *The Road* (1965), front cover. By permission of Oxford University Press

Figure 8.5 Wole Soyinka, *Three Short Plays* (1969), front and back covers. By permission of Oxford University Press

Figure 8.6 Wole Soyinka, *Collected Plays 2* (1973), front and back covers. By permission of Oxford University Press

on the spine, and a description of Soyinka's cultural achievements, together with extracts from reviews, were printed on the back covers; these editions reflected Soyinka's categorisation as a mainstream, canonical, Oxford author (Figure 8.6). Meanwhile, the controversial Three Crowns editions continued to be published for the African markets.

Marketing Soyinka

Due to its privileged status in Africa as an educational publisher with unrivalled supply routes and a secure, guaranteed place in the school market, investment in book promotion was minimal and the publisher relied instead on the established reputation of the OUP imprint and the non-competitive marketplace.[54] Soyinka's books were marketed simply by a few cheaply produced leaflets. The flyer promoting *A Dance of the Forests* quoted from Gerald Moore's review, in which the play was defined not as political satire, but as a mythical tale – a blend of African folklore and European literary traditions:

> The whole action of the play is set in a mysterious Forest, very like Shakespeare's Forest of the Comedies or the Heath of King Lear. ... If the Forest reminds us of Shakespeare (though its origin is more likely the 'Bush' of African folklore), the episodic but cumulative nature of the action and its 'total' embrace of acting, music, song and dance, have a somewhat Brechtian quality.[55]

A leaflet for *The Lion and the Jewel* likewise praises the play for merging African and Shakespearean literary traditions, arguing that Soyinka was 'dealing not just with rich folk material, but with the impact of the modern on tribal custom; to find any parallel for his work in English drama you have to go back to the Elizabethans'.[56] The Three Crowns promotional booklet described Soyinka's work in similar terms: 'his plays, mixing realistic and mythical elements, prose and verse, achieve a vivid and strongly local form of expression'.[57]

The publisher's epitext characterised Soyinka not as a satirist and political activist, but as an authentic African writer who drew on European – and especially Shakespearean – literary traditions. The book advertisements principally served to endorse Soyinka to OUP's main market in Africa – that is, the examination boards and the school teachers who would be selecting texts for the curriculum.

Selling Soyinka

James English argues that Soyinka's work, 'at times rather dense and obscure linguistically as well as avant-gardist in its formal procedures, had arguably succeeded better in Britain ... and on the Continent ... than in Africa'.[58]

However, the sales figures for Soyinka's OUP publications provide important evidence of the main readership of his plays in the 1960s and 1970s, and challenge the assumption that Soyinka was writing predominantly for the West.

Five Plays (1964) was the only Three Crowns book to be produced in hardback, which can be seen as an attempt to aid Soyinka's critical reception in the UK and US literary marketplaces. However, by 1967 this collected volume had sold only 336 copies in the UK (27 per cent of sales), 317 to the US (26 per cent) and 495 to African branches (40 per cent).[59] Collings also attempted to sell Soyinka's paperback editions in the UK trade market and through OUP's New York branch, but the same pattern of sales was discernible. During the financial year of 1967, 15 per cent of the books were sold in the UK and 11 per cent in the USA, while the majority (71 per cent) were sold to the African branches.[60] Over the period 1965–69, an average of only 15 per cent of the total sales of Soyinka's plays were in the UK.[61] In 1969 the Publisher, John Brown, concluded: 'There have been no significant sales in the UK even of Soyinka and it looks as if the market really has been supplementary readers.'[62] However, by 1971 the US market for the Three Crowns editions of Soyinka's plays had increased, and nearly 30 per cent of Soyinka's books were distributed by the New York branch, the main market in the USA being to black Americans.[63] Yet, the majority of Soyinka's books (56 per cent) were still being exported to Africa in this year.[64] The editors soon realised that the major market for Soyinka was the African school market, which constituted between 80 to 90 per cent of the total book market in East and West Africa in the 1960s and 1970s.[65]

Soyinka's plays were widely prescribed as examination texts throughout anglophone Africa. From 1969 to 1977 Soyinka's *The Lion and the Jewel* and *The Trials of Brother Jero* were prescribed in East Africa, Lesotho and Zimbabwe for the University of Cambridge local examination syndicate, where the plays were offered as an alternative to Shakespeare's *The Merchant of Venice*.[66] This is reflected in sales of these titles. In the period from 1964 to 1971, *The Lion and the Jewel* was the highest seller, selling nearly 39,000 copies, whereas *A Dance of the Forests*, which was not a set text, sold only 7300 copies during this period.[67] When *Kongi's Harvest* was prescribed for East Africa for 1971–72, an order of 15,000 copies was put through to London by the Nairobi branch. In Zimbabwe *The Lion and the Jewel* was prescribed for the O-level syllabus for 1987–90. The vast majority of sales of Soyinka's texts were, however, in his native Nigeria. As already noted, over 18,000 copies of *The Lion and the Jewel* were sold in 1970, and 15,000 of these were sold in Nigeria.[68]

Thus, Soyinka's books initially achieved high sales to the African school market, and only later achieved sales to the more prestigious literary and higher education market in the UK and USA. He therefore managed in a unique way within the series to achieve cultural and economic capital simultaneously, findings which problematise once again Bourdieu's theory of the fundamental 'opposition between the sub-field of restricted production and the sub-field of large-scale production'.[69] Evidently the marginalised and low-status schoolbook market in Africa was crucial in creating Soyinka's international reputation.

Reading Soyinka

Robert Darnton advocates a reconstruction of the social context of reading: 'the history of reading will have to take account of the way that texts constrain readers as well as the ways that readers take liberties with texts'.[70] Although evidence of readers' responses to the Three Crowns editions of Soyinka is limited, the letters of one Kenyan school pupil to the Press shed light on the way in which the readers of Soyinka's plays were constrained by the publisher.

In 1972, Robert Maviala, of Musingu High School in Kakemega, Kenya, wrote to Ron Heapy, editor of Three Crowns, about *Kongi's Harvest*: 'We are here with other students much puzzled to the beginning and the end of this book. So we are very much interested in your making it much simpler than it really is. ... I think if we can only get two copies much simplified we can be much happy.'[71] Although Heapy forwarded this letter to Soyinka, the schoolboy wrote again to him:

> Dear Heapy ... How we are anxious to hear more from this book entitled THE KONGI'S HARVEST. Just the way it begins and how it ends is a problem. Oh! I just think perhaps you have heard a word from the author himself. ... The following questions were set in our mock: Discuss the characters of Kongi's Harvest and how did he behave after receiving the new yam, why was the gunpowder fired immediately, was it a plan if so discuss. How anxious I am for the reply.[72]

Heapy replied to Maviala, 'There is something wrong with the mail. I have written again to the author on your behalf. I am sorry he did not reply before. I wish you the best of luck in all your examinations.'[73]

This was not simply one isolated reader's problem. Several years earlier, in 1966, Tani Solaru had written to London about the problems Soyinka's plays caused for some school pupils:

> From reports received from our travelers, there is increasingly interest and demand for plays written by Nigerian authors, especially those of Soyinka. It has been pointed out however that the language is often more difficult than students in the School's certificate can easily comprehend. One wonders whether an annotated edition for schools cannot be done.[74]

Anthony Toyne categorically rejected his proposal: 'Would not the annotation of poetic turns of phrase be open to charges of pedantry? And yet what else is there to annotate?'[75] The same issue was raised in 1974 by Jonathan Kariara, editor in Nairobi. He wrote to Heapy about the difficulty of *Kongi's Harvest* for Kenyan students, and added that there was a similar, although less serious problem with *The Lion and the Jewel*. Suggesting that additional information was required on Yoruba culture, he proposed an annotated edition of Soyinka. Permission was again refused in London by Bill Mitchell:

> In general, I am against Study Guides for commercial reasons (low revenue against relatively high editorial costs), and also ... with the tendency towards rote learning in markets like Kenya, the Guide probably results in less rather than more intelligent study and enjoyment of the text.[76]

Attempts by the branch editors to make the plays more accessible were thus vetoed by London, and the difficulty of Soyinka's texts for readers in schools across Africa was if anything exacerbated by the publication process. The decision to issue his plays without introductions, explanations or notes was taken deliberately, partly to save on editorial costs, but also to avoid 'rote learning' and 'charges of pedantry'. The publisher's main concern was evidently to promote Soyinka to African examination boards, as a writer whose complex plays warranted close critical analysis.

Conclusion

This chapter has focused on the role of a British publisher in the construction and dissemination of African literature; it has assessed the implications of the control and mediation of Soyinka's plays by a publisher that had been intrinsically involved in the colonial education system in Africa. In the case of Soyinka, the principal interventions of the publisher occurred not at the copy-editing stage but at the other stages of the communications circuit. Soyinka's plays – many of which he regarded as political satires in performance – were published with exotic and homogeneous paratext. Most significantly, his plays were selected for, edited, marketed and sold through the residual colonial-style distribution channels.

This study casts doubt on the interpretation of Soyinka as a writer alienated from his own market through the process of international publication. The Three Crowns editors were keen to court the prestigious UK and US literary marketplace for Soyinka, but in fact the African market was far more significant in economic terms. The editorial and production policies were highly successful in appealing to African examination boards: publicity materials proclaimed the publishers' authorisation of Soyinka's place in the European cultural and literary field, and the books, modelled on supplementary readers, were cheaply produced. This strategy led to the adoption of Soyinka in schools throughout anglophone Africa. He is now canonised in his own continent, and is referred to in the African press as 'Africa's Own William Shakespeare' and as 'Our own W. S'.[77]

Rather than implying authorial complicity with his British publisher, the archival evidence indicates instead that Soyinka was increasingly divorced from the publishing process at OUP and had little control over the publication of his books. Although he retained authorial control of the typescript, he had no control over the subsequent exoticising and universalising publishing processes. Soyinka was critical of the Western construction of African literature as a uniform entity, and he registered disaffection with OUP, first by objecting to editorial and design decisions, and by attempting to publish his work independently in Nigeria. His final course of action was to leave the Press, and ignore later correspondence.

This study considers that the publication of Soyinka in the Three Crowns series was crucial in the symbolic construction of the playwright not as writer-activist, but as a universal genius – as Africa's Shakespeare – an identity which was then affirmed by the Nobel prize committee and which has been reiterated in many recent critical studies.[78] Although, undoubtedly, both Soyinka and OUP benefited financially and in terms of prestige from OUP's publishing strategy, the archival evidence shows that the relationship between Soyinka and his first international publisher was not one of 'voluntary cultural servitude' and that the publisher's interventions were neither endorsed nor welcomed by the author.

9
Publishing Athol Fugard

Introduction

This chapter is concerned with the creation of Athol Fugard's plays not as performances or as texts, but as material objects: it explores how the social conditions of textual production and circulation have affected their interpretation. It charts the transformation of 'Fugard' into an increasingly valuable piece of literary property, on which different meanings have been inscribed.

From the 1970s, Oxford University Press became Fugard's preferred British publisher. It was the main publisher to exploit its legal advantage and seek British territorial rights for Fugard's texts and, by 1983, OUP had 12 of Fugard's major plays in publication. These have proved to be of enduring financial value for the Press, and are still in print. They have been included in and out of various series, packaged both individually and in collections, in paperback and hardback. They have been prescribed for school and university syllabuses worldwide, and have been published by OUP in London, Oxford, New York, Nairobi and Cape Town. While existing Fugard scholarship centres on the plays either as performance or as text, this is the first study of Fugard's publishing history, which focuses on seven of Fugard's plays published by OUP during the period 1968 to 1974.

A 'universal' or political dramatist?

The major question that OUP editors grappled with was how to interpret and promote Fugard. Was he a political, anti-apartheid dramatist or a writer of 'universal' truths? Was his work specific to South Africa or did it have a resonance beyond that country? In the late 1960s and early 1970s, Fugard was writing in the context of increasingly entrenched state repression and violence in South Africa. Following a state of emergency after Sharpeville and a crackdown on political opposition, resistance to apartheid was suppressed. The Terrorism Act of 1967 authorised the imprisonment of suspects without trial, and oppositional organisations were banned in 1968. The Black Homeland Citizenship Act of 1970 changed the status of black people in South Africa so that they became citizens of the Bantustans, rather than citizens of South Africa, resulting in enforced resettlement during the 1970s and the uprooting of almost one-third of a million black South Africans.[1] Fugard's published diary *Notebooks* charts his response to political events as they unfolded in Port Elizabeth in this period, and describes the local scene of devastation in July 1973 following evictions in nearby Salisbury Park under the Group Areas Act.[2] He deliberates at length on the role and responsibility of the writer in 'the troubled state of South Africa', formulating the opposition between art and politics as a 'tightrope between poetry and propaganda', and declaring that 'my life's work [was] possibly just to witness as truthfully as I could, the nameless and destitute (desperate) of this one little corner of the world'.[3]

Fugard scholarship has queried whether he should be regarded as a political writer or whether his writing transcends immediate politics. Stephen Gray wrote in 1982 of the 'universalism' of Fugard, suggesting, 'It is a kind of critical injustice ... to deal with Fugard's plays exclusively in terms of the political issues they dramatise,'[4] while Russell Vandenbroucke's *Truths the Hand Can Touch* (1985) focuses on how his works addressed the 'universal condition'. Dennis Walder in 1984 argued that Fugard's plays were undeniably about the 'inhuman facts of apartheid' and that such interpretations of him as 'universal' were simply attempts to make the writer institutionally acceptable: 'Fugard's plays are political. ... The South African reviewers and critics who make up the overwhelming majority of contributors to *Athol Fugard* have to pretend that this is not so.'[5] By contrast, Hilary Seymour, in 1980, regarded *Sizwe Bansi* as far from politically radical, contending that its 'image of the self-made man pulling himself up by his boot straps is a key concept in the mythology and ideological superstructure of industrial capitalist societies'.[6] Since the end of apartheid, critics have repeatedly argued that Fugard's plays transcend their specific political context. For example, André Brink's examination of *Sizwe Bansi* in 1993 reflects on ways in which Fugard 'aimed at transcending the "merely" sociopolitical'.[7] Likewise, Albert Wertheim (2000) insisted that while 'Fugard's plays have been milestones and signposts of apartheid's devastating progress, its demise, and the future that is unfolding in its wake', the issues he addresses 'extend well beyond the borders of his homeland'.[8] Harry Garuba (2001) positions *The Island* within the '"writing back" dimension of postcolonial discourse', in which 'issues of colonialism, of race and color, of political disenfranchisement and tyranny come to the fore';[9] and Walder (2003) argues that *The Island* 'transcends the immediate circumstances of its making' although he goes on to qualify this: 'But that is not the same as saying that it is "transcendent", much less universal.'[10]

This chapter charts the ways in which the publisher addressed and resolved this tension between Fugard as a political playwright and Fugard as a writer disclosing universal truths, which was part of a much broader academic debate in the 1960s about the definition of an aesthetic value system for African literature.[11] It examines the interventions of the publisher in the 'symbolic production' of Fugard's work. In particular, this case-study considers the role played by OUP in packaging and promoting Fugard as a 'universal' writer who transcended immediate social and political situations. A related concern is whether this was part of a strategy to 'universalise' the market for Fugard's plays. Amuta suggests that a universal market for literature is an automatic by-product of international publication: 'Once written and published, a literary work enters the domain of public discourse and the international market place. The audience of the work becomes universal.'[12] Yet, although an international market for literature is the aspiration of a publisher, it is not, as Amuta implies in this statement, something that is automatically obtained. Instead, it is the result of specific publishing strategies. Charting OUP's publishing strategy for Fugard's plays, this chapter questions whether the editorial concern for 'universalism' in African literature was simply an aesthetic judgement for the publisher, or was it an attempt to make his writing accessible to Anglo-American readers and palatable in apartheid South Africa?

Fugard and the Three Crowns series

By the late 1960s, Three Crowns was caught in the middle of conflicting demands and expectations. On the one hand, the series carried a certain cultural kudos – it represented Oxford University Press's literary engagement with postcolonial Africa and its attempt to create a new canon of African literature. On the other hand, as part of OUP's mass educational publishing strategy in Africa, the series was expected to deliver profits to the centre, and was not regarded as suitable for investment. The first three plays by Fugard that were acquired by OUP were all published in the Three Crowns series: *People Are Living There* (1970), *Hello and Goodbye* (1973) and *Boesman and Lena* (1973). The slow and involved acquisition process for these plays illustrates the difficulties of selecting texts to meet the complex demands of the series and demonstrates how the series identity had to shift to accommodate Fugard.

Fugard's *Hello and Goodbye* was first recommended to Jon Stallworthy in 1968, while he was series editor of Three Crowns, by Charles Lewis and Jonathan Kariara of the OUP Nairobi office. Lewis had sought the advice of the academic Bob Green, from the Department of Literature, University College, Dar es Salaam, who was enthusiastic about the idea: 'As you know I am a Fugard fan and I think it would be a marvellous idea if *Hello and Goodbye* were to come out in your "Three Crowns" list.'[13] Stallworthy then enlisted the help of David Philip in Cape Town to negotiate with Fugard over British territorial rights, and to locate the manuscripts of both *Hello and*

Goodbye and *People Are Living There*. Philip had great difficulty in achieving this, as Fugard's mail was intercepted by the authorities and letters from the South Africa branch were never received, but he finally managed to obtain from Fugard the manuscript for *People Are Living There*. It emerged that *Hello and Goodbye* had already been published in South Africa by A. A. Balkema of Cape Town in 1966.

There was an initial debate about whether Fugard was sufficiently African to fit into the Three Crowns series. Could the series accommodate a white writer? Although there were several non-fiction white authors, all the literary authors to date had been black Africans. Stallworthy wrote to David Philip to check on Fugard's ethnicity. Philip replied: 'Fugard is as white (or as coloured) as most white people in this country, and is officially classified as such.'[14] There was also concern about the appropriateness of the white South African subject matter in his plays. *Hello and Goodbye*, for instance, is a play about an Afrikaner brother and sister in Port Elizabeth, each considering their past and their future in the aftermath of their father's death. It was well received by the editor Carol Buckroyd, who wrote: 'Without being good at analysing why a play is good, I feel that this one certainly has considerable merit. It is gripping – in that one wants to read on – and it is memorable.'[15] Her one reservation was that 'There is nothing in the play specifically South African. Indeed, apart from occasional slang phrases and references to places and railways, anything that couldn't equally well have been written by an Englishman of England.'[16]

People Are Living There raised similar questions. This play centred on four 'poor white' lodgers in a Johannesburg boarding house and was considered to be too divorced from South African racial politics by Heapy. His report on the play was very positive, but he added: 'The only thing that bothers me is the South African setting. I can't honestly say whether people talk or behave in this way in Johannesburg. There's no question of race or colour anywhere. I wonder in fact whether one is meant to worry about the Johannesburg setting – whether the author means us to treat the characters as being not necessarily South African but as more universal.'[17] Stallworthy echoed this concern: 'Fugard's western treatment of a western theme leaves me unconvinced that it would be a success on its own as a Three Crown.'[18]

The third play, *Boesman and Lena*, was, however, very specifically about 'race and colour'.[19] The three characters in the play are coloured and Xhosa South Africans. According to Fugard's *Notebooks*, the play was inspired by his need to testify to the situation of the homeless, dispossessed South Africans, whom he encountered on a daily basis. 'Strangely no surprise at seeing Lena. Just a sense of the possibility of sacrilege, of the demand that the truth be told, that I must not bear false witness.'[20] The editors' concern in this case was whether the play was too specifically South African and whether it would have any significance beyond that country. The reader of the manuscript wrote a long report on 8 January 1970 that concluded that the play, while dealing with local issues, was universal in its themes: 'This play, like *The Blood Knot*, is firmly rooted in the South African situation and will undoubtedly have greater impact in that country than anywhere else. ... However, the play's theme is universal and its compassion and realism transcend national barriers.'[21] The reader concludes that the racial hierarchies and violence in the play were not unique to South Africa under apartheid: 'One can see in the situation many parallels in a society's structure; each level beating until, at the last, there is one insensate sufferer.'[22] Once again, the reader recommended publication, and there were no doubts about the quality of the plays: '*Boesman and Lena* has been performed in Cape Town, to judge by the glowing review in the *Cape Argus* with outstanding success. ... This play, like *People Are Living There*, is a work of great poignancy and deserves a larger audience than it is likely to receive.'[23]

A further consideration for acceptance in the series was whether the plays would sell well enough in Africa, and there were further delays while the opinion of the three African branches was sought. The Ibadan and Nairobi branches recommended that the plays be published singly and with the addition of an introduction, to make them more saleable to schools and more prescribable for examinations.[24] Fred Cannon, trade manager of OUP's Cape Town branch, was less encouraging, as he considered large sales in South Africa were unlikely: 'My immediate reaction to your enquiry as to whether we could sell approximately 3000 copies over three years at 10/- would be to say that we hadn't a hope. ... I think it would be a pity if we scrapped the idea of publishing "Boesman and Lena" at this stage but I do understand that the interest outside Southern Africa is likely to be small.'[25]

What finally settled the matter was Stallworthy's secondment to South Africa in 1970, during which time he contacted Fugard and became convinced that he should be acquired by OUP. In particular, he was highly impressed by the stage production of *Boesman and Lena* in Cape Town in July 1970, in which Fugard and Yvonne Bryceland acted the main roles. He wrote to Fugard: 'I was very sorry to be whirled away at the end of B and L before I could thank you and Yvonne for the most moving evening I have had at the theatre for a long time. I thought you were both – indeed all three – superb, and the play impressed me more than when I first read it.'[26] He urged his colleague at Ely House in London, Richard Brain, to press ahead with getting the agreement to publish Fugard: 'It really was stunning. Fugard is the real thing.'[27] Brain then read the playscript, and felt that it transcended its specific South African political situation in its universality and its use of allegory:

> Despite the assertion in the South African press that Fugard is not a political writer (which perhaps is made advisedly, for his sake), I interpret 'Boesman and Lena' myself entirely as a political allegory, relevant not only to the dominance patterns on ethnic lines in South Africa in particular,

> but also more widely to the social and economic world situation, with aspects of capitalism and communism, tiered exploitation and the third world, indicated. In such terms the tedious repetitiveness of much of the first act fits dramatically; as does the ending. As a psychological drama the play is coherent and honest also; but personally I see analogies with Brecht rather than with Beckett.[28]

Thus, the decision was finally made to publish all three books in Three Crowns, and Fugard's inclusion helped provide a new identity and lease of life for the ailing series. Evidently Fugard was regarded as a successor to Soyinka: a playwright who was 'universal', who was able to 'transcend national barriers' and who would draw in new authors and add prestige. However, the acquisition of Fugard for Three Crowns also helped define the series politically. As the Cape Town branch had moved away from oppositional publications, and was now focusing on producing and selling prescribed educational texts for segregated schools, Three Crowns acquired South Africa's foremost playwright, who regarded it as his life's work to 'bear witness' to the inhumanity of racist politics and laws in South Africa.[29] Fugard was one of Stallworthy's last acquisitions for OUP, and can be seen as part of his protest against the change of publishing policy in Cape Town.[30] The acquisition of Fugard for Three Crowns served to maintain a politically engaged, anti-apartheid cachet, which was particularly important for the reputation of the series in postcolonial Africa.

Acquiring rights in Fugard

Although Fugard assigned his rights to South African publishers as well as British and American publishers, these publishers were at a marked legal and economic disadvantage in reaching an international audience, because of the terms specified by the British Commonwealth Market Agreement.[31] Although South Africa had left the Commonwealth in 1961, it continued to be considered as part of the British package of territorial rights, which was automatically assigned to any British publisher.

Fugard had little understanding of legal matters in publishing. Blithely oblivious to the norms and protocols in dealing with agents and authors, he evidently entered into negotiations with any publisher who approached him, and assigned his copyright liberally. Fugard frequently assigned the same rights twice, leading to chaos amongst South African, British and US publishers, and triggering complex negotiations between them as they struggled to come to mutual agreements. This problem was intensified when he employed a US literary agent, Willliam Morris, who in turn had an arrangement with the agent Anthony Sheil in London. Instead of alleviating the problem, this led to further breakdowns in communication and greater confusion over rights ownership.

Failing to appreciate the competitive market for Fugard, OUP lost exclusive rights to publish his plays on several occasions due to the protracted deliberations and delays over each new acquisition. After months with no response from OUP, Fugard assumed the editors had decided not to publish *People Are Living There*, and assigned the rights to the Johannesburg-based publisher, Buren, for a South African edition of the play.[32] As a result, OUP was only able to acquire rights to this play outside South Africa, thus losing the book's major market.[33] The delay in reaching a decision about *Boesman and Lena* was equally costly for the Press. Fugard offered rights in the trilogy *Boesman and Lena, The Blood Knot* and *Hello and Goodbye* to Viking in the USA, and wrote to Stallworthy to explain the situation in October 1970: 'A slight misunderstanding on my side. Your last letter said the play was going to be submitted to your delegates at their next meeting, and that if they accepted it, I would be made an offer. I've heard nothing from London, and didn't know what happened.'[34] However, believing that the UK rights were still available, Fugard offered OUP the British territorial rights to all three plays:

> My association with OUP in connection with the publication of 'People Are Living There' was a very happy one for me personally. I would be extremely proud to have OUP bring out my other plays for the English and Commonwealth markets. I do hope that this will be possible.[35]

Unfortunately, Fugard forgot the fact that he had already assigned world rights to Penguin for the publication of *The Blood Knot* and he was evidently unaware that his agent had also assigned UK paperback publication rights in the whole trilogy to Penguin.[36] This prompted a complex series of negotiations, after which OUP acquired hardcover rights to the trilogy and acquired rights to publish *Boesman and Lena* and *Hello and Goodbye* (but not *The Blood Knot*) in Three Crowns for the British traditional market, on condition that they were priced at no less than 50p per play. As a series that was by this stage mainly for Africa, this was not considered to be a threat to Penguin's UK trade market.[37] Sheil then intensified the competition for rights in these plays by threatening to assign rights in *Boesman and Lena* and *Hello and Goodbye* to another publisher, Davis-Poynter, for his Playscripts series:

> As I told you, another publisher has been diligently pursuing Athol Fugard and I cannot just rule him out, even despite your persuasive arguments. I should like you ... to bear in mind the possibility of improving somewhat your offer for hardback rights. It may be that I shall ultimately have to leave it up to Fugard to decide which offer he wants to accept, taking into account his obvious inclinations to appear under your imprint.[38]

Fugard's preference for OUP evidently settled the matter, but not before OUP improved its advance and the royalty level.[39]

In the carve-up of Fugard's intellectual property rights, his literary agents failed to take into account the rights of the South African publishers. Only at the point of printing did Brain find out that Buren retained rights to print *Boesman and Lena* and that Balkema owned the exclusive rights to publish *Hello and Goodbye* in South Africa. OUP was forced to go ahead with the publications non-exclusively, meaning that its editions had to compete with the South African publishers' editions, and it had to compensate 'cunning old Balkema' by paying him a percentage of the royalties on the sales of OUP's editions of *Hello and Goodbye* within South Africa.[40] Brain wrote to Neville Gracie in exasperation: 'Really, it was easier to deal with unbusinesslike Fugard himself than with his slow and inefficient American/British agents!'[41]

By the late 1960s the market for Fugard's intellectual property was intense and competitive, involving publishers in South Africa, Britain and the United States. Rights in Fugard were managed and traded by international agents and publishers who effectively divided his works up for world consumption. Through this process, 'Athol Fugard' as a literary product quickly became disassociated from Fugard the individual. This process is, in Sarah Brouillette's view, typical for the postcolonial writer: 'whereas the romantic author-figure once lamented a commercial compromise in attaining widespread acclaim, for the postcolonial writer the problem is the politicisation of incorporation into a discredited global sphere'.[42] Fugard was geographically isolated from his main publishers, who were based in London and New York, while his South African publishers were unable to reach a world market due to the restrictions of international trade agreements. By the early 1970s, his plays were all disseminated from New York and London, and OUP in London became the locus for Fugard sales back to Africa.

Editing and producing Fugard in Three Crowns

People Are Living There was the first of the Three Crowns plays to be published by OUP. Published in 1970, a year after rights had been acquired, it was set in a Johannesburg boarding house. The play's foreward gives a summary of the play:

> There is Milly, the kind-hearted slovenly landlady; Don, a cynical student lay-about engaged in a permanent attempt to find himself and analyze others; and Shorty, a dim-witted postman, whose passions in life are boxing and silkworms. ... It is Milly's fiftieth birthday and, just jilted by the German lodger with whom she has lived for the past ten years, she asks the other two to join her in a wild birthday party – a gesture of defiance to prove to herself that she, too, is alive and can have a Good Time. The others rather reluctantly agree.

The publisher's paratext of this edition associates Fugard firmly with the Three Crowns series, with the front cover privileging the series name over the publisher's name (Figure 9.1).[43] Both the series name and colophon appear on the front cover, and the only reference to the imprint is the small 'OXFORD' at the base of the spine. Indeed, the cover design suggests a disassociation of OUP from the published product. The book was cheaply produced, without embellishment and, in common with other books in the series, contains no introduction. It was published in the usual crown octavo size (7½ x 5 in.), again resembling in format the *Oxford English Course* supplementary readers. Fugard's status as a South African writer is emphasised in the foreword, which quotes a *Cape Times* theatre review: '*People Are Living There* confirms Fugard's position as perhaps the most important writer in the country today and ensures for him a place of honour in the history of South African theatre.' The same newspaper is quoted again on the back-cover blurb: 'Athol Fugard is quite simply the best playwright South Africa has, or ever has had, and in his own way he is probably one of the best playwrights in the world.' The cover illustration is by the avant-garde cover designer Bill Botten, and is a black and white line-drawing of a long-haired white man sitting on a kitchen chair, printed on a white front cover (see Figure 9.1). Thus, the paratext carries a complex array of meanings: it signals Fugard's ethnicity, nationality, national acclaim and avant-garde popularity, whilst at the same time identifying him within an African writing tradition and indicating the book's destination for African schools.

Fugard registered his delight with the cover design and with the book as a whole.[44] Despite the loss of the South African market, this book sold fast: by March 1972, 2339 copies of *People Are Living There* had been sold, at the price of 35p per book. Brain concluded that 'These figures seem to me quite encouraging for the Three Crowns editions of Hello and Goodbye and Boesman and Lena.'[45]

Publication of *Hello and Goodbye* and *Boesman and Lena* in Three Crowns began in October 1971.[46] Editorially, little was done as the plays were reprints of previous editions: *Hello and Goodbye* was a reprint of the Balkema edition, and *Boesman and Lena* was a reprint of the Odyssey Press US edition, both of which had been approved by Fugard; Viking also sent a copy of Fugard's revised introduction to the plays and a glossary of the South African terms. The introduction was reserved for the hardback edition of the plays, but the glossary was adopted for *Boesman and Lena* for the Xhosa and Afrikaans words used in the play.

Fugard's *Hello and Goodbye* and *Boesman and Lena* were selected for redesign by Ruari McLean in 1971 (Figures 9.2 and 9.3). This new design branded the plays more obtrusively as part of Three Crowns: the series identity was promoted over the playwright's identity and the publisher's imprint. The play titles and author's name are somewhat overpowered by the bright primary red of the book cover, as each genre in the series was colour-coded.

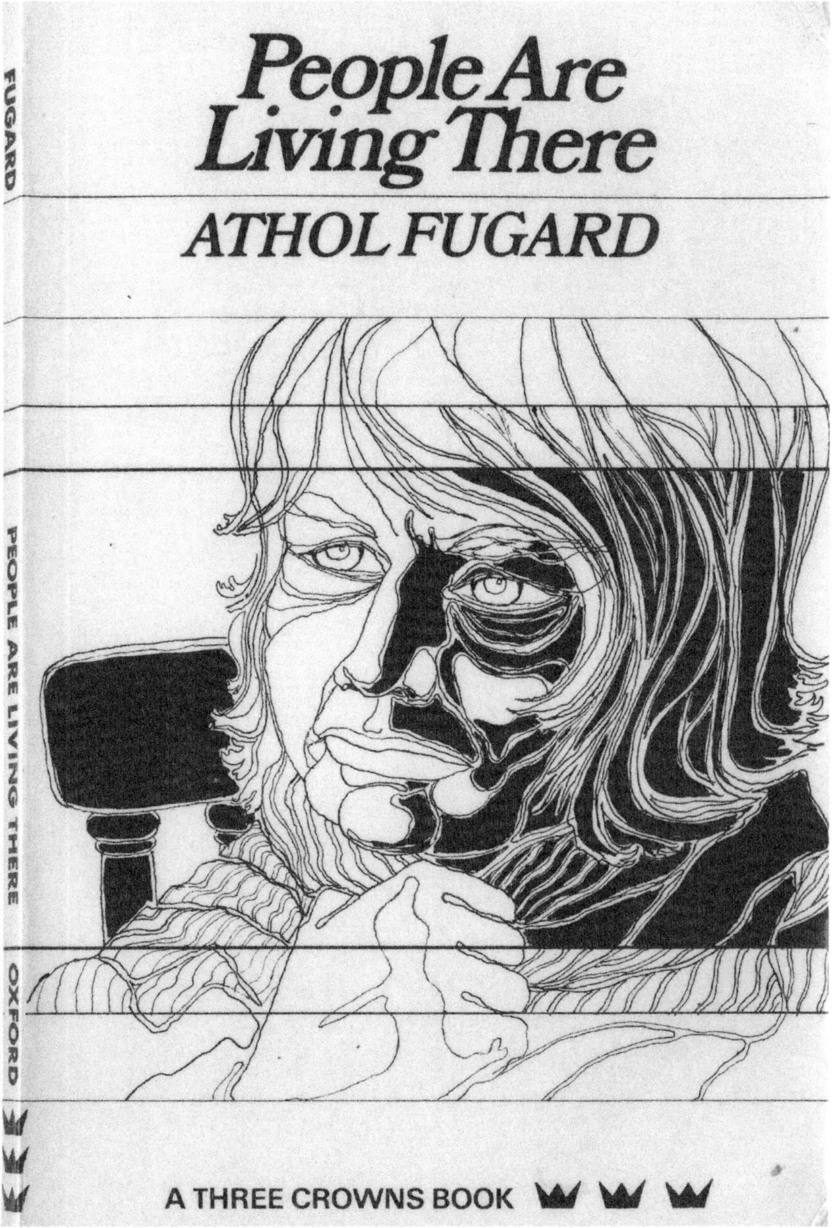

Figure 9.1 Athol Fugard, *People Are Living There* (1970), front cover. By permission of Oxford University Press

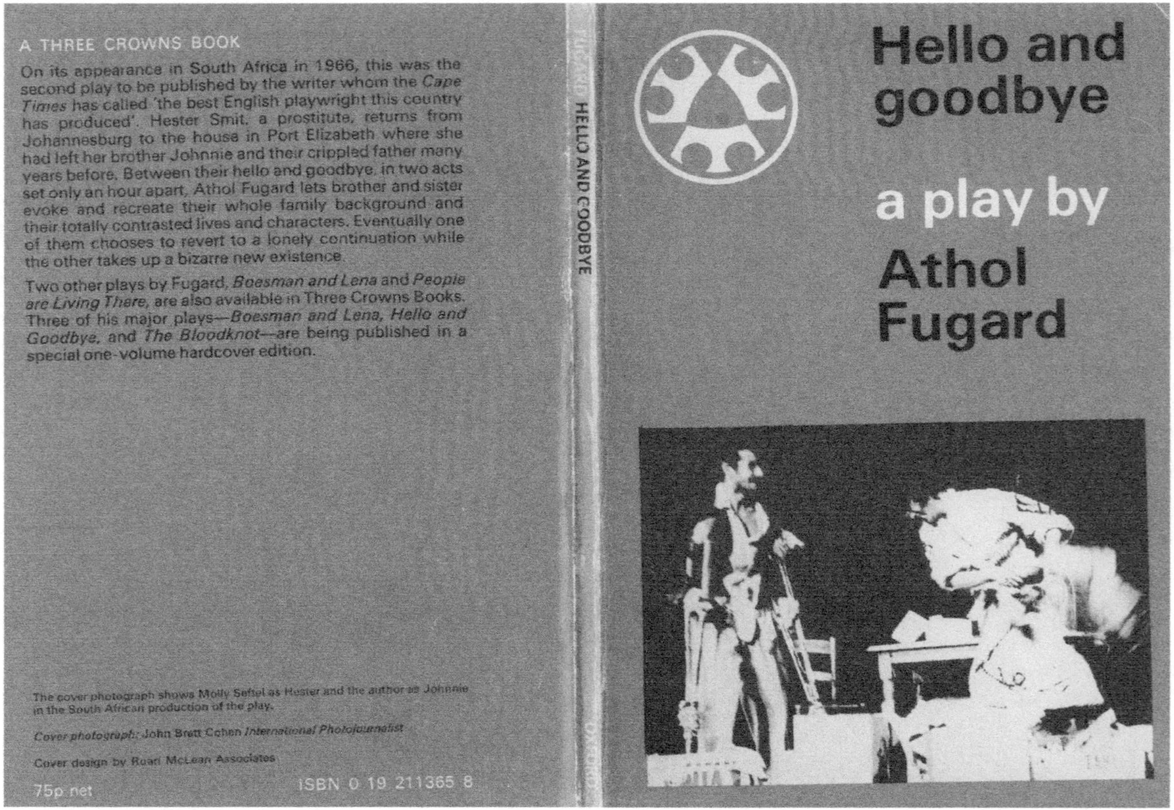

Figure 9.2 Athol Fugard, *Hello and Goodbye* (1973), front and back covers. By permission of Oxford University Press

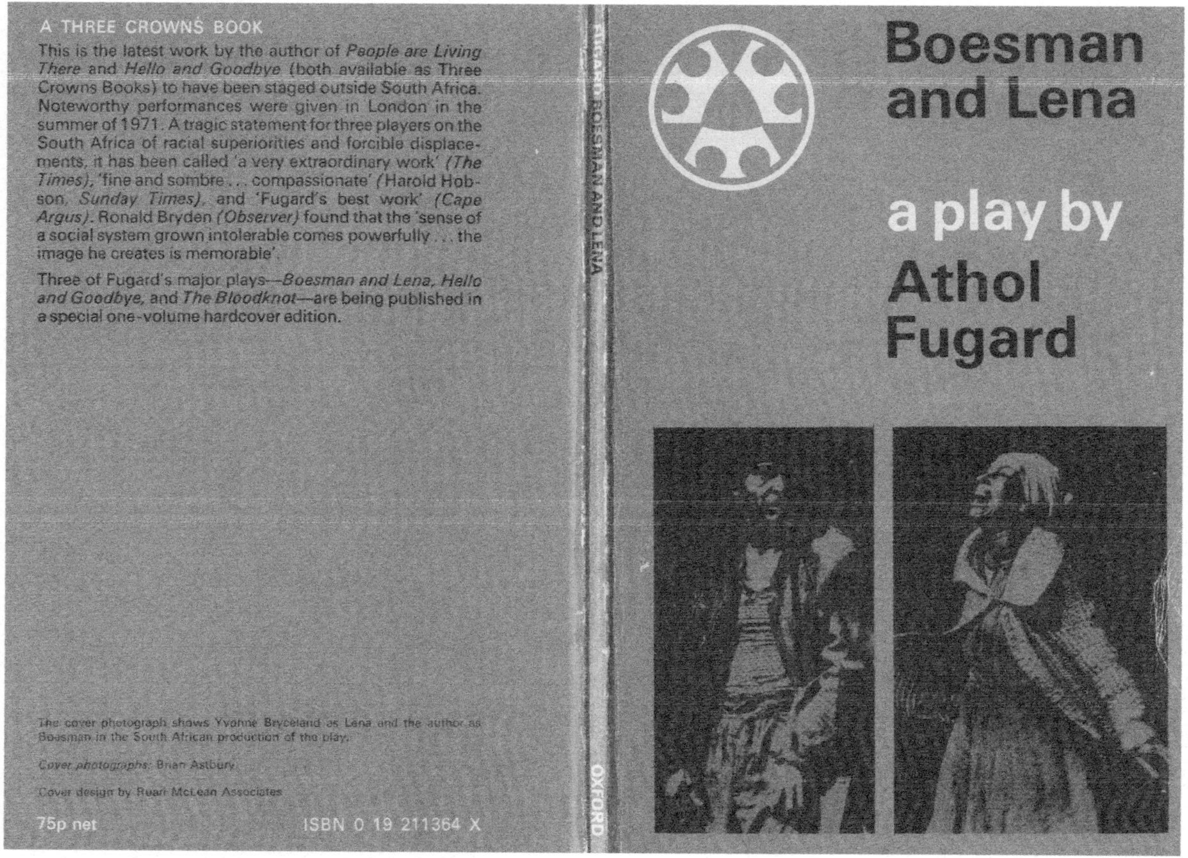

Figure 9.3 Athol Fugard, *Boesman and Lena* (1973), front and back covers. By permission of Oxford University Press

The name 'Oxford' only appears in small capitals on the spine, and the series colophon takes pride of place on the front cover. The use of the new design caused significant delays in the publication of Fugard's *Hello and Goodbye* and *Boesman and Lena*, and these delays were then exacerbated by delays in the production schedule, as the books were chosen to trial the new IBM computerised typesetting rather than using traditional hand-setting. Heapy complained about the quality of the books, and the photographs used on the covers were unclear. Heapy wrote, equivocally, to the Production department, 'As you say, the photography for *Hello and Goodbye* is blurred but it does look as though it is a play. ... Agreed, it would have been nice to have cut-outs of Boesman and Lena but as you say you cannot see where Boesman's head is really. It is very effective, though as it is and looks rather somber, which fits the play.'[47]

The back-cover blurb for *Boesman and Lena* referred directly to the forced displacements and racism in South Africa that underlie the play, and by using a montage of review quotes, readers were introduced to the political significance of the work:

> A tragic statement for three players on the South Africa of racial superiorities and forcible displacements, it has been called 'a very extraordinary work' (*The Times*), 'fine and sombre ... compassionate' (Harold Hobson, *Sunday Times*), and 'Fugard's best work' (*Cape Argus*). Ronald Bryden (*Observer*) found that the 'sense of a social system grown intolerable comes powerfully ... the image he creates is memorable'.[48]

For the postcolonial African market, Fugard's anti-apartheid political association was evidently an asset, whilst the use of fulsome reviews by international theatre critics promotes Fugard as suitable for prescription by examination boards. The blurb for *Hello and Goodbye* also asserts the literary status of the playwright by means of a quotation from the *Cape Times*. Fugard is described as 'the best English playwright this country has produced'. The books are again codified as part of a series of African writing for the African schools marketplace. Despite efforts to raise the design and production quality for the series, the books were in the event cheaply produced and printed. Yet, despite the poor-quality production and the inordinate delays in publishing these Three Crowns editions, Fugard was characteristically enthusiastic about the result. He wrote to Heapy in April 1973:

> The books were well worth waiting for! I can't tell you how pleased I am with them. I sincerely hope that sales will justify the choice that OUP took in publishing them. ... Once again, do please thank every body in Dover Street who had anything to do with the two books. Assure them that one very pleased and satisfied writer is tucked away down at the bottom of the world.[49]

Three years later, the Nairobi branch approached Brain and Heapy to discuss the publication of a single-volume edition of *The Blood Knot* as a Three Crowns text, following its recommendation as a set text for the East African A-level examinations in Kenya and Uganda: the branch predicted sales of 3000 copies to the East African schools market. Fugard was delighted about the idea of an African school edition, and wrote to Jonathan Kariara in Nairobi that he was happy to write an introduction:[50]

> Many thanks for your letter and the very good news regarding *The Blood Knot*. I am only too prepared to help the publication of a school edition of the play by writing an introduction along the lines you suggested. I will start thinking about it immediately and if all goes well, will have it in the post to you by the end of this month.[51]

However, Heapy was then unable to take it on for Three Crowns, despite the fact that it was a sure success, with a guaranteed, prescribed school market. He wrote to the Nairobi office: 'I can't really commit myself at the moment because there is a dismal lack of money around.'[52] He suggested instead that the book might be published in Nairobi as a Three Crowns text, but as there are no further references to this in the files, or in library records, it appears that this publication did not go ahead.

Through the Three Crowns series, Fugard was initially targeted to the African market and was identified as an African writer, which was an identity he valued. Despite the editors' initial reservations about placing a white South African author in Three Crowns, Fugard was the most enthusiastic of all the Three Crowns authors about his inclusion in the series. This was perhaps due to his close association with other playwrights in the series. He first became friends with Nkosi in 1957 in Sophiatown, when he had spent time with him in the offices of *Drum*, discussing the possibility of setting up a theatre group.[53] In addition, Fugard produced Soyinka's plays in London in 1966; he worked with a London-based theatre company of Africans that held workshops, leading to a production of Soyinka's *The Trials of Brother Jero* at the Theatre Royal in Brighton and then at the Hampstead Theatre Club in July 1966. He was excited about his books reaching the school market in Africa, and was also very satisfied with the quality of the books that were published in Three Crowns. However, within OUP there was a discomfort at the positioning of Fugard in this lowly series directed to the African educational market.

Three Port Elizabeth Plays – Fugard as an 'Oxford author'

During the initial acquisition process for Fugard's early plays, Richard Brain questioned whether the Three Crowns series was sufficiently prestigious for Fugard. As 'South Africa's leading playwright', he aimed to position Fugard as an 'Oxford author', and to give him a rightful place in the UK-based literary marketplace.[54] This objective was realised in the publication in 1974 of *Three Port Elizabeth Plays*, which was an out-of-series hardback volume of *The Blood Knot, Hello and Goodbye* and *Boesman and Lena*.

Brain was literary editor in the General division rather than the Educational division of the London business. In 1971, he secured hardback rights for the trilogy,[55] and following the publication of the Three Crowns plays, he began work on its publication.[56] His first concern was the title, which Fugard initially suggested should be called *The Family*.[57] Brian advised instead that it should be named either 'Three Plays', 'Three Plays for Two Players' or 'Three Port Elizabeth Plays'.[58] Fugard happily took his advice:

> I completely agree with your objections to some of the titles suggested. The one I personally like most both in terms of the other possibilities is Three Port Elizabeth Plays. That strange, ugly little town has been so decisive in my work so far that I couldn't think of a more accurate and honest title for a book containing the three plays which I have written out of my response to it. Yes, I definitely favour that.[59]

This was the first publication of *The Blood Knot* by OUP, and the play about the complex relationship between two coloured brothers living in Port Elizabeth – one who could pass for white, the other black – was the most explicitly anti-apartheid of Fugard's plays published so far by the Press. The introduction, written by Fugard in 1971, was part of the package it acquired from Viking, and its main concern was the origin of the three plays, their inspiration and the conditions under which these plays were performed.[60] Editorially, few changes were made to the texts: Brain proposed an expanded glossary, based on the *Boesman and Lena* playscript, which OUP would be responsible for compiling. He suggested that he should produce the blurb, unless Fugard preferred to do this himself (which he didn't), and also suggested that the play would be produced without photographs from performances.[61] The lack of scholarly, historical or critical apparatus in the edition was regarded as a major flaw by Dennis Walder. He writes of this edition, as well as of the previous Three Crowns editions, 'I thought them barely adequate reading copies, in a handy little format. But unhelpful without any personal or performance or historical/cultural/political context or notes, especially for readers outside South Africa.'[62]

Three Port Elizabeth Plays was an understated hardback edition issued primarily for the UK market. The series title-page made no reference to the Three Crowns series or earlier individual editions of the plays; it simply states: 'Also by Athol Fugard: *People Are Living There*'. This edition evidently sought to be disassociated from its poorer Three Crowns cousins. The title-page is centrally formatted with a serif typeface, denoting that this was a traditional publication. It was identified as an Oxford University Press book simply by means of the capitalised publisher's name at the base of the title-page. The book was not overtly promoted and authorised by the publisher by means of a foreword or blurb: the symbolic production of this book relied simply on the reputation of the imprint. Through this publication, Fugard became a mainstream 'Oxford author'.

The critical reception of *Port Elizabeth Plays* illustrated how this edition was a means by which Fugard was accredited as a significant international playwright. Publishing in hardback in the 1970s was essential for a book to gain reviews and library sales.[63] In 1977, a review by Derek Cohen in *Modern Language Studies* alluded to the 'stature' and 'acclaim' acquired by Fugard through being published by OUP:

> Although several of the handful of internationally-known South African writers have tried their hands at drama, only Athol Fugard remains a playwright of stature. Having won acclaim in the English-speaking world with some half dozen successful plays about South African life, Fugard stands assured of a place in dramatic history. ... His work has been published by Oxford University Press, and last year three of his first plays were published in a single collection under the title *Three Port Elizabeth Plays*. The plays there anthologised are *The Blood Knot, Hello and Goodbye,* and *Boesman and Lena*.[64]

The edition was significant in terms of Fugard's reputation, and was the means by which OUP helped legitimise the playwright and his works and assure his 'place in dramatic history'. *Three Port Elizabeth Plays* placed Fugard firmly within the 'field of restricted production', for, in terms of sales, it was unsuccessful, and four years after publication it was described as a 'slow selling hardback'.[65] This trilogy was the means by which OUP attempted to canonise Fugard not simply as an African writer for the mass educational market, but as an international writer of universal significance for the UK literary and academic marketplace.

Publishing *Statements: Three Plays*

From 1972, OUP in London began work on the acquisition of Fugard's plays *Sizwe Bansi is Dead, The Island* and *Statements after an Arrest under the Immorality Act,* which were published as a trilogy under the title *Statements: Three Plays,* in 1974. These were the first of Fugard's plays for which OUP was the original publisher. They were also the most overtly political of his plays, each directly addressing and attacking apartheid legislation and enforcement.

Sizwe Bansi and *The Island* were developed in improvisational workshops, in collaboration with John Kani and Winston Ntshona, who were both Xhosa actors in the Serpent Players theatre company. The process of creating these plays was itself illegal under South African law, involving as it did inter-racial interaction, and the plays had be rehearsed and performed surreptitiously. In addition, the plays directly address and attack apartheid legislation and enforcement. *The Island* concerns two prisoners on Robben Island who attempt to alleviate their situation through theatre, by a performance of *Antigone*. It was based on first-hand accounts of life in the maximum security jail of the Serpent Players actor Norman Ntshinga,[66] and specifically relates to Ntshinga's performance in prison of a two-man version of *Antigone* with the other Serpent Players actor, Sipho 'Sharkey' Mguqulwa.[67] *Sizwe Bansi* was written in response to the tightening of the Pass Laws in the 1960s; set in a photographic studio, the plot centres on Sizwe Bansi's dilemma in arriving in Port Elizabeth without a passbook and, therefore, being unable to obtain work. Ultimately, he adopts the passbook, and therefore the identity, of a dead man, by pasting over his own photograph. *Statements after an Arrest under the Immorality Act* was developed in improvisational workshops by Fugard with the actor Yvonne Bryceland. The play concerns inter-racial sexual relations in South Africa, and the annihilative impact of the state on a white librarian and a coloured school principal, caught in an illicit love affair.

Performances, 1972–76

As the most politically explicit of Fugard's plays, the performances of all three plays in South Africa were subjected to banning restrictions by the South African authorities. In 1972, the police informed Brian Astbury, owner of The Space Theatre in Cape Town, that *Sizwe Banzi* (as it was first spelt) could not play to open audiences, and the performance was cancelled. The only way to get round this was to run it as a private club event, although the police again tried to stop the show. *Statements after an Arrest* was also premiered in The Space Theatre in 1972, followed by performances of *The Island*, which played at the theatre to a private audience for three weeks from June 1973.[68] It had to be kept quiet because of the legal embargo against publicly discussing the South African prison situation, and the Robben Island subject of the play was disguised by the name *Hodoshe Span*.[69]

The actors were then invited to London's Royal Court Theatre for its 'South African Season'. *Sizwe Bansi* ran from 20 September 1973 for nine months, *The Island* ran from 12 December 1973 and *Statements after an Arrest* ran from 22 January 1974. Following critical acclaim and transfer to the West End in April 1974, there was a national tour and the plays were then performed in America, first at the Long Wharf Theatre in New Haven, Connecticut in October 1974, and then in repertory at the Edison Theatre on Broadway. The programme for the Royal Court was written by the Three Crowns author Mary Benson, a friend of Fugard's exiled from South Africa for her anti-apartheid activism. It promoted the plays as specifically political, anti-apartheid plays, describing them as 'a response to the realities of the South African scene'.[70] The programme cover resembled a passbook, with passport photos of each of the actors on the front; it included explanatory material about the political, legal and penal context in South Africa (see Figure 9.4). The Edison Theatre adapted the same programme, adding a photograph of Kani's actual passbook. The programme also emphasised the plays' collaborative authorship. Whereas the cover announced, 'Directed by Athol Fugard', inside *Sizwe Bansi* and *The Island* are described as 'products of ... experiments in play-making', and are credited as 'devised by Athol Fugard, John Kani and Winston Ntshona'.

Two years later, Kani and Ntshona went on tour in the Transkei. A performance of *Sizwe Bansi* in the small town of Butterworth took place on 8 October 1976, two weeks before the Transkei was due to become independent. According to a report in *The Star* the actors used the opportunity to convey their opposition to Bantustans: 'The reason for the strong reaction to the play is believed to have been references in the Umtata and Butterworth performances – in which the actors have scope to improvise – to the Transkei being a dumping ground for dispossessed urban blacks and wholesale bloodshed following its independence.' The actors were promptly imprisoned; Chief George Mantanzima, the Transkei Minister of Justice, declared that the performance of the play was 'vulgar, abusive and highly flammable'.[71] Kani and Ntshona spent 15 days in solitary confinement and were only released after a campaign in the UK led by Benson, the Royal Shakespeare Theatre and the Royal Court Theatre. The writers wrote in a letter to the Royal Court: 'we wish to assure you all, that were it not for your involvement and support we would never have been released as our release had no precedent'.[72] Following this brief overview of the authorship, performances and early reception of these three plays, this chapter now considers the publication process of these plays.

Acquisition

In April 1972 Fugard approached Sally Carpenter, editor at the Cape Town branch of the Press, and offered her *Statements after an Arrest* for publication. Hearing news of this, Richard Brain, literary editor in the General division of OUP London, immediately wrote to Fugard, even before he had read the manuscripts, requesting world rights and urging him to inform his agent that OUP should have first option.[73] Ron Heapy also worked behind the scenes to obtain rights to Fugard's other new plays for the series. In March 1973, he wrote: 'I read, by chance, in a cutting from some South African magazine that you have "knocked into shape" a play called *Sizwe Banzi is Dead*. Could there be any chance of us having a look at this? Do you think that *Statements* is ready for publication yet?'[74] Brain then heard about the productions of the plays at the Royal Court, and

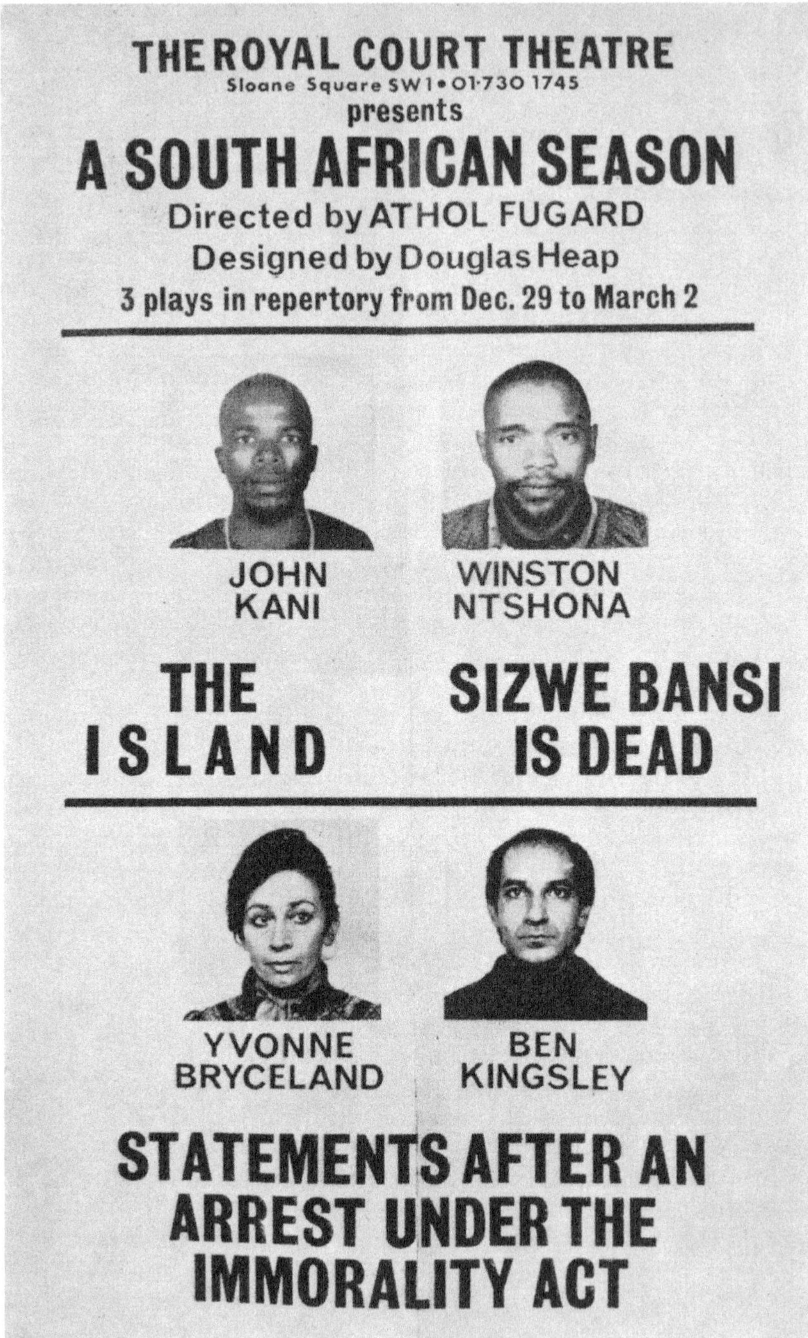

Figure 9.4 Royal Court Theatre, *A South African Season*, programme cover (1974). By permission of the Royal Court Theatre

wrote to Fugard, 'we can look forward to seeing both your new pieces, Sizwe Banzi is Dead and The Hodoshe Span at the Theatre Upstairs; what I've heard of your "Experiments in Playmaking" makes me very eager'.[75] However, it was not until the end of the Royal Court Season that Fugard contacted OUP. Upon his return to Port Elizabeth in February 1974, he wrote to Ron Heapy:

> Sincerest apologies for my appalling neglect of OUP's interest in the South African Season. My last three weeks in London were unbelievably noisy. The past two weeks back home, unbelievably depressing. It happens every time – a theatrical equivalent of post-coital deflation. I've come out of the doldrums now though.[76]

Fugard explained that the *Sizwe Bansi* script had already been published in *Plays and Players* and was available to OUP in that format. He added that the *Statements after an Arrest* script was clean, and just needed minor tidying up, whereas *The Island* needed about an additional month's work.

By this time, Fugard was, in the words of Heapy, 'hot property'.[77] His tour had attracted a great deal of publicity in the UK, and on 13 March 1974 *Sizwe Bansi* was shown on British television. OUP was keen to capitalise on this, and agreed to generous terms. Anthony Sheil, Fugard's literary agent, insisted that Fugard should be getting a better deal from OUP than its proposed 7.5 per cent royalty on the paperback, and successfully argued for the royalty to be increased to 10 per cent and the advance to be raised to £500 from the proposed £200.[78] Fugard stipulated that all royalties on *The Island* and *Sizwe Bansi is Dead* should be evenly divided between himself, Kani and Ntshona.[79]

There was a notable lack of discussion among OUP editors about the potential political repercussions of publishing the three plays in South Africa, considering the risks associated with the publication or importation of anti-apartheid literature at the time.[80] Despite the constraints on branch publishing, Gracie urged rapid publication of the book in London: 'We are delighted that you are to publish Fugard's three new plays. ... I am not sure that I would have selected a single three-in-one volume but at any rate I am pleased that it is in paperback. There will be an excellent market in South Africa for this title and I hope that you will be able to publish before the end of this year.'[81] The new publications notice referred to the anticipated market in South Africa: 'South African interest – unless there is any political incident between now and then – will certainly be high (1000 copies initially?).'[82] Evidently the most important consideration was the book's marketability: there was no expectation that the book would be banned, and Fugard was regarded as a profitable acquisition for the Press.

Series identity

The initial plan was to publish the new plays in Three Crowns, but Brain was keen to move Fugard out of the series, and into the more prestigious Oxford Paperbacks series. The series was targeted to the UK student market, with a list that concentrated on reprints of classics from English literature, academic non-fiction and the occasional new edition. In the event, the decision to move Fugard into the new series was made without consulting the author. He was simply informed by Heapy, 'The general plan (I think) is that the three plays and the introduction should come out as an Oxford Paperback. Text of the other three may come out as individual Three Crowns.'[83] The individual Three Crowns editions never did come about, and thereafter Fugard was published only in Oxford Paperbacks: *Dimetos, Nongogo and No-Good Friday* and a new edition of *Boesman and Lena and Other Plays* in 1978, *A Lesson from Aloes* in 1981 and *Master Harold and the Boys* in 1983.

Bourdieu's discussion of the publisher's involvement in the symbolic production of literature – the 'meaning and value of a work' – suggests that a publisher's imprint determines the field of production in which a literary text circulates.[84] In the case of Fugard, however, the symbolic capital accrued to an author by publication was determined not simply by the publisher's imprint but also by the *series* in which the book was published: the series determined the book's editing, design, production and promotion strategy and, ultimately, its end market, and therefore its distribution and reception. The decision to move Fugard out of a series for the African market and into a 'mainstream' series for the UK market had a determining impact on the publication of these three plays, and positioned Fugard at the centre rather than the margins of OUP's publishing strategy. Although in Bourdieu's analysis the size of the audience is an indicator of the position of the author in the cultural field, this case-study suggests that with respect to postcolonial literature, the dichotomy was not simply one of 'large-scale production' (offered by Three Crowns) in contrast to 'restricted production' (offered by Oxford Paperbacks), for the Oxford Paperbacks was also a mass-paperback series in which Fugard's plays achieved high volume sales.[85] The distinction between the two series was predominantly geographical: despite the author's satisfaction with the series, he was removed from Three Crowns mainly because it was too closely associated with the less prestigious East and West African markets. The association of Three Crowns with the African periphery ultimately meant that it was regarded by his publisher as an unworthy home for the playwright.

Editing *Statements: Three Plays*

In his introduction to the trilogy Fugard muses: 'I have always regarded the completed text as being only a half-way stage to my ultimate objective – the living performance and its particular definition of space and silence.'[86] In a later interview, Fugard observed again that his interest was in the play as performance not as a static textual product: 'The thing for me is, a play is not so many words on paper; a play is an experience in a theatre. I have absolutely no reverence for words on paper, texts.'[87] Fugard thus registered an awareness of his distinct contrast in attitude towards his plays as performances and as texts. It is interesting to consider the editing process of the three *Statements* plays in the light of his comments.

The text of *Sizwe Bansi* remained largely unaltered from the previously published edition by *Plays and Players*. Brain agreed with Fugard that the text should be 'printed exactly as in Plays and Players, cockroaches, doom and all'. However, Carol Buckroyd carried out extensive editorial work on the manuscripts of *Statements after an Arrest* and *The Island*.[88] Her editorial annotations focused on the stage directions in particular, as well as the play-scripts' phrasing, grammar and punctuation. In a letter to Buckroyd, Fugard gratefully acknowledges her editorial work in helping him to transform *The Island*, an unstable improvisation, into a fixed typescript:

> 'The Island'. It has really not been easy putting this together. I had to work from two recordings, a mess of notes and scraps of paper. The truth of the matter is that I need the responses of an objective but loving outsider as you so generously provided in the case of Statements. I look forward to hearing your comments on 'The Island' text. I really can't thank you enough for the trouble and care you've taken in trying to get the South African Season into print. You make my debt of gratitude to Oxford University Press very formidable.[89]

The choice of introduction was the main concern of the two editors, Heapy and Brain. Ron Heapy advised Fugard to write a 'straightforward Preface saying what actually happened (that is describing how you and the actors worked at the idea and produced drafts and revised drafts) rather than plain theory'.[90] Brain initially anticipated that the plays would have an introduction explaining the plays' political context, in a similar form to the Royal Court programme, and he wrote to Benson: 'I'll certainly suggest to Athol that the longer version of the background material you provided that went into the programme notes for the South African Season might be included in the book, whether as a Foreword or an Appendix or whatever.'[91] In the event, this idea was not pursued.[92] Brain visited Fugard in Port Elizabeth to discuss the publication of the plays, and Fugard agreed to write a new introduction himself.[93]

Fugard's introduction to *Statements: Three Plays* concentrated not on the specific South African political context but on his 'experiment with improvised theatre', his views on 'the pure theatre experience' and attempts to put into practice Grotowski's theories of drama. André Brink observed: 'Significantly, in the seven-page introduction that precedes the three *Statements* plays, he concerns himself with some of the dramaturgical and philosophical problems he confronted in them, without a single reference to their ideological or sociopolitical context.'[94] It is not clear whether the subject matter of the introduction was the decision of the publisher or the author, but the end result served to promote Fugard as a serious member of the literary elite, rather than as a political commentator, for his introduction bears the essential marks of a cultural work, as characterised by Bourdieu:

> Few works do not bear within them the imprint of the system of positions in relation to which their originality is defined; few works do not contain indications of the manner in which the author conceived the novelty of his undertaking or of what, in his own eyes, distinguished it from his contemporaries and precursors.[95]

Fugard dwells in his introduction on the way in which he broke with scriptwriting norms and attempted a new type of playwriting in the creation of the three plays. The improvisational workshop collaboration with Ntshona and Kani has been regarded by critics as a radical attempt – in terms of both form and politics – to blur authorial boundaries and cross racial divisions. Gray, for example, describes *Sizwe Bansi* and *The Island* as experimental attempts to create new South African theatre, describing them as 'impromptu inventiveness'. According to him, 'The collaborative plays ... call into question the concept of unique authorship and the copyrighting of communal experience.'[96] Walder regards this playwriting process as an important 'alternative to the dominant, Western, conventional hierarchy of author-text-production', but nonetheless reflects on the inevitable difficulties in the relationship: 'For Fugard, the task has been to cross the divide, a move which, like all serious transgression, involves difficulty, even danger, producing fear and guilt on one side, but also anger and resentment on the other.' He writes 'that the near-total hegemony of the white minority created by apartheid has meant that white liberals and other dissidents such as Fugard are part of the structures of domination they oppose'.[97] Walder's analysis relates to the process of collaborative writing of these plays, but it might also be applied to the process of publication, which provoked significant tension between the authors.

Fugard used the introduction to reflect on the authorship process for the three improvisational plays, and to carefully differentiate between his role as writer and that of the actors:

> I would just like to make one point clear: we did not jettison the writer. It was never a question of coming together with the actors on a 'let's make a play' basis. The starting-point to our work was always at least

> an image, sometimes an already structured complex of images about which I, as a writer, was obsessional. In all three of these plays the writer provided us with a mandate in terms of which the actors then went on to work. ...
>
> These initial mandates from the writer were also not his final contribution. He kept pace with us as fast as we discovered and explored ... sometimes as no more than a scribe, but at other times in a much more decisive way. The final dramatic structure of each play, for example, was his responsibility. Looking back on the three experiences now, it was as if instead of first putting words on paper in order to arrive eventually at the stage and a live performance, I was able to write directly into its space and silence via the actor.[98]

Slipping between use of the first and the third person to describe himself, Fugard self-consciously positions himself as 'the writer', who exercised a 'decisive' role in providing the 'initial mandates' to the actors, giving 'dramatic structure' to the work, and writing 'via the actor'. This version of the plays' origins and writing process was later contested by John Kani, who claimed in an interview that he and Ntshona were the main creators of the plots and dialogue of the plays and that Fugard had worked with them only one day a week devising the play: 'it was not until the London production as we prepared for a wider and more sophisticated audience that we enlisted Mr. Fugard as director. That is when he took over completely.'[99] With regard to *The Island,* Kani stressed the actors' significance in the play's creation: 'Again it was one day with Fugard, six days with us because we can't exceed a certain number of hours visiting a white man. We had an eighty per cent contribution. In *Sizwe Bansi,* he was the overseer. *The Island* is where we worked directly with him in the creation of the play.'[100] Kani and Ntshona were not given the opportunity by the publisher to approve Fugard's introduction or to add their own version of events.

This consideration of the editing of *Statements: Three Plays* suggests that there was a clear distinction between Fugard's approach to the plays in writing and performance and in publication. The playwright evidently monitored the performances of his plays with precise detail, frequently directing and acting in his own plays, yet he willingly handed over his playscripts to OUP for extensive copy-editing, adopting a more casual attitude to the printed form of the book. Moreover, in contrast to the writing process, the editing process for these plays was far from collective. Fugard entered into negotiations with the Press without Kani and Ntshona's involvement, he transcribed the plays and made changes to the manuscripts without consulting them, and the introduction presents his voice and interpretation alone. Fugard acted as spokesman for his silent co-authors; he alone assumed the role as 'the writer'.

Designing *Statements: Three Plays*

A controversy that manifested itself in the evolving paratext of the book related to how Kani and Ntshona should be credited. OUP initially expected to credit Fugard alone on the front cover. It was only after prompting from Anthony Sheil – acting on behalf of Kani and Ntshona as well as Fugard – that OUP made changes to the cover, title-page and contract to acknowledge the plays' joint authorship. In April 1974, Sheil wrote to Buckroyd to notify her that he had made arrangements to become Kani and Ntshona's agent, and to complain that Fugard had licensed his work to OUP without the permission of his co-authors:

> I received a visit from John Kani and Winston Ntshona from which it emerges that Athol is not much better at communications with his colleagues than with his publisher. ... it came as a complete surprise to them that he had agreed terms and that a contract was about to be signed because he told them nothing about details that had been arranged. Their main sources of concern are first, that the authorship of the plays should be clearly attributed and joint copyright attributed in the case of the two plays of which they can legitimately be regarded, as well as wanting to see proofs and read the introduction.[101]

Sheil insisted that changes should be made to the title-page to include their names. Buckroyd replied, resisting the idea of making changes to the front cover:

> I am surprised to hear that Athol did not tell John Kani and Winston Ntshona about the publication plans for these three plays. All along he has been very anxious that the proper credit and return should go to them. They shall also see proofs of the cover, when I have them. We plan to use a marvellous photograph of them on it. ON the front, however, we shall not include their names, but simply the wording 'Athol Fugard Statements'. You must see the problem here; if we listed all the plays and all the authors, the cover would be far too cluttered to be effective at all.[102]

The publisher's need for an individual, recognisable celebrity author evidently militated against joint authorship. Buckroyd's concern was that the cover was branded with Fugard's name alone, lest the cover become 'far too cluttered to be effective'. For, as Juliet Gardiner observes, 'The culture that circulates the author's name in Britain today is one that is suffused with a Romantic reading of authorship as singular, individual, confessional.'[103] Kani and Ntshona were to be seen but not heard: a visual spectacle realised by a 'marvellous photograph', but deprived of authorial attribution.

Buckroyd then contacted Kani and Ntshona to reassure them that 'everything is in order',[104] and then wrote to Fugard to complain about the interventions of his agent:

> I've just received a rather tiresome letter from your rather tiresome agent, and enclose a photocopy of it, together with a copy of my reply to him and a copy of a letter I sent off to John and Winston. I feel certain that Sheil must be stirring things up, but as equally certain there's no need and no harm done.[105]

Despite Buckroyd's indignation, changes were made. The copyright notice was altered to incorporate Kani and Ntshona's names, OUP sought to get them included in the contract, and there were attempts to liaise with them over publication of the text. However, OUP received no reply; the authors' signatures were not obtained on the contract, and indeed three years after the book's publication, it still remained unsigned, and their royalties had begun to accumulate, unclaimed.

In the 1974 edition of *Statements: Three Plays*, the co-authors are listed on the front cover, albeit in a smaller-sized typeface and positioned below Fugard's name (see Figure 9.5). The size of the authors' names is significant, for as Genette cogently notes: 'On the cover the name may be printed in varying sizes, depending on the author's reputation.'[106] The title-page has Fugard's name in capitals across the top; Kani and Ntshona are listed as 'devisors' of the workshop productions in a smaller typeface below (Figure 9.6). The copy on the back cover was also amended to include a reference in parenthesis to the fact that they were 'workshop productions, devised by John Kani, Winston Ntshona, and Athol Fugard'. However, the spine of the book, described by Genette as 'a narrow site but one with obvious strategic importance', contains Fugard's name alone.[107] The paratext of the published book thus signals a distinct hierarchy of authorship.

The final book design for *Statements: Three Plays* branded Fugard as an 'Oxford' author. The Oxford imprint was becoming increasingly prominent, with its connotations of academia, conservatism and permanence. The back cover had the words 'Oxford Paperbacks/Drama', categorising the text within the series and genre, while the imprint name was repeated at the base. The quality of production was good, in terms of both paper quality and typography. Published in a traditional serif typeface, the typography contrasted with the more avant-garde sans-serif typography of the Three Crowns editions. In comparison with the poor photographic reprints on the front covers of *Hello and Goodbye* and *Boesman and Lena*, *Statements: Three Plays* carried a well-produced front-cover illustration of Kani and Ntshona, which was taken from the Royal Court performance (see Figure 9.5).

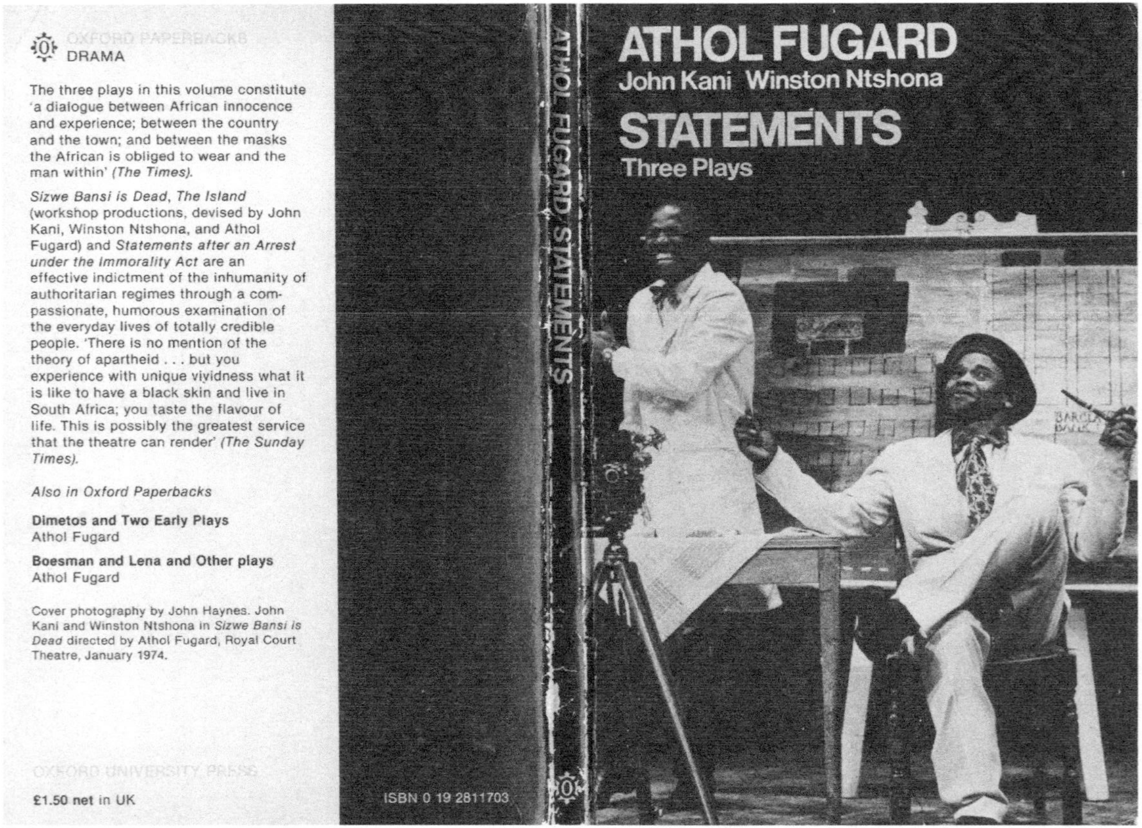

Figure 9.5 Athol Fugard, John Kani and Winston Ntshona, *Statements: Three Plays*. Oxford Paperback edition (1974), front and back covers. By permission of Oxford University Press

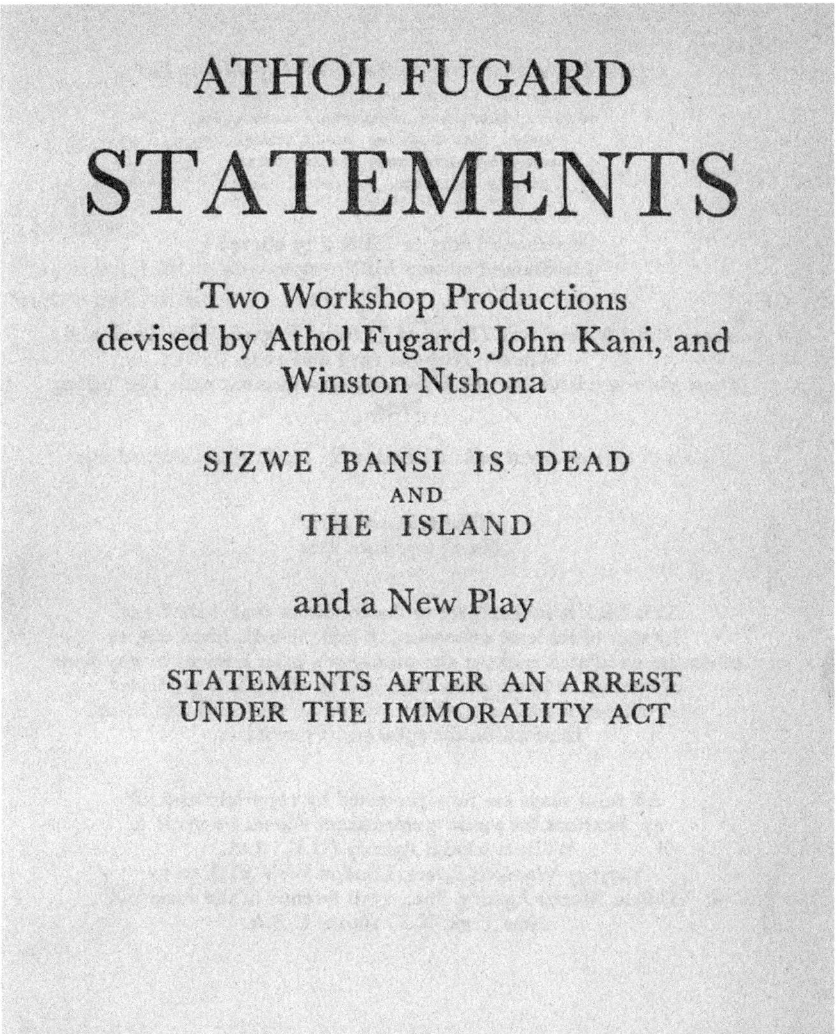

ATHOL FUGARD

STATEMENTS

Two Workshop Productions
devised by Athol Fugard, John Kani, and
Winston Ntshona

SIZWE BANSI IS DEAD
AND
THE ISLAND

and a New Play

STATEMENTS AFTER AN ARREST
UNDER THE IMMORALITY ACT

OXFORD UNIVERSITY PRESS

OXFORD NEW YORK TORONTO MELBOURNE

Figure 9.6 Athol Fugard, John Kani and Winston Ntshona, *Statements: Three Plays* (1974), title-page. By permission of Oxford University Press

The back-cover blurb for the trilogy was written by Buckroyd, and demonstrated her concern to promote the plays as literary works:

> The three plays in this volume constitute 'a dialogue between African innocence and experience; between the country and the town; and between the masks the African is obliged to wear and the man within' (*The Times*). *Sizwe Bansi is Dead, The Island* (workshop productions, devised by John Kani, Winston Ntshona, and Athol Fugard) and *Statements after an Arrest under the Immorality Act* are an effective indictment of the inhumanity of authoritarian regimes through a compassionate, humorous examination of the everyday lives of totally credible people. 'There is no mention of the theory of apartheid ... but you experience with unique vividness what it is like to have a black skin and live in South Africa; you taste the flavour of life. This is possibly the greatest service that the theatre can render' (*The Sunday Times*).[108]

Thus, the reader of these most overtly political of Fugard's plays was reassured at the threshold of the book that 'there is no mention of the theory of apartheid' in the plays. Employing an allusion to Blake, the reader was instead assured that the politics of the plays were tempered by literary abstraction. The specific South African content was not denied, but the plays were promoted as more widely significant, as representations of 'Africa' and the 'African experience'. This generalisation served as an important promotional strategy, and as a means of maximising the book's market. This edition – destined particularly for the international literary and academic market in the UK, USA and South Africa – sought to downplay the specific anti-apartheid message which, in contrast, had been highlighted in the Royal Court plays.

Sales and distribution

Statements: Three Plays became the most successful of Fugard's publications for the Press. The book was published on 14 November 1974 and it was decided that 2000 copies of the cloth edition would be published at £3.50, with the paperback retailing at £1.25.[109] However, sales increased substantially after *Sizwe Bansi* was included in the Open University's Modern Drama course on the recommendation of Dennis Walder. As a result the book was adopted as a set text, which guaranteed sales of 1500 per annum.[110] By the end of 1975, it had sold 1965 copies, rising to 2230 in 1976. A reprint of 7000 copies was ordered in June 1976, and by 1980 it had gone into four editions.[111] There was some competition for US rights in the plays. In 1974 Viking gained US rights to the two joint-authored plays, which were published as the single-volume *Sizwe Bansi is Dead and The Island* in 1976. OUP New York then published *Statements: Three Plays* in January 1978, estimating initial sales of 11,000 copies.[112]

The South African office was a major outlet for the book and 1000 copies were ordered for it at the outset. OUP had for the first time exclusive rights for the South African market, as Fugard did not have a South African publisher for the three plays. Three years after the publication and successful importing of *Statements: Three Plays* into South Africa, it attracted the attention of the customs officials. In August 1977, Neville Gracie reported that the book had been referred to the Directorate of Publications as possible 'imported undesirable literature'; a temporary embargo was placed on the import and sale of the books while a decision over possible prosecution was made.[113] However, there are no further references to this in the file; evidently the ban was lifted and *Statements: Three Plays* continued to sell freely in South Africa.

The publication of the *Statements* trilogy by OUP resulted in a more individualistic work than the plays in performance in the early 1970s, and through publication these improvised pieces were moulded into stable products. The concept of collaborative authorship was at odds with the individualistic one promoted by the publisher: the editors proceeded to publish the plays as if they had been written by Fugard in isolation, and Fugard was considered to be the sole author in terms of all editorial and contractual decisions. This conventional model of authorship applied by OUP undermined the inter-racial partnership between Fugard, Kani and Ntshona – indeed, the publication process served to expose and exacerbate the divisions between the authors of the plays.

The distinction between Fugard's works as published products and as performances was most acute in the case of the *Statements* plays. In performance, the plays were regarded as radical and subversive by the South African state as well as by audiences and critics. The South African security police monitored, regulated and sometimes banned Fugard's performances in South Africa. However, in sharp contrast, his work was made safe in the published books: they were packaged as universal, literary and commercial products that circulated freely in South Africa.

Conclusion

This chapter has considered the impact of OUP on Athol Fugard's early plays, and assessed how the publisher influenced their symbolic production. In 1984, Dennis Walder made some perceptive comments on the contrast between Fugard's plays in performance and in publication:

> All twelve plays (excluding ephemera, film scripts, and the minimal text, Orestes) are currently in print, courtesy of Oxford University Press; his latest, *'Master Harold' and the Boys*, is doing phenomenally well both in America, where it was premiered, and in South Africa. Thus does the poet of the dispossessed and disinherited, the culturally marginal, become

> assimilated. ... Perhaps the process is inevitable: this review participates in it, of course. But it does make the power, the demand, of the original theatrical experience, which is after all the raison d'être of the whole business, seem rather a long way away.[114]

This distinction between publication and performance was partly a result of Fugard's geographical separation from his publisher. International copyright legislation meant that a British publisher was necessary for Fugard to be published outside South Africa. In the hands of international publishers – via the mediation of literary agents – Fugard became a valuable literary commodity, to be bartered over and carved up. This trade in 'Athol Fugard' as a piece of literary property occurred with little reference to the playwright himself. In fact, Fugard's involvement in the publishing process as a whole was minimal. The distance between author and publisher meant that communication regularly broke down and he frequently failed to respond to correspondence. In addition, Fugard's lack of 'reverence for words on paper, texts' meant that he did not take control of the publication: he tended to follow his editors' advice regarding the choice of introduction, titles, editorial changes and glossaries. As a result, the publisher had a determining impact on the finished product. In particular, crucial decisions about which series his works should be assigned to were made without consultation with Fugard.

This 'elevation' of Fugard from the Three Crowns series into the Oxford Paperbacks literary canon had marked consequences for the way that his plays were edited and packaged. Through Three Crowns, Fugard had been associated with black African playwrights and with anti-apartheid South African authors, and his plays were sold predominantly in the African educational marketplace. However, as OUP recognised Fugard's international acclaim, he was moved into mainstream Oxford publishing, and the Oxford imprint was increasingly prominent in the branding of Fugard's texts, with its connotations of academia, conservatism and permanence. By these strategies, the publisher played a decisive role in neutralising the political impact of the plays and in successfully incorporating Fugard into the literary establishment in the UK, the USA and South Africa under apartheid.

Conclusion

This book recounts the previously untold stories of individuals who sought to serve African literature, culture and education through publishing. Specifically, it describes the OUP editors in Africa and Britain who contributed to the work of Three Crowns, defended it in the face of threats of closure and went to great lengths to discover new authors. Their sense of mission was in some respects a secular version of the missionary enterprise in Africa; their aim was to bring books to the continent, to give Africans a voice, to find the best of African literature and to deliver it to a world market. While the achievements of these impressive and dedicated individuals are undoubtedly part of the story of OUP in Africa, this study has also explored the economic and cultural inequalities that shaped the institutions and practice of colonial and postcolonial publishing. For, as Said writes, the 'civilising mission ... was always accompanied by domination'.[1]

In analysing the model of cultural production instituted by OUP in Africa in the twentieth century, I have argued that the relationship between OUP's metropolitan centre and its African branches involved an elaborate system of cross-subsidisation of cultural, symbolic and economic capital. Sales of educational books to Africa supported academic and scholarly publishing in the UK and generated substantial economic capital, whilst the Oxford University brand name conferred symbolic capital on the school textbooks and the Three Crowns literary texts alike for publications in Africa. Within this broader publishing strategy, Three Crowns was integral to OUP's 'narrative of redemption' in Africa. The Press veiled its profit motive in Africa partly through its geographical separation from the main profit centres in the former colonies, but also by producing a series of carefully constructed narratives to describe its cultural mission in Africa. In Bourdieu's terms, OUP perceived African literary publishing as a means of 'avoiding the crudest forms of mercantilism and ... abstaining from fully revealing their self-interested goals'.[2] The Three Crowns series was an important part of OUP's self-representation as a patron of African culture, and African literary publishing was a means by which the Press sought to occlude its commercial interests in postcolonial Africa and in South Africa under apartheid.

With respect to discussions about postcolonial authorship, I have aimed to contribute to debates on the vexed question of the 'assimilated postcolonial author'. Literary assimilation is widely regarded as the postcolonial author's response to domination of the international literary field, as encapsulated in Casanova's argument: 'Not every writer proceeds in the same way, but all writers attempt to enter the same race, and all of them struggle, albeit with unequal advantages, to attain the same goal: literary legitimacy.'[3] With regard to Three Crowns, however, there are indications of a more complex relationship between the African writer and the British cultural establishment. The case-studies of Fugard, Soyinka and Mtshali in particular demonstrate that they had little knowledge of or interest in the publication process. In the case of Soyinka and Fugard, they avowed that their main priority was the play in performance and all three writers had minimal influence in deciding how their literature should be published and promoted. It seems that they were primarily concerned about the local cultural and political context and not the finer details of the literary establishment in Europe or the USA. Rather than suggesting authorial complicity and assimilation, the archival evidence indicates instead that they were divorced from the publishing process. Evidently the authors in question did not know, did not want to know or actively contested the 'rules of the game'. Without denying the agency of individual African authors in getting their work published, I have argued that theorisations in postcolonial literary studies about the 'assimiliated and compromised' African author overemphasise the power of the author and ignore the influence of the publisher in the construction of the authors' texts and literary personae. Furthermore, the focus on the formal qualities of the literary text and the figure of the author diminishes the influence of transnational cultural and economic relations on the constitution of their literature.

Regarding the role of the editor, this study contests the construction of the European editor as a simple 'champion' and 'supporter' of the African writer. Instead, the role is shown to be more interventionist. As one of the leading publishers in anglophone Africa, OUP wielded significant power over constituting African literature in English. The editorial management policy for Three Crowns established and enforced a centre–periphery model of publishing, in which London-based editors and readers acted as agents of 'consecration' and 'legitimisation' for African literature. A literary hierarchy was devised in which the 'superior' African literature was directed to Three Crowns in London, whereas rejected literature was permitted to be published by the African branches. Although challenged by the branches, British-based authorisation of the literature was a principle that was upheld throughout Three Crowns' history. During the acquisition process, British-based editors and readers acted as 'gatekeepers' in determining the type of

African literature that should be published. The evidence of these author case-studies confirms Casanova's argument, that authors from 'literarily dominated' nations faced additional, and often insuperable, barriers in entering the literary field.[4]

Positioned at the interface between the author and the published book, the editor evidently acted as a 'filter' to the selected author's work, by redefining and re-representing it through paratextual interventions. The editor's interpretation of the text resulted in the creation of paratext that was designed to appeal to an international market through 'exotic' and 'primitive' representations of Africa, and through the promotion of the literature as universal and transcendent in its themes. The paratext also promoted the books to African examination boards as African equivalents of canonical Western texts and, as such, as worthy of being prescribed for use in school classrooms in Africa. The resulting publisher's paratext was at times in direct conflict with the author's text, most strikingly perhaps in the case of Soyinka's *A Dance of the Forests*. Written as a satire of the new colonial government in Nigeria, and presenting a damning portrayal of precolonial rule in Nigeria, it was promoted as an African *A Midsummer Night's Dream*, and given a primitive front cover evoking African myth and folklore.

With regard to the production processes, the material form of the postcolonial book symbolised the cultural and commercial demands that were brought to bear on the literature. The destination market was reflected in the books' resemblance to the familiar supplementary reader, and thus the Three Crowns books continued a long tradition at OUP of literary publishing for Africa. The supplementary reader was the most enduring – and financially successful – colonial and postcolonial literary form. OUP was instrumental in the creation of this product, and in the widespread dissemination of these books throughout Africa. Indeed, the English-language textbooks and accompanying readers were crucial elements in OUP's economic success throughout the twentieth century. Ironically, the books that Rex Collings planned as a departure from OUP's mainstream publishing practices in Africa ended up being compared with the mass-produced schoolbooks that he disparaged: the new canon of African writing was encased in the form of books that were not really books, but which, instead, resembled the denigrated and humble supplementary reader. Three Crowns books were ultimately regarded as an embarrassment by OUP editors and managers worldwide. There were objections to the fact that the best of African literature was being produced in this cheaply produced, second-rate form.

Finally, with respect to the sales and distribution of postcolonial African literature, the symbolic value of African literature was evidently influenced by the location of its market.[5] The Three Crowns editors envisaged a hierarchical literary marketplace in which the Western market accrued greater symbolic capital for literature than the African market. The initial *raison d'être* for Three Crowns was that, as a London-based series, the literature could be sold to the prestigious Anglo-American literary marketplace. However, this ambition soon had to be abandoned as the books in Three Crowns were increasingly expected by the Press management to yield similar profits to schoolbooks. As a result, the series was targeted primarily to the less prestigious but more profitable mass educational market, and increasingly titles were selected according to the likelihood of their being prescribed by examination boards. The series struggled throughout its history to serve these diverse markets. Although the African school market was denigrated by Three Crowns editors, the case-studies here suggest that this marginalised and low-status schoolbook market in Africa was crucial in creating the international reputation of several authors. In the case of Soyinka, in particular, it appears that OUP's promotion of the writer as an African Shakespeare to the examination boards, and its distribution of his books to the African school market, were crucial factors in his renown and canonisation in his own continent.

Therefore, in its task to 'represent Africa' through Three Crowns, OUP entered a 'battle for Africa' which was fought out on several fronts.[6] The most prominent battle was over whether the series should be regarded as part of OUP's cultural mission in Africa, or as part of its commercial enterprise. In the end, and in spite of significant opposition, commerce prevailed. Three Crowns was integrated into OUP's educational publishing programme in Africa, and the series was subjected to the same financial expectations as schoolbooks for these markets. Secondly, on an institutional level, there was a struggle over the 'power to consecrate' African literature,[7] which took place between the African branches and the metropolitan centre, and which resulted in entrenched international literary hierarchies, with London at the apex. Finally, with regard to the texts themselves, there was a constant conflict over which discourse on Africa should be supported and circulated, and in the transition of the new postcolonial writing from manuscript to printed book, it was filtered through, and frequently subsumed by, the residual colonial discourse, reinforced by the books being distributed through colonial sales channels.

This book sheds light on some of the ways in which persistent cultural and economic inequalities became entrenched in the global literary marketplace in the twentieth century, and to address how they affected the emergence of postcolonial African literature both institutionally and in terms of the material form of the book in this particular period of postcolonial history. I have argued for a historically and geographically contextualised study of the establishment of African literature, which moves beyond an analysis of the text and the author to a consideration of the institutions and processes behind literature's production, and in doing so have proposed some preliminary ways in which the asymmetrical relationship between the publisher and author might be understood, in respect to the creation, constitution and reception of postcolonial African literature.

Notes

Introduction

1. See James Currey, *Africa Writes Back: The African Writers Series and the Launch of African Literature* (Oxford: James Currey, 2008), Appendix '1962–2003: African Writers Series by Year of Publication', pp. 301–10.
2. Hans M. Zell and Helene Silvers, *A Reader's Guide to African Literature* (London: Heinemann Educational Books, 1972). This contains a bibliography of African literature published before 1972, from which this list of publishers is drawn.
3. Elleke Boehmer, *Colonial and Postcolonial Literature* (Oxford: Oxford University Press, 1995), p. 184.
4. Juliet Gardiner, 'What is an Author? Contemporary Publishing Discourse and the Author Figure', *Publishing Research Quarterly* 16:1 (2000), p. 67.
5. For example, Alan Hill's account of Heinemann Educational, *In Pursuit of Publishing* (London: John Murray, 1988), Philip Wallis's history of Longman, *At the Sign of the Ship* (Harlow: Longman, 1974), Peter Sutcliffe's *The Oxford University Press: An Informal History* (Oxford: Oxford University Press, 1978), as well as publishers' memoirs, such as David Philip, 'Book Publishing under and after Apartheid', in *Book Publishing in South Africa for the 1990s: Proceedings of a Symposium Held at the South African Library*, Cape Town, 22–23 November 1990 (Cape Town: South African Library, 1991).
6. Charles Larson, *The Ordeal of the African Writer* (London: Zed, 2001), p. 71.
7. Phaswane Mpe, 'The Role of the Heinemann African Writers Series in the Development and Promotion of African Literature', *African Studies*, 58 (1999), pp. 105–22.
8. Hans Zell, 'Publishing in Africa', unpublished paper, Oxford Brookes University Library Special Collection on African Publishing, *c*. 1992, p. 8.
9. Chinweizu, Jemie Onwuchekwa and Madubuike Ihechukwu, *Toward the Decolonization of African Literature: African Fiction and Poetry and their Critics* (London: KPI, 1980), pp. 16 and 7.
10. Aijaz Ahmad, *In Theory: Class, Nations, Literatures* (London: Verso, 1992), p. 45.
11. D. F. McKenzie, *Bibliography and the Sociology of Texts* (London: British Library, 1986), and Jerome McGann, *The Textual Condition* (Princeton, NJ: Princeton University Press, 1991).
12. Robert Darnton, 'What is the History of Books', in *The Kiss of Lamourette: Reflections in Cultural History* (New York: W. W. Norton, 1990), pp. 107–36.
13. The study of African readers and reading communities is an important and expanding field of study that has been significantly shaped by recent scholarship; for example: Isabel Hofmeyr's *The Portable Bunyan: A Transnational History of the Pilgrim's Progress* (Princeton, NJ: Princeton University Press, 2004); Stephanie Newell's *Literary Culture in Colonial Ghana: 'How to Play the Game of Life'* (Manchester: Manchester University Press, 2002) and *West African Literatures: Ways of Reading* (Oxford: Oxford University Press, 2006); Karin Barber (ed.), *Africa's Hidden Histories: Everyday Literacy and Making the Self* (Bloomington: Indiana University Press, 2006); and Archie Dick's *The Hidden History of South Africa's Book and Reading Cultures* (Toronto: University of Toronto Press, 2012).

14. Sarah Brouillette, *Postcolonial Writers in the Global Literary Marketplace* (Basingstoke: Palgrave Macmillan, 2007), p. 3.
15. See David Johnson, *Shakespeare and South Africa* (Oxford: Oxford University Press, 1996), pp. 90–7.
16. Ngũgĩ wa Thiong'o, *Penpoints, Gunpoints and Dreams: Towards a Critical Theory of the Arts and the State in Africa* (Oxford: Oxford University Press, 1997).
17. Chidi Amuta, *The Theory of African Literature: Implications for Practical Criticism* (London: Zed Books, 1989), pp. 2–3, 29, 34–6.
18. Pascale Casanova, *The World Republic of Letters*, trans. M. B. Debevoise (Cambridge, MA: Harvard University Press, 2004), p. 208.
19. Ibid.
20. Ibid., p. 209.
21. Graham Huggan, *The Postcolonial Exotic: Marketing the Margins* (London: Routledge, 2001), p. 54.
22. Brouillette, *Postcolonial Writers*, pp. 7 and 175.
23. See Pierre Bourdieu, 'The Production of Belief', in *The Field of Cultural Production*, ed. Randal Johnson (Cambridge: Polity Press, 1993), pp. 103–5, for a discussion of the role of the publisher in 'consecrating' literature.
24. See Pierre Bourdieu, *The Rules of Art: Genesis and Structure of the Literary Field*, trans. Susan Emanuel (Cambridge: Polity Press, 1996), pp. 142–6, for a general examination of the institutions of publishing and the different fields of cultural production, and Bourdieu, *Field of Cultural Production*, pp. 36–7 for an explanation of the role of the publisher in the symbolic production of a work of literature.
25. Casanova, *World Republic of Letters*, p. 39.
26. Shafquat Towheed, 'Two Paradigms of Literary Production: The Production, Circulation and Legal Status of Rudyard Kipling's Departmental Ditties and Indian Railway Library Texts', in *Books without Borders*, vol. II: *Perspectives from South Asia*, ed. Robert Fraser and Mary Hammond (Basingstoke: Palgrave Macmillan, 2008), p. 133. This study identifies the existence of a 'segregated readership' in colonial India, in which new Indian readers were widely ignored by authors, for example Rudyard Kipling.
27. See Gérard Genette, *Paratexts: Thresholds of Interpretation* (Cambridge: Cambridge University Press, 1997), pp. 3 and 16.
28. Huggan, *The Postcolonial Exotic*, pp. 53 and 54.
29. James English, *The Economy of Prestige: Prizes, Awards and the Circulation of Cultural Value* (Cambridge, MA: Harvard University Press, 2005), p. 298.
30. Casanova, *World Republic of Letters*, pp. 115 and 119.
31. Brouillette, *Postcolonial Writers*, p. 58.
32. Nourdin Bejjit, 'The Publishing of African Literature: Chinua Achebe, Ngũgĩ wa Thiong'o and the Heinemann African Writers Series, 1962–1988', unpublished Ph.D. thesis, Open University (2009).
33. Previous studies of Three Crowns are my own history of the series 'Postcolonial Publishing: Oxford University Press and the Three Crowns Series, 1962–1976' published in *Book History* (2005), my Ph.D. thesis, 'Postcolonial Literary Publishing: Oxford University Press in Africa and the Three Crowns Series' (Open University, 2010), and Gail Low's informative chapter on the series in *Publishing the Postcolonial: West African and Caribbean Writing in the UK, 1950–1967* (Abingdon: Routledge, 2011), pp. 26–57.
34. Janice Radway, *A Feeling for Books: The Book-of-the-Month Club, Literary Taste, and Middle-Class Desire* (Chapel Hill: University of North Carolina Press, 1997), p. 76.

35. Bourdieu, *Rules of Art*, p. 142.
36. See Radway, *Feeling for Books* for a detailed examination of the relationship between cultural and economic capital in publishing with respect to the US Book-of-the-Month Club.
37. The relationship between Oxford University Press and Oxford University will be explained in Chapter 1, p. 19.
38. E. C. Parnwell, report to the OUP, 25 September 1932, 'The Biological Approach to Education', Africa and India Branch Books (1927–35), File: IB/14, Archives of Oxford University Press (henceforth cited as AOUP). Access to the archive was kindly provided by Dr Martin Maw, OUP Archivist. There is a 30-year embargo on access to archival documents, so files up to 1982 were consulted for this research. All archival references and quotations are reprinted by permission of the Secretary to the Delegates of Oxford University Press.
39. Edward W. Said, *Culture and Imperialism* (London: Vintage, 1994), pp. 158–9.
40. 'Publisher's Speech at the Warehouse Opening', 14 October 1970, West Africa Branch, Ibadan, Nigeria Misc., 286/322, AOUP.
41. Said, *Culture and Imperialism*, p. 82.
42. Collings to Neale, 24 June 1962, Three Crowns Series, 1967–71, LG29/221–1, AOUP.
43. Collings to Neale, 4 July 1962, Soyinka: Lion and the Jewel, OP1619/12161, AOUP.
44. It should also be noted that my enquiry is confined to a study of the African branches of OUP and the Three Crowns archival records: it does not encompass the African Studies list of the Clarendon Press in London, or the parallel series entitled the Oxford Library of African Literature, which was a series of literature with an anthropological tendency – including African folklore, mythology and oral literature – that was translated into English and published from Oxford.
45. It is archival policy to remove records of rejected manuscripts; the archive does not retain author manuscripts or typescripts and so it is not possible to chart the transition of manuscript to final published book; jacket designs and page proofs are not retained; and, in addition, several editorial files are missing and some correspondence has gone astray.
46. Ann Laura Stoler, 'Colonial Archives and the Arts of Governance: On the Content in the Form', in Francis X. Blouin Jr and William G. Rosenberg (eds), *Archives, Documentation, and Institutions of Social Memory: Essays from the Sawyer Seminar* (Ann Arbor: University of Michigan Press, 2006), p. 269.
47. Stoler, 'Colonial Archives', p. 272. Note that Antoinette Burton uses similar terms to describe the task facing the historian in reading 'backstage of archives': Antoinette Burton (ed.), *Archive Stories: Facts, Fictions and the Writing of History* (Durham, NC: Duke University Press, 2005), p. 6.

1 The Vision for OUP in Africa

1. Parnwell to Sisam, 19 October 1928, p. 9, South Africa Branch, 165 (1) AOUP.
2. Jenny Lee, 'Exploiting the Imprint', in David Carter and Anne Galligan (eds), *Making Books: Contemporary Australian Publishing* (St Lucia: University of Queensland Press, 2007), p. 26.
3. See Graeme Johanson, *Colonial Editions in Australia, 1843–1972* (Wagga Wagga: Elibank Press, 2000), p. 1.
4. Priya Joshi, *In Another Country: Colonialism, Culture and the English Novel in India* (New York: Columbia University Press, 2002), pp. 98 and 102.

5. See Rimi B. Chatterjee, *Empires of the Mind: A History of the Oxford University Press in India under the Raj* (Delhi: Oxford University Press, 2006), chap. 1 (pp. 17–44) for an informative overview of the background to the establishment of the India publishing programme and an overview of the work of the branches in India in the first half of the twentieth century.
6. Chatterjee, *Empires of the Mind*, pp. 10 and 376.
7. Said, *Culture and Imperialism*, p. 130.
8. Bourdieu, *Rules of Art*, p. 145.
9. Riette Hart, 'Cape Town Branch: The Story of Oxford University Press Southern Africa' (1992), p. 1. David Philip's copy of this unpublished branch history is lodged in the National English Literary Museum, Grahamstown (hereafter NELM); 2006.30.2.12, File: OUP CTB After 1969. A further copy is housed at the OUP Archive (UK), and is available as a public domain document.
10. Parnwell to Milford, 8 April 1943, South Africa branch, 165 (1), AOUP.
11. Sisam to Milford, 25 August 1943, South Africa branch, 165 (1), AOUP.
12. Jeffrey Peires, 'Lovedale Press: Literature for the Bantu Revisited', *History in Africa*, 6 (1979), pp. 155–75.
13. Walton Johnson, 'Education: Keystone of Apartheid', *Anthropology & Education Quarterly*, 13:3 (1982), p. 217.
14. Jonathan Hyslop, *The Classroom Struggle: Policy and Resistance in South Africa, 1940–1990* (Pietermaritzburg: University of Natal Press, 1999), p. 2.
15. Ibid., p. 3.
16. *Oxford House, Ibadan* (Oxford: Oxford University Press, 1954), p. 10, West Africa Branch, Ibadan, Nigeria Misc., 286/322, AOUP.
17. Parnwell's Report on meeting with Rivers-Smith, 16 September 1927, Africa and India Branch Books (1927–35), File: IB/14, AOUP.
18. Ibid.
19. Ibid.
20. Ibid.
21. Parnwell to Goffin, Bombay, 14 October 1927, Africa and India Branch Books (1927–35), File: IB/14, AOUP.
22. Parnwell to Goffin, Bombay, 23 April 1928, in ibid.
23. Parnwell to K. Sisam, 19 October 1928, 165 (1), May 1928–July 1975, South African Branch.
24. Parnwell to India Branch, 11 February 1932, File: Africa and India Branch Books (1927–35), File: IB/14, AOUP.
25. Thomas Jesse Jones, *Education in Africa: A Study of West, South, and Equatorial Africa* (New York: Phelps-Stokes Fund, 1922) and his *Education in East Africa* (New York: Phelps-Stokes Fund, 1925).
26. Quoted in Sybille Küster, '"Book Learning" versus "Adapted Education": The Impact of Phelps-Stokesism on Colonial Education Systems in Central Africa in the Interwar Period', *Paedagogica Historica*, 43:1 (2007), pp. 79–97, at p. 85.
27. E. C. Parwell Report to the OUP, 25 September 1932, 'The Biological Approach to Education', File: Africa and India Branch Books (1927–35), File: IB/14, AOUP.
28. N. B. Hunter, *A First Course in Geography and History for African Schools* (London: Oxford University Press, 1931), vol. 1, p. 24.
29. Ibid., vol. 2, p. 37.
30. Ibid., vol. 1, p. 62.
31. Mabel Mellor, *A Practical Modern Geography*, West African edition (London: Oxford University Press, 1934), Book II, p. 36.

32. A. V. Murray, *The School in the Bush: A Critical Study of the Theory and Practice of Native Education in Africa* (London: Longmans, Green, 1929), p. 361. See also David Johnson's 'From the Colonial to the Post-Colonial: Shakespeare and Education in Africa', in Ania Loomba and Martin Orkin (eds), *Post-Colonial Shakespeares* (London: Routledge, 1998), pp. 218–34, at pp. 222–3, for a more detailed analysis of Murray's response to this educational policy in relation to its implications for a literary education.
33. Küster, '"Book Learning" versus "Adapted Education"', p. 93.
34. Ruth Makotsi and Lily Nyariki, *Publishing and the Book Trade in Kenya* (Nairobi: East African Educational Publishers, 1997), p. 36. A counter-argument is put forward by Peter Kallaway that the policy had little impact beyond these countries, as 'despite the rhetoric, little policy development of this kind took place outside of isolated experimental situations in Kenya, Southern Rhodesia and Nyasaland'. See Peter Kallaway, 'Welfare and Education in British Colonial Africa and South Africa during the 1930s and 1940s', *Paedagogica Historica*, 41:3 (2005), pp. 337–56, at p. 345.
35. Johnson, 'From the Colonial to the Post-Colonial', p. 222.
36. Bourdieu, *Rules of Art*, p. 141.
37. Sutcliffe, *The Oxford University Press*, p. 214.
38. Richard C. Smith, *Teaching English as a Foreign Language, 1912–1936: Pioneers of ELT* (London: Routledge, 2003), pp. x–xii.
39. A. P. R. Howatt, *Warwick ELT Archive Launch Lecture*, 7 May 2005, http://www2.warwick.ac.uk/fac/soc/al/research/collect/elt_archive/launch/lecture/.
40. Bourdieu, *Rules of Art*, p. 142.
41. New Oxford English Course for East Africa, Books I–VI, Pupils' and Teachers' Notes, CA48/LOCA002512–23, and New Oxford English Course for Nigeria, Books 1–VI, Teachers' and Pupils' Notes, CA48/LOCA002494–250, AOUP.
42. See Chatterjee, *Empires of the Mind*, pp. 346–50, for further details of the development of the *Oxford English Course*, in relation to OUP's unsuccessful attempt to form a partnership with Longmans, Green in 1934 and in relation to the details of Faucett's English-language teaching scheme.
43. Further titles in the course were abridged versions of: Edgar Allan Poe, *The Purloined Letter* (1933), Nathanial Hawthorne, *The Great Stone Face* (1933), Thomas Hughes, *Tom Brown's Schooldays* (1934), Washington Irving, *Rip Van Winkle* (1936) and G. C. Latham's *David Livingstone in East Africa* (1936).
44. Charles Granston Richards, 'No Carpet on the Floor: Recollections and Reflections on the Work of Forty Years, 1935–1975, in the Development of Literature and Publishing', unpublished memoir (1991, University of Witwatersrand Library), p. 58.
45. Further titles in the series were: *The Tortoise of Koka, and Other Stories* (1949), Jessie Hertslet's *The Story of an African Boy* (1942) and *The Story of an African Girl* (1948), Alec Ernest Haarer's *The Chief's Shadow* (1950) and Harold Beken Thomas's *The Story of Uganda* (1955).
46. See, for example, Thomas Mofolo, *Chaka the Zulu* (London: Oxford University Press, 1949), back cover.
47. Said, *Culture and Imperialism*, p. 96.
48. Mofolo, *Chaka the Zulu*, Introduction, p. 1. Note that OUP published the first edition of Thomas Mofolo's *Chaka* in 1931, followed by his second novel, *The Traveller of the East*, in 1934.
49. J. Grenfell Williams, *Moshesh, the Man on the Mountain* (London: Oxford University Press, 1950), p. 147.

50. Stephanie Newell, *Ghanaian Popular Fiction: 'Thrilling Discoveries in Conjugal Life' and Other Tales* (Oxford: James Currey, 2000), p. 114.
51. John Nottingham, 'Establishing an African Publishing Industry: A Study in Decolonization', *African Affairs*, 271:68 (1969), pp. 139–44, at p. 141.
52. Note that a further example is provided by Stephanie Newell, in *Literary Culture in Colonial Ghana*, pp. 89–90, in which she analyses the report of a Gold Coast students' reading competition in 1935 and, in particular, a report on *Lamb's Tales from Shakespeare*, an OUP reader, rated by the student as 'the second book to the Holy Bible'.
53. Ngũgĩ wa Thiong'o, *Moving the Centre: The Struggle for Cultural Freedom* (Oxford: James Currey, 1993), pp. 34–5.
54. Joseph O. O. Okpaku, 'Publishing and Public Enlightenment in Africa', in Edwina Oluwasanmi, Eva McLean and Hans Zell (eds), *Publishing in Africa in the Seventies* (Ife: University of Ife Press, 1975), pp. 233–7, at p. 235. Note that Okpaku went on to found the New York publishing house Third Press.
55. Ibid., p. 236.
56. Note that Rimi Chatterjee's overview of the *Oxford English Course* supplementary readers that were exported to India in the late 1930s draws similar conclusions: 'the series was still selling an image of an ideal and idyllic Europe in the guise of education, presumably for more or less imperialistic reasons'. Chatterjee, *Empires of the Mind*, p. 350. See also Johnson's *Shakespeare and South Africa* for an in-depth examination of the institutions of English literary education in relation to the politics of British colonial rule and the educational system under apartheid in South Africa.
57. Parnwell, 'Africa: Post-War Organization', 165 (1), May 1928–July 1975, South African Branch, AOUP.
58. Norrington to Milford and Parnwell, 31 August 1943, 165 2 (1) May 1928–July 1975, South African Branch folder C: 1943–8, AOUP.
59. P. J. Cain and A. G. Hopkins, *British Imperialism: Crisis and Deconstruction* (London: Longman, 1993), pp. 275–9.
60. Henry Chakava, 'East and Central Africa', *Journal of Commonwealth Literature*, 13:3 (1979), pp. 10–17, at p. 12.
61. See John Hench, *Books as Weapons: Propaganda, Publishing, and the Battle for Global Markets in the Era of World War II* (Ithaca, NY: Cornell University Press, 2010), p. 212.
62. Bourdieu, *Field of Cultural Production*, p. 125.
63. James Currey lists the major publishers involved in African literature in *Africa Writes Back*, pp. 14–15.
64. Sutcliffe, *The Oxford University Press*, p. 266.
65. 'Report of the Committee on the University Press', *Oxford University Gazette*, 100 (1970), Supplement no. 7, pp. 24–5.
66. Bell to Lewis, 31 July 1969, and Burton to Brown, 11 July 1969, Three Crowns Series, 1967–72, LG29/221–3, AOUP.
67. Bell to Lewis, 31 July 1969, in ibid.
68. 'Report of the Committee on the University Press', p. 114.
69. Ibid., para. 234.
70. George B. Richardson to Inland Revenue for Exemption Status from Corporate Tax, 24 March 1977, http://www.btinternet.com/~akme/75dcm2.html.
71. Ibid.
72. Ibid., p. 6.

2 'The Obligation to Be Profitable': OUP in West Africa

1. John Brown, Publisher, 'Speech at the Warehouse Opening', 14 October 1970, West Africa Branch, Ibadan, Nigeria Misc., 286/322, AOUP. This speech was then quoted at length in the *Nigeria Tribune* and *Daily Sketch*, Nigeria, 15 October 1970 (see cuttings in file).
2. Jomo Kenyatta, *My People of Kikuyu* (Nairobi: Oxford University Press, 1966). Kenyatta writes in his introduction: 'When I look back to 1942, there seemed then no end to the explication of my people, to the creed of Colonial domination, to the hypocrisy of an alien rule which used the gloss of altruism to cover ambition and greed' (p. 1).
3. In publishing terminology, the 'book supply chain' is the process by which a book travels from author via agent, publisher, printer, distributor to retailer or institution. See John Thompson, *Merchants of Culture: The Publishing Business in the Twenty-First Century* (Cambridge: Polity Press, 2010), pp. 14–22, for an analysis of the 'publishing chain'.
4. Bourdieu, 'The Production of Belief', pp. 78–9.
5. Casanova, *World Republic of Letters*, p. 86.
6. Ibid., p. 108.
7. Ibid., p. 115.
8. Ibid., pp. 111 and 109.
9. Huggan, *The Postcolonial Exotic*, pp. 34 and 54. See the Introduction for further discussion of this issue.
10. Bejjit, 'The Publishing of African Literature', p. 7.
11. Currey, *Africa Writes Back*, p. xxiv.
12. Gareth Griffiths also observes that the educational market in Africa had an 'incalculable influence on the development of African writing in English'. Gareth Griffiths, *African Literatures in English: East and West* (Harlow: Pearson Education, 2000), p. 76.
13. See Huggan, *The Postcolonial Exotic*, p. 36.
14. Newell, *Ghanaian Popular Fiction*, p. 90.
15. Ibid., p. 91.
16. Ibid., p. 90.
17. Robert Fraser, *Book History through Postcolonial Eyes: Rewriting the Script* (London: Routledge, 2008), pp. 166–7.
18. *Oxford House, Ibadan* (Oxford: Oxford University Press, 1954), p. 12, West Africa Branch, Ibadan, Nigeria Misc., 286/322, AOUP.
19. T. T. Solaru, Nigerian Branch Annual Managerial Report, 1967/8. Note that, in addition, the branch acted as agent for the Edinburgh University Press, Cambridge University Press, Faber & Faber and Cape, as outlined in T. T. Solaru, Nigerian Branch Annual Managerial Report, 1968/9, Nigeria Branch Accounts, AOUP.
20. A. Aseidu-Akrofi, 'Education in Ghana', in A. Babs Fafunwa and J. U. Aisiku (eds), *Education in Africa: A Comparative Survey* (London: George Allen & Unwin, 1982), chap. 5, see p. 100.
21. Victor Nwankwo, 'Nigeria', in Philip G. Altbach and Edith S. Hoshino (eds), *International Book Publishing: An Encyclopedia* (London: Routledge, 1995), p. 398.
22. New Oxford English Course for East Africa, Books I–VI, Pupils and Teachers Notes, CA48/LOCA002512–23 and New Oxford English Course for Nigeria, Books 1–VI, Teachers and Pupils Notes, CA48/LOCA002494–250, AOUP.

23. Don Dodson and Barbara Dodson, 'Publishing Progress in Nigeria', *Scholarly Publishing*, 4:1 (1972), pp. 61–72, at p. 68.
24. T. T. Solaru, Nigerian Branch Annual Report, 1970, p. 2, Nigeria Branch Accounts, AOUP.
25. Oluwasanmi et al. (eds), *Publishing in Africa in the Seventies*, p. 4.
26. G. O. Onibonoje, 'Wanted! A Cultural Revolution, Not a Dialogue', in Oluwasanmi et al. (eds), *Publishing in Africa in the Seventies*, p. 275. G. O. Onibonoje was managing director of Onibonoje Press and Book Industries in Nigeria.
27. Solaru, Annual Managerial Report 1967/8 and Branch Annual Report, September 1970, p. 1, Nigeria Branch Accounts, AOUP.
28. Solaru, Annual Managerial Report, 1967/8, Nigeria Branch Accounts, AOUP.
29. See Thomas Biersteker, *Multinationals, the State and Control of the Nigerian Economy* (Princeton, NJ: Princeton University Press, 1987), chaps 2 and 4 for details of the indigenisation decrees.
30. Solaru, Branch Annual Managerial Report, 1968/9, Nigeria Branch Accounts, AOUP.
31. Dodson and Dodson, 'Publishing Progress in Nigeria', p. 64.
32. Quoted in Per I. Gedin, 'Private Enterprise Publishing in Africa: Why and How it Should be Fostered', *Logos*, 2:3 (1991), pp. 133–9, at p. 135.
33. Nicholas Balabkins, *Indigenization and Economic Development: The Nigerian Experience* (Greenwich, CT: JAI Press, 1982), p. 163.
34. Nwankwo, 'Nigeria', p. 398.
35. Solaru, Annual Managerial Report, 1973–4, Nigeria Branch Accounts, AOUP.
36. A. B. Fafunwa, *History of Education in Nigeria* (London: George Allen & Unwin, 1974), p. 193.
37. Ukeje Onyerisara and J. U. Aisiku, 'Education in Nigeria', in A. Babs Fafunwa and J. U. Aisiku (eds), *Education in Africa: A Comparative Survey* (London: George Allen & Unwin, 1982), p. 231.
38. See the reference to the prescription of Joe de Graft's *Sons and Daughters*, described in Chapter 5, p. 97.
39. Zell, 'Publishing in Africa', p. 6.
40. Solaru, Annual Managerial Report 1968/9, Nigeria Branch Accounts, AOUP.
41. OUP's main competitors in academic and scholarly publishing in Nigeria were the African Universities Press, the University of Ife and the University of Ibadan Press.
42. This data is drawn from British Library records of books that were published at the Ibadan branch from 1954 to 1980, and that were subsequently deposited in the British Library.
43. By 1970, it was publishing for the Royal Institute of International Affairs, the International African Institute, the Institute of Race Relations, the Nigerian Institute for Social and Economic Research and the University of Nigeria, Nsukka. OUP Ibadan was also the publisher of the *West African Journal of Archaeology* for the University of Ibadan, and *ODU*, the cultural journal of the Department of African Studies of Ife University, as reported in the *Daily Sketch* (Nigeria), 14 October 1970, West Africa Branch, Ibadan, Nigeria Misc., 286/322, AOUP.
44. Robert Fraser, 'War and the Colonial Book Trade: The Case of OUP India', in Robert Fraser and Mary Hammond (eds), *Books without Borders*, vol. II: *Perspectives from South Asia* (Basingstoke: Palgrave Macmillan, 2008), pp. 146–7.
45. Butcher to Bell, 18 September 1969, Three Crowns Series, 1967–72, LG29/221–3, AOUP.
46. Mitchell to Bell, 17 November 1971, p. 3, in ibid.
47. Ibid.

48. Burton to Bell, 11 July 1969, Three Crowns Series, 1967–72, LG29/221-3, AOUP.
49. Handwritten note of 2 October 1973, Soyinka: Lion and the Jewel, OP1620/12164, AOUP.
50. Heapy to Otesanya, 4 November 1975, Clark: Ozidi, OP1620/12168, AOUP.
51. Memo from Bell to Branch Managers, 29 November 1971, Three Crowns Series, 1967–72, LG29/221-3, AOUP. Note that Ely House was the name of the building that housed OUP London. Originally it had been based in Amen House.
52. Neal Burton reported to Rex Collings on 1 May 1963, 'Certainly the universities as a whole are going to study African writing wherever this reaches a moderate standard of quality,' Three Crowns Series, 1967–72, LG29/221-3, AOUP.
53. T. T. Solaru to the Delegates, 'Nigerian Branch Annual Managerial Report 1967/68', Nigeria Branch Accounts, AOUP.
54. Philip Chester, Editorial General Session, Editorial Assistance to the branches, June 1971, in Three Crowns Series, 1967–72, LG29/221-3, AOUP.
55. Accounts Report, 1963, Nigeria Branch Accounts, AOUP.
56. Delegates of the University Press, 'Annual Report, 1 April 1975–31 March 1976', *Oxford University Gazette*, November 1976, Supplement no. 1, p. 15.
57. Nwankwo, 'Nigeria', p. 398.
58. Delegates of the University Press, 'Annual Report, 1 April 1976–31 March 1977', *Oxford University Gazette*, December 1977, Supplement no. 1, p. 7.
59. Ibid.
60. Ibid., p. 16.
61. Eva-Maria McLean Rathgeber, 'Nigerian University Presses: Problems and Prospects', *The African Book Publishing Record*, 5:1 (1979), pp. 13–18, at p. 14.
62. Delegates of the University Press, 'Annual Report, 1 April 1977–31 March 1978', *Oxford University Gazette*, November 1978, Supplement no. 1, p. 6.
63. 'University Press Limited Annual Report 1979', p. 6, Nigeria Accounts 1962–80, AOUP.
64. Delegates of the University Press, 'Annual Report, 1 April 1978–31 March 1979', *Oxford University Gazette*, November 1979, Supplement no. 1, p. 7.
65. Bernth Lindfors, 'Bibliography: Africa Western', *The Journal of Commonwealth Literature*, 20:2 (1985), pp. 6–18, at p. 6.
66. In 1968, a UNESCO Book Development meeting was held in Accra, Ghana; in 1973 the Ife Conference on Publishing and Book Development in Africa took place; in the 1980s, the Dag Hammarskjöld Foundation seminars on indigenous publishing development were held in Arusha, Tanzania; in 1991 a Conference on Publishing in the Third World was organised at the Rockefeller Conference Centre in Bellagio, Italy, resulting in Altbach's *Publishing and Development in the Third World*. See Hans Zell's *African Publishing Companion: A Resource Guide* (Lochcarron: Hans Zell, 2002) for further information on African publishing development.
67. Gedin, 'Private Enterprise Publishing in Africa', p. 134.
68. Casanova, *World Republic of Letters*, p. 115.
69. Said, *Culture and Imperialism*, p. 75.

3 'The Call to Duty': OUP in East Africa

1. Richards, 'No Carpet on the Floor', p. 58.
2. Said, *Culture and Imperialism*, pp. 130–1.
3. Richards, 'No Carpet on the Floor', pp. 21–2.
4. Ibid., p. 65.

5. *Oxford House, Ibadan* (Oxford: Oxford University Press, 1954), p. 12, West Africa Branch, Ibadan, Nigeria Misc., 286/322, AOUP. Charles Richards took over from the first representative at the office, Simon Abbott. Longman was the first British commercial publisher to establish an office in Nairobi in 1950. OUP were then followed by Macmillan, Evans and Nelson, who established sales outlets for their UK publications.
6. Richards, 'No Carpet on the Floor', p. 66.
7. Chakava worked at Heinemann Educational Books in Nairobi from 1972 and became managing director in 1977.
8. Henry Chakava, 'Kenyan Publishing: Independence and Dependence', in Philip Altbach (ed.), *Publishing and Development in the Third World* (London: Hans Zell, 1992), pp. 119–50, at pp. 119–21. Charles Richards's memoir contains a seven-page section entitled 'Comments on errors' relating to Chakava's chapter, which he considers to be 'based on untrue statements'. He added this to his memoir in April 1993.
9. Ibid., p. 129.
10. Makotsi and Nyariki, *Publishing and the Book Trade in Kenya*, pp. 22–3.
11. Charles Lewis, 'Annual Report, 1965', p. 2, Eastern African Branch Accounts 1964–73, AOUP.
12. This investigation of new titles from Nairobi is based on British Library records. While many texts from the Nairobi and Ibadan branches were deposited in the British Library, there are certain notable omissions, for example only one of the New Fiction from Africa series was deposited in the British Library or the Bodleian. However, the number of books in the British Library that were published in Nairobi in this period corresponds reasonably well with references in the East Africa branch annual reports.
13. Zell, 'Publishing in Africa', p. 6, Chakava, 'Kenyan Publishing', pp. 122–3.
14. Filomina Indire, 'Education in Kenya', in A. Babs Fafunwa and J. U. Aisiku (eds), *Education in Africa: A Comparative Survey* (London: George Allen & Unwin, 1982), pp. 115–39, at p. 122.
15. Ibid., p. 130.
16. Herme Joseph Mosha, 'A Reassessment of the Indicators of Primary Education Quality in Developing Countries: Emerging Evidence from Tanzania', *International Review of Education*, 34:1 (1988), pp. 17–45, at p. 25.
17. Roger Houghton, Eastern Africa Branch Annual Report, 1968/9, Eastern African Branch Accounts 1964–73, AOUP.
18. Indire, 'Education in Kenya', p. 132.
19. Nottingham, 'Establishing an African Publishing Industry', p. 140.
20. Gedin, 'Private Enterprise Publishing in Africa', p. 134.
21. It should be noted that in Kenya, net profits were subject to a high tax rate of 40 per cent.
22. Chakava, 'Kenyan Publishing', pp. 119–24.
23. Charles Lewis, 'Annual Report, 1965', p. 1, Eastern African Branch Accounts, 1964–73, AOUP.
24. Roger Houghton, Eastern Africa Branch Annual Report, 1968/9, p. 2, Eastern African Branch Accounts 1964–73, AOUP.
25. See 'Eastern Africa Branch Annual Report 1965–6', 'Eastern African Branch Annual Managerial Report 1967–8', 'Eastern African Branch Annual Report 1968–9', in Eastern African Branch Accounts, 1964–73, AOUP.
26. Chakava, 'Kenyan Publishing', pp. 121–4.

27. Charles Lewis, 'Annual Report, 1965', p. 2, Eastern African Branch Accounts, 1964–73, AOUP. Note that Harold Macmillan, British Prime Minister from 1957 to 1963, became Chairman of Macmillan Publishers in 1964 after retiring from politics. He was the grandson of the founder, Daniel Macmillan, and he had previously worked at the firm from 1920 to 1940.
28. Macmillan helped form the Uganda Publishing House (1966), the Tanzania Publishing House (1966), the Kenneth Kaunda Foundation, in Zambia (1967), the Ghana State Publishing Corporation (1965) and the Northern Nigeria Publishing Corporation (1972). Macmillan did not find a willing state publisher to work with in Kenya, however, and set up an independent branch there in 1971 under the registered name of (Macmillan) Books for Africa. An analysis of Macmillan's work in Ghana is provided in Newell's *Ghanaian Popular Fiction*, pp. 92–3.
29. Zell, 'Publishing in Africa', p. 7.
30. Anon., 'East Africa', Macmillans in Africa: 1967–8, File: 8380, AOUP.
31. 'Statement by the Publishers Association on State Monopoly Publishing and Distribution and the Erosion of Copyright', *The Bookseller*, 27 April 1967 and 'Macmillans in Africa: The Plot Thickens', *The Sunday Times*, 30 April 1967, Macmillans in Africa: 1967–8, File: 8380, AOUP.
32. John Nottingham, quoted in *The Bookseller*, 20 May 1967, p. 2274, Macmillans in Africa: 1967–8, File 8380, AOUP.
33. 'Material for a Press Statement in Nairobi', May 1967, in ibid.
34. Charles Lewis, Eastern Africa Branch Annual Managerial Report 1967–8, East Africa/Nairobi Branch Accounts 1966–75, AOUP.
35. Roger Houghton, 'Eastern Africa Branch Annual Report 1968/9', Eastern African Branch Accounts, 1964–73, AOUP.
36. 'Eastern African Branch Capital', undated (*c.* 1970), Eastern African Branch Accounts, 1964–73, AOUP.
37. Houghton, 'Eastern African Branch Annual Report 1971/2', p. 2, Eastern African Branch Accounts, 1964–73, AOUP.
38. Chakava, 'Kenyan Publishing', pp. 122–3.
39. Lewis, 'Annual Report, 1965', p. 1, File: Eastern African Branch Accounts, 1964–73, AOUP.
40. Richards, 'No Carpet on the Floor', p. 68.
41. David Birmingham, *The Decolonization of Africa* (London: UCL Press, 1995), pp. 49–52, and Julius Nyerere, 'Africa and the Debt Crisis', *African Affairs*, 84:337 (1985), pp. 493–5.
42. Roger Houghton, Eastern Africa Branch Annual Report 1972/3, p. 1, East Africa/Nairobi Branch Accounts, 1966–75, AOUP.
43. Ibid., pp. 2–3.
44. Roger Houghton, 'Eastern Africa Branch Annual Report 1 April 1973–31 March 1974', p. 2, East Africa/Nairobi Branch Accounts, 1966–75, AOUP.
45. Charles Lewis, 'Eastern Africa Branch Annual Report 1965–1966', p. 1, East Africa/Nairobi Branch Accounts, 1966–75, AOUP.
46. Richards, 'No Carpet on the Floor', p. 30.
47. Lewis to Toyne, 31 October 1966, Three Crowns Series, 1967–71, LG29/221-1, AOUP. Ely House was at this time the location of the OUP offices in London.
48. Ibid.
49. Murray Carlin, *Not Now, Sweet Desdemona* (Nairobi: Oxford University Press, 1969), back cover.

50. Austin S. Bukenya, 'East and Central Africa', *Journal of Commonwealth Literature*, 7:2 (1972), pp. 15–25, at p. 15.
51. R. N. Ndegwa, 'Africa: East and Central', *Journal of Commonwealth Literature*, 16:2 (1982), pp. 9–11, at p. 10.
52. Chris Wanjala, 'East and Central Africa', *Journal of Commonwealth Literature*, 8:2 (1973), pp. 14–22, at p. 14.
53. Note, however, that Three Crowns texts relating to East Africa were co-published in Nairobi: Derek Hollingworth's *They Came to Mauritius* and Barbara Kimenye's *Kalasanda* and *Kalasanda Revisited*.
54. Kariara to Veronica C., Oxford Paperbacks, 6 February 1970, Three Crowns Series, 1967–72, LG29/221–3, AOUP.
55. Stallworthy to Chester, 20 February 1970, Three Crowns Series, 1967–72, LG29/221–3, AOUP.
56. Houghton to Burton, 14 May 1970, Three Crowns Series, 1967–72, LG29/221–3, AOUP.
57. Ibid.
58. Lewis to Crowther, 19 September 1966, Three Crowns Series, 1967–71, LG29/221–1, AOUP.
59. Lewis to Bell, 7 July 1969, Three Crowns Series, 1967–72, LG29/221–3, AOUP.
60. Ibid.
61. Bell to Lewis, 31 July 1969, Three Crowns Series, 1967–72, LG29/221–3, AOUP.
62. Bukenya, 'East and Central Africa', p. 15.
63. Ibid.
64. Ibid.
65. Marjorie Macgoye's prize-winning novel *Coming to Birth* was later published by Heinemann Kenya, see Chakava 'Kenyan Publishing', p. 132.
66. Charles Mungoshi, *Coming of the Dry Season*, rev. edn (Harare: Zimbabwe Publishing House, 1981), p. 6. Note that the original OUP edition of Charles Mungoshi's *Coming of the Dry Season* (1972) is not available in the British Library or Bodleian Library.
67. Ibid., p. 44.
68. Ibid., p. 48.
69. Ibid., p. 56.
70. Ibid., p. 58.
71. E. W. Krog, 'The Progress of Shona and Ndebele Literature', http://www.mazwi.net/essays/the-progress-of-shona-and-ndebele-literature.
72. These extracts from the Censor Board's files have been copied from Patricia Alden, 'Competing Interpretations: Charles Mungoshi's "The Accident"', *Zambezia*, 21:2 (1994), pp. 107–22, at p. 111. She quotes from files kept in the Department of English, University of Zimbabwe. Alden goes on to contrast black and white Zimbabwean students' readings of 'The Accident' in two Harare schools in 1994.
73. 'The Appeal from the Department of English' and 'The Response of the Censor Board', quoted in Alden, 'Competing Interpretations', p. 113.
74. Brown to branch managers, 12 October 1971, Three Crowns Series, 1967–72, LG29/221–3, AOUP.
75. Bell to branch managers, 29 November 1971, in ibid.
76. Jon Stallworthy, personal interview, 3 July 2002, Wolfson College, Oxford University.
77. Bukenya, 'East and Central Africa', p. 15.
78. Lewis to Bell, 16 December 1971, Three Crowns Series, 1967–72, LG29/221–3, AOUP.

79. Chakava, 'Kenyan Publishing', p. 125.
80. Ibid.
81. Chakava, 'East and Central Africa', pp. 11–12.
82. The East African Publishing House was a non-profit-making arm of the East African Community, and was the publisher of the literary journals *Buscara, Dhana, Joiso, Maktaba, Mawaza* and *Umma*.
83. Ndegwa, 'Africa: East and Central' 16:2 (1982), pp. 10–11. This survey related to books published in 1980, in which the only one published by a British-owned publisher was Koigi wa Wamwere's *A Woman Reborn*, published by Heinemann Educational Books, Nairobi (which was by then locally incorporated).
84. R. N. Ndegwa, 'Africa: East and Central', *Journal of Commonwealth Literature*, 17:2 (1982), pp. 2–8, at p. 2.
85. Quoted in R. N. Ndegwa, 'Africa: East and Central', *Journal of Commonwealth Literature*, 21:2 (1986), p. 2.

4 Publishing under Apartheid: OUP in South Africa

1. Examples include M. Trump (ed.), *Rendering Things Visible: Essays on South African Literary Culture* (Johannesburg: Ravan Press, 1990); G. E. de Villiers (ed.), *Ravan: Twenty-Five Years, 1972–1997: A Commemorative Volume of New Writing* (Randburg: Ravan Press, 1997); Geoffrey V. Davis and Holger G. Ehling, 'Levelling the Playing Fields: An Interview with David and Marie Philip', in Geoffrey V. Davis (ed.), *South African Writing: Voyages and Explorations* (Amsterdam: Rodopi, 1994), pp. 133–42; Glenn Moss, 'The Life and Changing Times of an Independent Publisher in South Africa', *Logos*, 4:3 (1993), pp. 144–6; G. Friedman and R. Blumenthal (eds), *A Writer in Stone: South African Writers Celebrate the 70th Birthday of Lionel Abrahams* (Cape Town: David Philip, 1998); and A. Donker, 'English-Language Publishing in South Africa', *English in Africa*, 10:1 (1983), pp. 29–35.
2. Sutcliffe, *The Oxford University Press*, inside book jacket.
3. Bell to Lewis, 31 July 1969, Three Crowns Series, 1967–72, LG29/221-3, AOUP.
4. Marquard to Milford, 29 January 1945, OUP CTB after 1969, File: 2006.30.2.1, NELM.
5. Randolph Vigne, *Liberals Against Apartheid: A History of the Liberal Party of South Africa, 1953–1968* (London: Macmillan, 1997), p. 21.
6. Christopher Merrett, *A Culture of Censorship: Secrecy and Intellectual Repression in South Africa* (Cape Town: David Philip, 1995), pp. 21 and 34.
7. Philip, 'Book Publishing under and after Apartheid', p. 11.
8. Ibid.
9. Z. Ngwane, 'Apartheid under Education: Schooling, Initiation, and Domestic Reproduction in Post-Apartheid Rural South Africa', in Peter Kallaway (ed.), *The History of Education under Apartheid 1948–1994: The Doors of Learning and Culture Shall Be Opened* (Cape Town: Pearson, 2002), pp. 276–7.
10. Johnson, 'Education', p. 219.
11. Verwoerd's speech to the House of Assembly on 17 September 1953 is quoted in ibid.
12. Peter Kallaway, 'An Introduction to the Study of Education for Blacks in South Africa', in Peter Kallaway (ed.), *Apartheid and Education: The Education of Black South Africans* (Johannesburg: Ravan Press, 1984), p. 4.
13. Ibid., p. 11.

14. Johnson, 'Education', p. 220.
15. Muriel Horrell, *A Decade of Bantu Education* (Johannesburg: South African Institute of Race Relations, 1964), p. 149.
16. Johnson, *Shakespeare and South Africa*, p. 164.
17. Marquard to Mary Benson, 8 March 1955, BC587, C129.7, CTU.
18. Alan Paton to Marquard, 17 March 1955, BC587, C129.8, CTU.
19. David Philip, 'Notes relating to meeting with the Delegates, the Publisher, E. Parnwell and D. Neale', 30 August 1957 and 'Report by Anthony Toyne of Ely House (OE) after Extended Visit 1969', p. 1, File 2006.3.2.11, Cape Town Branch to 1969, Folder 2, NELM.
20. Phaswane Mpe and Monica Seeber, 'The Politics of Book Publishing in South Africa: A Critical Overview', in *The Politics of Publishing in South Africa*, ed. Nicholas Evans and Monica Seeber (London: Holger Ehling Publishing, 2000), pp. 15–42, at pp. 20–1.
21. Peires, 'Lovedale Press', p. 160.
22. Ibid.
23. See Pam Christie and Colin Collins, 'Bantu Education: Apartheid Ideology or Labour Reproduction', *Comparative Education*, 18:1 (1982), pp. 59–75, at p. 60.
24. Mpe and Seeber, 'The Politics of Book Publishing', p. 20.
25. A. S. Gérard, *African Language Literatures: An Introduction to the Literary History of Sub-Saharan Africa* (Washington, DC: Three Continents Press, 1981), p. 207.
26. Johnson, *Shakespeare and South Africa*, p. 170.
27. L. Marquard to D. Neale, 21 February 1962, File 2006.3.2.11, David Philip Collection, NELM.
28. Inspector of Bantu Education to Chairman of the Central Book Committee, 6 March 1961, File 2006.3.2.11, NELM.
29. Kallaway, 'Introduction', pp. 14–15.
30. 'Rebusoajoang', 'Education and Social Control in South Africa', *African Affairs*, 78:311 (1979), p. 235.
31. Hyslop, *The Classroom Struggle*, pp. 65–81.
32. Ibid., p. 97.
33. Mary Benson, *Chief Albert Lutuli of South Africa* (Oxford: Oxford University Press, 1963), p. 25.
34. Philip, 'Book Publishing under and after Apartheid', p. 12.
35. J. van der Vyver, 'General Aspects of the South African Censorship Laws', in T. Coggin (ed.), *Censorship: A Study of Censorship in South Africa* (Johannesburg: South Africa Institute of Race Relations, 1983), pp. 21–2.
36. Merrett, *A Culture of Censorship*, p. 50.
37. Paul B. Rich, *Hope and Despair: English-Speaking Intellectuals and South African Politics 1896–1976* (London: British Academic Press, 1993), p. 206.
38. Titles included B. A. Pauw, *The Second Generation: A Study of the Family among Urbanized Bantu in East London* (Cape Town: Oxford University Press, 1963); S. T. van der Horst, *African Workers in Town: A Study of Labour in Cape Town* (Cape Town: Oxford University Press, 1964); P. Carsten, *The Social Structure of a Cape Coloured Reserve: A Study of Racial Integration and Segregation in South Africa* (Cape Town: Oxford University Press, 1966); and D. Welsh, *The Roots of Segregation: Native Policy in Natal, 1845–1910* (Cape Town: Oxford University Press, 1971).
39. R. Collings to D. Philip, 11 September 1962, Benson: Chief Albert Lutuli, 12031, AOUP.
40. Benson, *Chief Albert Lutuli of South Africa*, p. 16.
41. Ibid., pp. 19, 33 and 31.

42. 'Three Crowns books' (sale sheet), January 1971, Three Crowns Series, 1967–72, LG29/221–3, AOUP.
43. Philip, 'Book Publishing under and after Apartheid', p. 12.
44. Merrett, *A Culture of Censorship*, p. 63.
45. Interview with David and Marie Philip by Caroline Davis, 5 April 2007, Cape Town.
46. Leo Marquard, 'Writing under Permit', Rhodes University, 30 August 1962, BC587, H2.33, CTU.
47. Isabel Essery, 'Politics and Publishing in South Africa: Interviews with Two Pioneers', *Logos*, 17:3 (2006), p. 154.
48. Collings to Neale, 1 May 1963, Nkosi: The Rhythm of Violence, OP2005/15123, AOUP.
49. Cannon to Neale, 5 February 1964, Nkosi: The Rhythm of Violence, OP2005/15123, AOUP.
50. A. Van Wyk to the Secretary for Customs and Excise, 17 March 1964, File: Lewis Nkosi, 201/64 BCS 41, Cape Town Archives Repository (hereafter CTAR).
51. John Brown to the Secretary, 13 February 1968. Brown quotes from a memo sent by Cannon, in a handwritten postscript, South Africa Branch, 165 (1), AOUP.
52. F. Cannon to J. Kruger, Publications Control Board, 18 March 1970, File: BCS 100, 41/70, CTAR.
53. Objectionable Literature: Various Publications Published by Oxford University Press Southern Africa, BCS 100, 41/70, CTAR.
54. Peter McDonald, *The Literature Police: Apartheid Censorship and its Cultural Consequences* (Oxford: Oxford University Press, 2009), pp. 105–6.
55. Hart, 'Cape Town Branch', pp. 14, 17.
56. Fred Cannon to the Delegates, 'South African Branch Annual Report 1968/9', November 1969, South Africa Branch Accounts 1928–1981, AOUP.
57. Neville Gracie to the Delegates, 'Southern African Branch Annual Report 1970–71', 9 September 1971, in ibid.
58. John Brown to the Delegates, 'South Africa Branch Trading Account Year Ended 31 March 1969', December 1969, in ibid. Henry Blagden was the 'number two' who was offered the position and turned it down (Paul Cannon to Caroline Davis, email correspondence, 14 September 2011).
59. Stallworthy to Egbuna, 3 March 1970, Egbuna: Daughters of the Sun, OP9/8138, AOUP.
60. Hart, 'Cape Town Branch', p. 17.
61. Fred Cannon, 'South African Branch Trading Account Summary, Year Ended 31st March 1961'; Fred Cannon 'South African Branch Trading Account Summary: Year Ended 31st March 1968', South Africa Branch Accounts 1928–81, AOUP.
62. Hart, 'Cape Town Branch', p. 18.
63. The Manager of the New York branch to David Philip, 21 October 1970, South Africa Branch, 165 (1), AOUP.
64. Brown to Roberts, 13 April 1970, in ibid.
65. Roberts to Brown, 14 April 1970, in ibid.
66. Brown to Roberts, 16 April 1970, in ibid.
67. Bell to Lewis, 31 July 1969, Three Crowns Series, 1967–72, LG29/223, AOUP.
68. 'Report of the Committee on the University Press', *Oxford University Gazette*, 100 (May 1970), Supplement no. 7, p. 24.
69. Ibid., p. 27. According to Sutcliffe, *The Oxford University Press*, p. 268, 75 per cent of the Press's income was derived from exports and overseas branch income in 1967.
70. Hart, 'Cape Town Branch', p. 17.
71. Philip, 'Book Publishing under and after Apartheid', p. 13.

72. Philip, personal interview, 5 April 2007, Cape Town.
73. Philip died on 16 February 2009; see obituary by R. Vigne, 'David Philip: Publisher Who Resisted Apartheid', *The Independent*, 10 March 2009, available at http://www.independent.co.uk/news/obituaries/david-philip-publisher-who-resisted-apartheid-1641047.html.
74. Lionel Morrison, *Evening Standard*, 3 July 1973, p. 10, Mtshali: Sounds of a Cowhide Drum, OP1619/12159, AOUP. See Chapter 6 for a more detailed case-study, pp. 137–40.
75. Bell to Philip, 4 July 1971 (emphasis in original), File 2006.30.2.16, NELM.
76. Paton to Brown, 6 November 1973, File 2002.33.6.1: Paton and Alexander: Campbell: Selected Poems (Donker) 1982, NELM.
77. Brown to Paton, 23 November 1973, in ibid.
78. Stallworthy to Roberts, 8 June 1972, South Africa Branch, 165 (1), AOUP.
79. Hart to Roberts, 7 June 1972, in ibid.
80. Roberts to Hart, 9 June 1972, in ibid.
81. Roberts to Thompson, 9 June 1972, in ibid.
82. Mpe and Seeber, 'The Politics of Book Publishing', p. 22.
83. David Philip's copy of this history is lodged in the National English Literary Museum (NELM) in Grahamstown and there is a public-domain copy also available in the OUP (UK) archive. This is my main source of information about OUP's history from 1980 to 1990.
84. Hart, 'Cape Town Branch', p. 22.
85. Gracie to the Finance Committee, 31 July 1972, 'South African Branch Annual Report 1971/2', South Africa Branch Accounts 1928–1981, AOUP.
86. Neville Gracie, 16 September 1974, 'Southern African Branch Annual Report 1973/4', in ibid.
87. Gracie to Binding, 10 March 1977, South Africa Branch Accounts 1928–1981, LG12/96 Cape Town (General), AOUP.
88. Gracie to Bossy, 18 November 1975, in ibid.
89. Hart, 'Cape Town Branch', p. 21.
90. Neville Gracie to the Finance Committee, 'Annual Report 1972/3', South Africa Branch Accounts 1928–1981, AOUP.
91. Neville Gracie, 16 September 1974, 'Southern African Branch Annual Report 1973/4', in ibid.
92. Victor Pohl, *Farewell the Little People* (Cape Town: Oxford University Press, 1968), preface.
93. Gracie to Sutcliffe, 30 December 1975, Southern African Branch, 165 (2), From 1976, AOUP.
94. Gracie to Sutcliffe, 9 August 1976, in ibid.
95. Gracie to Sutcliffe, 25 November 1976, in ibid.
96. Philip, personal interview, 5 April 2007, Cape Town.
97. Hart, 'Cape Town Branch', p. 23.
98. Neville Gracie to the Finance Committee, South African Branch Annual Report 1971/72, 31 July 1972, p. 1, South Africa Branch Accounts 1928–1981, AOUP.
99. Colin Roberts to Gracie, 22 June 1973, South Africa Branch, 165 (1), AOUP.
100. Neville Gracie, 'Annual Report 1973/4', South Africa Branch Accounts 1928–1981, AOUP.
101. Hart, 'Cape Town Branch', p. 25.
102. 'Trading Account for Year to 31 March 1982', South Africa Branch Accounts 1928–1981, AOUP.

103. John Brown to the Delegates, December 1969, 'South African Branch Trading Account Year Ended 31 March 1969', South Africa Branch Accounts 1928–1981, AOUP. Brown writes 'profits on the sales in the area accrue in the UK accounts and not the Branch accounts, which reflect profits on local publishing only'.
104. Philip Chester, 'Editorial General Session, Editorial Assistance to the Branches', June 1971, Three Crowns Series, 1967–72, LG29/221-3, AOUP.
105. Eastern African Branch Accounts 1964–73, AOUP.
106. 'Annual Report 1 April 1976–31 March 1977, *Oxford University Gazette* (1977), Supplement.
107. Hart, 'Cape Town Branch', p. 29.
108. Ibid., p. 31.
109. Ibid., p. 30. The investigation team consisted of Professor Sir Roger Eliot (then Chairman of the Finance Committee, subsequently Secretary to the Delegates of the Press), Sir George Richardson (Secretary) and Roger Boning.
110. Hart, 'Cape Town Branch', p. 30.
111. Ibid., p. 32.
112. *Chancellor, Masters and Scholars of the University of Oxford* v. *Commissioner for Inland Revenue, Republic of South Africa Cape Provincial Division*, 31 March and 13 June 1994, before Berman J. Tax Cases, volume 57, SATC 231; also cited as 1995 (3) SA 258, http://www.btinternet.com/~akme/berman.html.
113. Ibid.
114. C. J. Corbett, 'Judgement in Case no. 385/94 in the Supreme Court of South Africa (Appellate Division), in the matter between The Chancellor, Masters and Scholars of the University of Oxford and the Commissioner for Inland Revenue', 30 November 1995, p. 9, http://www.saflii.org/za/cases/ZASCA/1995/157.pdf.
115. Bourdieu, *Rules of Art*, p. 142.
116. N. Gracie, 'Southern Africa Branch Annual Report 1969–1970', South Africa Branch Accounts 1928–1981, AOUP.
117. Bourdieu, *Rules of Art*, p. 145.
118. Ibid., p. 142.

Conclusion to Part I

1. Bell to Lewis, 31 July 1969, Three Crowns Series, 1967–72, LG29/221-3, AOUP. This was an instruction from the Delegates of the OUP.
2. Sutcliffe, *The Oxford University Press*, p. 268.
3. 'Report of the Committee on the University Press', *Oxford University Gazette*, 100 (May 1970), Supplement no. 7, p. 27. In 1970, Ibadan branch total sales were £469,322 and Nairobi branch total sales were £504,120. Note that these figures exclude the sale of books from the UK to Africa.
4. Delegates of the University Press, 'Annual Report, 1 April 1976–31 March 1977', *Oxford University Gazette*, December 1977, Supplement no. 1, p. 15.
5. Ibid.
6. Neville Gracie, 'Annual Report of 1969–70', Southern African Branch, Cape Town, AOUP.

5 The History of Three Crowns

1. Collings to Neale, 2 July 1962, Soyinka: Lion and the Jewel, OP1619/12161, AOUP.
2. Neale to Collings, 2 July 1962, in ibid.

3. Collings to Neale, 4 July 1962, in ibid.
4. Bourdieu, 'The Production of Belief', p. 78.
5. Collings to Solaru, July 1962, Soyinka: Lion and the Jewel, OP1619/12161, AOUP.
6. Currey, *Africa Writes Back*, p. 14.
7. Collings to Neale, 4 July 1962, Soyinka: Lion and the Jewel, OP1619/12161, AOUP.
8. Memo from Neale to the managers of the branches in Toronto, New York and Melbourne, January 1963, Three Crowns Series, 1967–71, LG29/221–1, AOUP.
9. Low, *Publishing the Postcolonial*, pp. 35–6.
10. 'UK Sales Expressed as a Percentage of Total Sales', Three Crowns Series, 1967–71, LG29/221–1, AOUP.
11. 'Three Crowns: Towards a Definition of Policy', 19 September 1966, Section B, in ibid.
12. Robert Fraser with Nourdin Bejjit, 'The Tiger that Pounced: The African Writers Series (1962–2003) and the Online Reader', *Chadwyck Healey's African Writers Series Online*, September 2005.
13. Memo from Neale to the managers of the branches in Toronto, New York and Melbourne, January 1963, Three Crowns Series, 1967–71, LG29/221–1, AOUP.
14. Collings to Neale, 26 June 1962, Easmon: Dear Parent and Ogre, PB/ED 8149/911066, AOUP.
15. Three Crown Books publicity brochure, September 1964, Three Crowns Series, 1967–71, LG29/221–1, AOUP.
16. See Bourdieu, 'The Field of Cultural Production, or: The Economic World Reversed', in *Field of Cultural Production*, pp. 52–3.
17. Chakava, 'Kenyan Publishing', p. 128 and Rathgeber, 'Nigerian University Presses', p. 14.
18. James Currey, personal interview, 6 November 2003, Oxford Brookes University.
19. West African Exams Council to Burton, 13 March 1963, Three Crowns Series, 1967–71, LG29/221–1, AOUP.
20. Bourdieu defines symbolic capital as 'a kind of "economic" capital denied but recognised and hence legitimate – a veritable credit' in *Rules of Art*, p. 142.
21. See Bourdieu, 'The Production of Belief', p. 104 for a discussion of the dual economy of commercial and cultural publishing in publishing.
22. Note that correspondence from the author Tsegaye Gabre-Medhin indicates that Collings handed in his notice without a job to go to. The author asks: 'where would you work when you are through with OUP? Pankhurst tells me that you did not seem to have any idea judging from your letter to him; do you know now?' Letter from Tsegaye Gabre-Medhin to Collings, 12 June 1965, Gabre-Medhin: Oda-Oak Oracle, 2006/15128, AOUP.
23. Currey, personal interview, 6 November 2003, Oxford Brookes University.
24. Toyne to OUP Nairobi, 26 September 1966, Three Crowns Series, 1967–71, LG29/221–1, AOUP.
25. The terms on which the books in the series were sold changed from General (A1 net) to Educational (E3 Net) by Toyne in 1966. This had the effect of reducing the discount on UK sales but increasing it on African branch sales. Toyne to G. W. Taylor, 4 August 1966, Three Crowns Series, 1967–71, LG29/221–1, AOUP.
26. Toyne to Lewis, 26 September 1966, Three Crowns Series, 1967–71, LG29/221–1, AOUP.
27. Chester to Bell, 29 January 1968, Three Crowns Series, 1967–72, LG29/221–3, AOUP.
28. Currey, *Africa Writes Back*, p. 14.
29. Currey, personal interview, 6 November 2003, Oxford Brookes University.

30. 'Three Crowns Meeting, 16 February 1968', Jonathan Croall to Toyne, 19 February 1968, Three Crowns Series, 1967–71, LG29/221-1 and Chester to Toyne, 2 April 1968, Three Crowns Series, 1967–72, LG29/221-3, AOUP.
31. Lewis to Toyne, 31 October 1966 and Lewis to Bell, 16 January 1968, Three Crowns Series, 1967–71, LG29/221-1, AOUP.
32. 'Three Crowns: Towards a Definition of Policy', 19 September 1966, p. 6, Three Crowns Series, 1967–71, LG29/221-1, AOUP.
33. Ibid.
34. James Currey, 'African Writers Series: 21 Years On', *African Book Publishing Record,* 11 (1985), pp. 11–13, at p. 11.
35. Publisher's Agreement, 6 November 1969, Das: Larins Sahib, OP2005/15120, AOUP. Note that James Currey observes that 10,000 copies was the normal number for getting on to one of the big paperback printing machines at this time. See Currey, *Africa Writes Back*, p. 12.
36. During his posting to Cape Town and his one-year sabbatical immediately on his return, Richard Brain and Carol Buckroyd took over editorial responsibilities for Three Crowns.
37. Burton to Bell, 11 July 1969, Three Crowns Series, 1967–72, LG29/221-3, AOUP.
38. 'Report of the Committee on the University Press', *Oxford University Gazette*, vol. c (May 1970), Supplement no. 7.
39. Lewis to Bell, 7 July 1969, Three Crowns Series, 1967–72, LG29/221-3, AOUP.
40. Lewis to Bell, 7 July 1969, in ibid.
41. Jon Stallworthy, 'Session, Editorial General II, Branch Publishing, Section C, Fiction: Three Crown Books', March 1971, Three Crowns Series, 1967–72, LG29/221-3, AOUP.
42. Brown to Bell, 7 December 1970, Three Crowns Series, 1967–71, LG29/221-1, AOUP.
43. Jon Stallworthy, 'Session, Editorial General II, Branch Publishing, Section C, Fiction: Three Crown Books', March 1971, Three Crowns Series, 1967–72, LG29/221-3, AOUP.
44. Stallworthy, personal interview, 3 July 2002, Wolfson College, Oxford University.
45. In 1967, 73 per cent of the sales of Three Crowns titles were for the export (branch) market, 15 per cent for the UK market and 11 per cent for the US market. See letter from Smith to Lewis, April 1967, Three Crowns Series, 1967–72, LG29/221-3, AOUP.
46. Stallworthy to Bell, 3 March 1971, Three Crowns Series, 1967–72, LG29/221-3, AOUP.
47. Chester to Bell, 4 February 1971, in ibid.
48. Chaucer Pkt 86 1962 CG11/CPGE/54, AOUP.
49. Handwritten note of 2 October 1973, Soyinka: Lion and the Jewel, OP1620/12164, AOUP.
50. John Brown to branch managers, 12 October 1971, Three Crowns Series, 1967–72, LG29/221-3, AOUP.
51. 'Three Crowns: Towards a Definition of Policy', 19 September 1966, Section b, p. 7, Three Crowns Series, 1967–71, LG29/221-1, AOUP. This document was evidently drawn up by James Currey, Toyne and David Neale (see Neale to Currey, 4 August 1965, Three Crowns Series, 1967–71, LG29/221-1, AOUP).
52. Bell to Lewis, 31 July 1969, in ibid.
53. Bell to Branch Managers, 29 November 1971, in ibid.
54. Roger Houghton to Bell, 16 December 1971, in ibid.

55. Note that from 1970 to 1979, Oxford University Press was the publisher of the *Journal of Commonwealth Literature* in combination with Leeds University.
56. Roger Houghton to Bell, 16 December 1971, Three Crowns Series, 1967–72, LG29/221-3, AOUP.
57. Bell to Roger Houghton, 6 January 1972, in ibid.
58. Currey, personal interview, 6 November 2003, Oxford Brookes University.
59. Bell to Mr Trainer, 15 June 1973, Three Crowns Series, 1971–74, LG29/222, AOUP.
60. Heapy to Delhi OUP office, June 1973, Raja Rao: The Policeman and the Rose, OP1620/12172, AOUP.
61. Arthur Ravenscroft to Bell, 29 November 1972, Three Crowns Series, 1967–72, LG29/221-3, AOUP.
62. Ron Heapy, personal interview, 3 July 2002, Oxford University Press.
63. David Attwooll, personal interview, 16 February 2003, Oxford Brookes University.
64. Heapy to MOA, Nigeria, 30 August 1973, Three Crowns Series, 1971–74, LG29/222, AOUP.
65. In 1976, the entire Overseas Education division, consisting of 75 staff, was moved from London to Oxford, where it was split into English Language Teaching (ELT) and Oxford Educational (OE). In addition, three of the five departments of the General division (General Editorial, Children's Books and Paperbacks) were moved from London to Oxford, leaving only the Bible and Music departments. At this stage, there were only 18 employees in the International division, but 769 were employed in the overseas branches. See Delegates of the University Press, 'Annual Report, 1 April 1976–31 March 1977', *Oxford University Gazette*, 103 (December 1977), Supplement no. 1, p. 15.
66. Heapy to Keith Rose, Addis Ababa, 4 February 1975, Gubegna: Defiance, 1943/911093, AOUP.
67. 'Three Crowns: Minutes of a Meeting Held on Friday 24 April 1976', Three Crowns Series, 1971–74, LG29/222, AOUP.
68. Three Crowns books published from Delhi were: Nissim Ezekiel, *Hymns in Darkness* (1976); Keki N. Daruwalla, *Crossing of Rivers* (1976); A. K. Ramanujan, *Samskara: A Rite for a Dead Man* (1976); A. K. Ramanujan, *Selected Poems* (1976); Shiv K. Kumar, *Subterfuges* (1976); R. Parthasarathy (ed.), *Ten Twentieth-Century Indian Poets* (1976); Kaleem Omar (ed.) *Wordfall: Three Pakistani Poets* (1977); Keki N. Daruwalla, *The Keeper of the Dead* (1982); Nissim Ezekiel, *Latter-day Psalms* (1982); Jayanta Mahapatra, *Life Signs* (1983); Saros Cowasjee and Shiv K. Kumar (ed.), *Modern Indian Short Stories* (1983); Arvind Krishna Mehrotra, *Middle Earth* (1984); Patrick Fernando, *Selected Poems* (1984); Nirmal Verma, *Maya Darpan and Other Stories* (1986); A. K. Ramanujan, *Second Sight* (1986); Patrick Fernando, *Selected Poems* (1986); Jayanta Mahapatra, *Selected Poems* (1987); Ashok Mahajan, *Goan Vignettes and Other Poems* (1986).
69. Ndegwa, 'Africa: East and Central', 17:2 (1982), p. 2.
70. From 1970 to 1981, an average of 16 books annually were published in the series, but this was reduced to only four new titles a year in the remainder of the 1980s and six new titles a year in the 1990s. The series finally closed in 2003. See: '1962–2003: African Writers Series by Year of Publication', in Currey, *Africa Writes Back*, pp. 301–10.
71. Lindfors, 'Bibliography: Africa Western', p. 7. This was the last review of West African literature published in the journal until 2011.
72. Henry Chakava, 'A Decade of Publishing in Kenya', *African Book Publishing Record*, 14:4 (1988), pp. 235–42, at pp. 235–7.

73. Note Charles Lewis's speech on OUP's need to avoid charges of 'neo-colonialist exploitation'. Charles Lewis, 'Annual Report, 1965', p. 2, Eastern African Branch Accounts 1964–73, AOUP. This is discussed in Chapter 3, p. 50.
74. These arguments by Hans Zell and Charles Larson are summarised in the Introduction.

6 Judging African Literature

1. Collings to Ivor Wilkes, 11 January 1963, Three Crowns Series, 1967–71, LG29/221-1, AOUP.
2. Bernth Lindfors, *Long Drums and Canons: Teaching and Researching African Literatures* (Trenton, NJ: Africa World Press, 1995), p. 130.
3. Mpe, 'The Role of the Heinemann African Writers Series', p. 117.
4. Loretta Stec, 'Publishing and Canonicity: The Case of Heinemann's African Writers Series', *Pacific Coast Philology*, 32 (1997), pp. 140–9, at p. 146.
5. Amuta, *The Theory of African Literature*, p. 2.
6. Pascale Casanova makes this point about postcolonial novels and the Booker prize. See: Casanova, *World Republic of Letters*, p. 119.
7. Claire Squires, *Marketing Literature: The Making of Contemporary Writing in Britain* (Basingstoke: Palgrave Macmillan, 2007), p. 71.
8. David Cook, 'East and Central Africa', *Journal of Commonwealth Literature*, 4 (1969), pp. 9–18, at p. 10.
9. Collings to Lewis, 15 September 1964, Gabre-Medhin: Oda-Oak Oracle, 2006/15128, AOUP.
10. See Chapter 3, p. 58 for examples of this.
11. Collings to Neale, 26 March 1963, Clark: Three Plays, OP1619/12157, AOUP.
12. Richards to Neale, 16 March 1964, Kimenye: Kalasanda, OP2006/15131, AOUP.
13. As discussed in Chapter 3, p. 59.
14. See Bourdieu, 'The Production of Belief', pp. 103–5
15. Harold Bloom, *The Western Canon: The Books and School of the Age* (London: Macmillan, 1994). For a critique of Bloom's canon, see Anon., 'Black Writers and Harold Bloom's Literary Canon', *Journal of Blacks in Higher Education*, 6 (1994–95), pp. 24–5.
16. Mpe, 'The Role of the Heinemann African Writers Series', p. 116.
17. Clive Wake to Collings, 5 March 1962, Wake (ed.): Prose and Poetry, OP1947/775, AOUP.
18. See L. G. Mitchell, 'Bowra, Sir (Cecil) Maurice (1898–1971)', *Oxford Dictionary of National Biography*, Oxford University Press, online edn, May 2005.
19. C. M. Bowra to Bell, 6 July 1962, Wake (ed.): Prose and Poetry, OP1947/775, AOUP.
20. Burton to Bell, 30 May 1962, in ibid.
21. M. Usborne to Bell, 7 June 1962, in ibid.
22. Collings to Neale, undated, in ibid.
23. Collings to Dr Clive Wake, 31 July 1962, Senghor: Selected Poems, OP1103/211248, AOUP.
24. Note that the royalty rate for all Three Crowns books was calculated on the list price (the retail price) of the books, rather than the net receipts (the revenue to the publisher after discounts have been calculated, which is nowadays the more usual arrangement).

25. 'Three Crowns Books Sales', 1971, Three Crowns Series, 1967–72, LG29/223, AOUP.
26. Léopold Sédar Senghor, *Prose and Poetry*, selected and translated by John Reed and Clive Wake (London: Oxford University Press, 1965), p. 151.
27. Ibid., p. 135.
28. Ibid., p. 99.
29. Ibid., p. 71.
30. Bourdieu, 'The Production of Belief', p. 77.
31. Casanova, *World Republic of Letters*, pp. 40 and 42–3.
32. Amuta, *The Theory of African Literature*, p. 108. See also Anthony Arnove, 'Pierre Bourdieu, the Sociology of Intellectuals, and the Language of African Literature Author(s)', *NOVEL: A Forum on Fiction*, 26:3 (1993), pp. 278–96, at pp. 283 and 285–6 for a related discussion of the impact of an elitist colonial education on the careers of Chinua Achebe and Ngũgĩ wa Thiong'o.
33. Abdul R. Yesefu, 'Mbari Publications: A Pioneer Anglophone African Publishing House', *The African Book Publishing Record*, 8 (1982), pp. 53–7.
34. Collings to Neale, 26 March 1963, Clark: Three Plays, OP1619/12157, AOUP.
35. Fraser, *Book History through Postcolonial Eyes*, p. 88.
36. See Bourdieu, *Field of Cultural Production*, pp. 40–3 for a discussion of the struggle over which agents are 'legitimately entitled to designate legitimate writers or artists' (p. 41).
37. Marion Bieber to Collings, 19 April 1962, Easmon: Dear Parent and Ogre, PB/ED8149/911066, AOUP. The Congrès pour la Liberté de la Culture, or the Congress for Cultural Freedom, was an anti-communist advocacy movement founded in 1950, which, as it later emerged, was covertly funded by the CIA. See Greg Barnhisel and Catherine Turner, *Pressing the Fight: Print Propaganda and the Cold War* (Amherst and Boston, MA: University of Massachusetts Press, 2010), pp. 11–15.
38. Raymond Sarif Easmon, *Dear Parent and Ogre* (Oxford: Oxford University Press, 1964), pp. 3–4.
39. Reader's Report, undated (signed 'RS'), Easmon: Dear Parent and Ogre, PB/ED8149/911066, AOUP.
40. Brain to Collings, 6 July 1962, in ibid.
41. Keith Sambrook to Collings, 8 May 1964, in ibid.
42. Collings to Neale, 10 September 1963, in ibid.
43. 'Publishing Agreement', 25 September 1963, in ibid.
44. 'Three Crowns Books Sales', 1971. Three Crowns Series, 1967–72, LG29/221–3, AOUP. This is the last profit-and-loss statement available for the series.
45. Collings to Neale, 10 September 1963, Easmon: Dear Parent and Ogre, PB/ED8149/911066, AOUP. The play was later published by Longman in 1965.
46. See David M. White, 'The "Gatekeeper": A Case-Study in the Selection of News', in Lewis A. Dexter and David M. White, *People, Society and Mass Communications* (New York: Free Press of Glencoe, 1964), pp. 160–72, which was the first study of the practice of 'gatekeeping' in journalism. The theory of gatekeeping is applied to the publishing industry in Lynne Spender's polemical *Intruders on the Rights of Men: Women's Unpublished Heritage* (London: Pandora Press, 1983).
47. Squires, *Marketing Literature*, p. 57.
48. Immanuel Kant, *Critique of Judgment*, rev. edn (New York: Cosimo, 2007), p. 82.
49. Ibid., p. 56.
50. Ibid., p. 28.
51. Ibid., p. 51. On the tension between the need for art to fit exemplary models whilst also being original, Kant wrote: 'We consider some products of taste as

exemplary. Not that taste can be acquired by imitating others; for it must be an original faculty' (p. 51).

52. Chinweizu et al., *Toward the Decolonization of African Literature*, pp. 7 and 16.
53. Amuta, *The Theory of African Literature*, p. 36.
54. 'Three Crowns: Towards a Definition of Policy', 19 September 1966, p. 6, Three Crowns Series, 1967–71, LG29/221–1, AOUP.
55. Ibid.
56. Heapy to Arthur Ravenscroft, 16 January 1974, Raja Rao: The Policeman and the Rose, OP1620/12172.
57. Currey to Mr Johnson-Davies, 29 March 1966, Three Crowns Series, 1967–71, LG29/221–1, AOUP.
58. Chester to MBD, 5 April 1967, 'Three Crowns', in ibid.
59. Toyne to Stallworthy, 2 April (no year given, but probably 1968), in ibid.
60. Toyne to Brench, 23 July 1968, in ibid.
61. Heapy to Keith Rose, 8 June 1973, Gubegna: Defiance, 1943/911093, AOUP.
62. Heapy to Keith Rose, 4 February 1975, in ibid.
63. John Pepper Clark-Bekederemo at this time published under the name John Pepper Clark.
64. Review of John Pepper Clark, *Poems* (Ibadan: Mbari, 1962), in *Times Literary Supplement*, 10 August 1962. Quoted in a letter from Collings to Neale, 26 March 1963, Clark: Three Plays, OP1619/12157, AOUP.
65. Collings to Neale, 26 March 1963, Clark: Three Plays, OP1619/12157, AOUP.
66. Ibid.
67. The African Writers Series aimed for a 7.5 per cent royalty for paperback books and 10 per cent for hardcover books. See Currey, *Africa Writes Back*, p. 12.
68. 'Three Crowns Books Sales', 1971, Three Crowns Series, 1967–72, LG29/221–3, AOUP.
69. Memorandum, 3 July 1972, Clark: Three Plays, OP1619/12157, AOUP.
70. 'Three Crowns Books brochure', September 1970, Three Crowns Series, 1967–71, LG29/221–1, AOUP. This project was the beginning of a long-term project to record the Ozidi legend in its entirety, which was eventually published in 1977 jointly between Oxford University Press Nigeria and Ibadan University Press as *The Ozidi Saga*.
71. 'Three Crowns Books Sales', 1971, Three Crowns Series, 1967–72, LG29/223, AOUP.
72. Heapy to T. Otesanya, 4 November 1975, Clark: Ozidi, OP1620/12168, AOUP.
73. Bourdieu, 'The Production of Belief', p. 74.
74. Collings to Neale, 4 July 1962, Easmon: Dear Parent and Ogre, PB/ED8149/911066, AOUP.
75. It should be noted that the reduction in acqusitions began in 1965, while the African markets were still buoyant. However, it was further exacerbated by the collapse of the book market in East Africa in the mid-1970s. The series was moved to Ibadan before the economic crash in Nigeria.
76. Said, *Culture and Imperialism*, p. xiii.

7 Editing Three Crowns

1. Ngũgĩ wa Thiong'o, *Penpoints, Gunpoints and Dreams*, p. 127.
2. Ngũgĩ wa Thiong'o, *Decolonising the Mind: The Politics of Language in African Literatures* (Oxford: James Currey, EAEP, Heinemann, 1986), pp. 69–71.

3. Becky Clarke, 'The African Writers Series – Celebrating Forty Years of Publishing Distinction', *Research in African Literatures*, 34 (2003), pp. 163–74, at pp. 171, 165 and 168.
4. Lefevere, André, 'The Historiography of African Literature Written in English', in Bill Ashcroft, Gareth Griffiths and Helen Tiffin (eds), *Key Concepts in Post-Colonial Studies* (London: Routledge, 1998), pp. 465–70, at p. 466.
5. Ibid., p. 469.
6. Gail Low, 'The Natural Artist: Publishing Amos Tutuola's *The Palm-Wine Drinkard*', *Research in African Literatures*, 37 (2006), pp. 15–33. See also Bernth Lindfors, 'Amos Tutuola: Debts and Assets', *Cahiers d'Etudes Africaines*, 10:38 (1970), pp. 308–34.
7. Huggan, *The Postcolonial Exotic*, p. ix.
8. Ibid., p. 53.
9. Bejjit, 'The Publishing of African Literature', p. 7.
10. Stallworthy to Lionel Abrahams, 25 October 1971, and Buckroyd to Joseph Okpaku, Third Press, 5 January 1972, Mtshali: Sounds of a Cowhide Drum, OP1619/12159, AOUP.
11. Huggan, *The Postcolonial Exotic*, p. 53.
12. See Edward W. Said, *Orientalism* (London: Penguin, 2003), for definitions of the 'exotic' (p. 72) and for a consideration of universalising discourses on the Orient (pp. 38–40). See also Huggan, *The Postcolonial Exotic* for an analysis of exoticising discourses (p. 27).
13. Gabre-Medhin to Collings, 18 January 1964, Gabre-Medhin: Oda-Oak Oracle, 2006/15128, AOUP.
14. Tsegaye Gabre-Medhin, *Oda-Oak Oracle* (Oxford: Oxford University Press, 1965), p. 3.
15. Ibid., p. 37.
16. John Reed, Reader's Report, undated, Gabre-Medhin: Oda-Oak Oracle, 2006/15128, AOUP.
17. Collings to Gabre-Medhin, 30 April 1964, in ibid.
18. Gabre-Medhin to Collings, 14 May 1964, in ibid.
19. Gabre-Medhin to Collings, 4 June 1964, in ibid.
20. Collings to George Shepperson, 22 June 1965, in ibid.
21. Gabre-Medhin to Collings, 12 June 1965, in ibid. However, this was not the end of their literary association: Collings later published Gabre-Medhin's historical drama *Collision of Altars* in 1977, under his own imprint.
22. Huggan, *The Postcolonial Exotic*, p. 54.
23. See Chapter 6, p. 119 for further examples of texts from Ethiopia being rejected from Three Crowns on account of the small local book market.
24. 'Three Crowns Books Sales', 1971, Three Crowns Series, 1967–72, LG29/221–3, AOUP.
25. Genette, *Paratexts*, p. 1.
26. Ibid., p. 16.
27. Ibid., p. 11.
28. Collings to Neale, 26 June 1962, Easmon: Dear Parent and Ogre, PB/ED8149/911066, AOUP.
29. Huggan, *The Postcolonial Exotic*, p. 53.
30. Genette, *Paratexts*, p. 22.
31. 'Three Crowns Meeting, 16 February 1968', Jonathan Croall to Toyne, 19 February 1968, Three Crowns Series, 1967–71, LG29/221–1, AOUP.
32. Genette, *Paratexts*, p. 22.

33. Memorandum from Heapy to OUP branches in Kuala Lumpar, Ibadan, Nairobi, Delhi, Karachi, Cape Town, 5 May 1972, Fugard: Boesman and Lena, OP2007/15136, AOUP.
34. Ibid.
35. This is discussed further in the case-study of Athol Fugard in Chapter 9.
36. Heapy, personal interview, 3 July 2002, Oxford University Press.
37. Heapy, memorandum to Production department, 19 September 1972, Fugard: Boesman and Lena, OP2007/15136, AOUP.
38. Genette, *Paratexts*, p. 34.
39. See Nancy J. Schmidt, 'The Writer as Teacher: A Comparison of the African Adventure Stories of G. A. Henty, Rene Guillot, and Barbara Kimenye', *African Studies Review*, 19:2 (1976), pp. 69–80, at p. 75.
40. Barbara Kimenye, *Kalasanda* (Oxford: Oxford University Press, 1965), p. 7.
41. Ibid., p. 1.
42. Ibid., p. 2.
43. Richards to Collings, 16 March 1964, Kimenye: Kalasanda, OP2006/15131, AOUP.
44. Collings to Neale, 22 April 1964, in ibid.
45. 'Publishing Agreement', 28 May 1964, in ibid.
46. Barbara Kimenye to Collings, 24 May 1964, in ibid.
47. Barbara Kimenye to Collings, 30 November 1964, in ibid.
48. Toyne to Barbara Kimenye, 28 July 1965, in ibid.
49. Peter Nazareth, *Literature and Society in Modern Africa: Essays on Literature* (Nairobi: East African Literature Bureau, 1972), p. 171.
50. Edgar Wright, 'East and Central Africa', *Journal of Commonwealth Literature*, 2 (1967), pp. 10–14, at p. 11.
51. Hebe Welbourn, 'Village Gossip: *Kalasanda* by Barbara Kimenye', *Transition*, 24 (1966), p. 56.
52. 'Three Crowns Books Sales', 1971, Three Crowns Series, 1967–72, LG29/221–3, AOUP.
53. Bridget Egbuna to Stallworthy, 1 November 1968, Egbuna: Daughters of the Sun, OP9/8138, AOUP.
54. Obi B. Egbuna, *Daughters of the Sun and Other Stories* (Oxford: Oxford University Press, 1970), p. 92.
55. Ibid., p. 106.
56. Liz Stanley to Stallworthy, 30 September 1969, Egbuna: Daughters of the Sun, OP9/8138, AOUP.
57. Gareth Reeves, Report on Obi B. Egbuna's 'The Little Boy of Brussels', pp. 4–5, in ibid.
58. Egbuna, *Daughters of the Sun*, back cover.
59. Obi Egbuna to Stallworthy, 7 March 1970, Egbuna: Daughters of the Sun, OP9/8138, AOUP.
60. Ibadan editor to Stallworthy, 7 July 1970, Egbuna: Daughters of the Sun, OP9/8138, AOUP.
61. 'Three Crowns Books Sales', 1971, Three Crowns Series, 1967–72, LG29/221–3, AOUP.
62. Squires, *Marketing Literature*, pp. 176 and 54, and Juliet Gardiner, 'Recuperating the Author: Consuming Fictions of the 1990s', *Papers of the Bibliographical Society of America*, 94:2 (2000), pp. 255–74, at p. 274.
63. See Bourdieu, 'The Production of Belief', pp. 103–5, for a discussion of the degrees of consecration of different publishers.

64. Oswald Mbuyiseni Mtshali, 'Men in Chains', in *Sounds of a Cowhide Drum* (Oxford: Oxford University Press, 1972), p. 8.
65. 'Always a Suspect', in ibid., p. 28.
66. 'An Abandoned Bundle', in ibid., p. 60.
67. 'Nightfall in Soweto', in ibid., p. 42.
68. See Chapter 4, pp. 73–4 for a discussion of censorship legislation in this period.
69. Guy Butler to Lionel Abrahams, 28 October 1970, Oswald Joseph Mtshali Correspondence relating to Oswald Mtshali from Guy Butler, File: PL086–PL089 (2), NELM.
70. Ibid.
71. See Ann McClintock, '"Azikwelwa" (We Will Not Ride): Politics and Value in Black South African Poetry', *Critical Inquiry*, 13:3 (1987), pp. 597–623, at p. 612, for a brief discussion of the publication of this book by Lionel Abrahams in South Africa. Note that in this Renoster edition, Mtshali published under the name of 'Oswald Joseph Mtshali' but in the Three Crowns edition, under the name of 'Oswald Mbuyiseni Mtshali'.
72. Stallworthy to Lionel Abrahams, 26 July 1971, Mtshali: Sounds of a Cowhide Drum, OP1619/12159, AOUP.
73. Stallworthy to the Secretary, Clarendon Press, 26 August 1971, CPGE, File: 000069 CGB, Pkt 91(7), AOUP. At this time, all new acquisitions had to be approved by the Delegates, and Stallworthy here sought permission in advance of the Delegates' meeting.
74. Publishing Agreement, 28 October 1971, Mtshali: Sounds of a Cowhide Drum, OP1619/12159, AOUP.
75. P. R. Newman to Lionel Abrahams, 24 November 1971, in ibid.
76. See Chapter 1, p. 28 for more information on the British Commonwealth Market Agreement.
77. New Book Announcement, undated, Mtshali: Sounds of a Cowhide Drum, OP1619/12159, AOUP.
78. Blurb, undated, in ibid.
79. Stallworthy to Charles Osborne, 9 January 1972, in ibid.
80. Burton to Bell, 12 June 1973, in ibid.
81. Lionel Morrison, *Evening Standard*, 3 July 1973, p. 10, in ibid.
82. Bourdieu, 'The Production of Belief', pp. 103–5.
83. Charles H. Rowell, '"With Bloodstains to Testify": An Interview with Keorapetse Kgositsile', *Callaloo*, 2 (1978), pp. 23–42, at p. 36.
84. McClintock, '"Azikwelwa"', p. 614.
85. Ibid., p. 613.
86. Royalty rates for competitors and other paperback series at OUP at this time were evidently considerably lower: as mentioned, the African Writers Series offered a 7.5 per cent royalty rate on paperbacks (see Currey, *Africa Writes Back*, p. 12), OUP's Oxford Paperback series gave royalty rates of 5 per cent for exports and 7.5–8.75 per cent for the UK market (see Catherine Carver to JLIW, 8 August 1969, Oxford Paperbacks Misc., 1962–1974, LG25/195, AOUP), and OUP's NewYork-based Galaxy paperback series offered a 5 per cent royalty rate (see Toyne to Ibadan Branch, 5 September 1968, Soyinka: Three Short Plays, OP1620/12167, AOUP).
87. For example, Gabre-Medhin was subject to censorship in Ethiopia, and Lewis Nkosi and Mary Benson's books were banned in South Africa. Mtshali and Fugard's books were also considered vulnerable to being banned in South Africa.

88. Under their own imprints, James Currey and Collings frequently co-published works with David Philip, providing him with a vital sales outlet for books banned in South Africa.

8 Publishing Wole Soyinka

1. Nobel Prize in Literature Presentation Speech 1986, http://nobelprize.org/nobel_prizes/literature/laureates/1986/presentation-speech.html.
2. Suman Gupta writes: 'The Nobel Prize is now widely regarded as giving a stamp of universal literary value that is untainted by commercial considerations or insular social or political affiliations,' Suman Gupta, 'Samuel Becket, *Waiting for Godot*', in David Johnson (ed.), *The Popular and the Canonical* (Abingdon: Routledge, 2005), pp. 210–61, at p. 211.
3. Biodun Jeyifo, *Wole Soyinka: Politics, Poetics, and Postcolonialism* (Cambridge: Cambridge University Press, 2004), p. 8.
4. Mumia Abu-Jamal, 'Soyinka's Africa: Continent of Crisis, Conflict and Cradle of the Gods', *Black Scholar*, 31:1 (2001), pp. 31–42, at p. 39. Mumia Abu-Jamal is a prominent African American activist and journalist, who has been on death row in Pennsylvania since 1982, for allegedly shooting a police officer. Soyinka has campaigned for his release, and met him in 2000.
5. Recent critical studies of Soyinka as a writer-activist include Francis Ngaboh-Smart's analysis of *The Interpreters* as a complex exploration of the 'dilemma of the modern Nigerian nation', Francis Ngaboh-Smart, 'Re-narrating the Nation: Soyinka's *The Interpreters*', *Journal of Postcolonial Writing*, 46:1 (2010), pp. 42–52, at p. 51, and Lyndsey Green-Simms's exploration of the juxtaposition of 'universal questions of life and death' and 'the precariousness of postcolonial life' in *The Road*, Lindsey Green-Simms, '"No Danger No Delay": Wole Soyinka and the Perils of the Road', *Journal of Postcolonial Writing*, 46:1 (2010), pp. 53–64, at pp. 53–4.
6. Brief discussions of the publication of Soyinka have been published previously in my own history of Three Crowns, 'Postcolonial Publishing', pp. 227–8 and 237, in Low, *Publishing the Postcolonial*, pp. 40–2, and in relation to Soyinka's later publication in the African Writers Series, in Currey, *Africa Writes Back*, p. 22.
7. Darnton, 'What is the History of Books', p. 113.
8. Genette, *Paratexts*, p. 26.
9. Chinweizu et al., *Toward the Decolonization of African Literature*, pp. 163 and 171.
10. Oyenlyi Okunoye, 'Captives of Empire: Early Ibadan Poets and Poetry', *Journal of Commonwealth Literature*, 34:2 (1999), pp. 105–23, at p. 109. Note that Stephanie Newell in *West African Literature: Ways of Reading* (pp. 160–3) explores these debates in some detail, writing of the tension between Soyinka's satirical playwriting and overtly political travelling theatre work, and the tendency in West African Marxist criticism to describe Soyinka as 'apolitical and inaccessibly irrelevant', and engaged in a 'bourgeois desire for stylistic experimentation and aesthetically pleasing form' (p. 161).
11. Wole Soyinka, *Ibadan: The Penkelemes Years – A Memoir, 1946–1965* (London: Methuen, 1994), pp. 67 and 65.
12. James Gibbs, 'Soyinka in Zimbabwe: A Question and Answer Session, James Gibbs 1981', in Biodun Jeyifo (ed.), *Conversations with Wole Soyinka* (Jackson: University Press of Mississippi, 2001), pp. 82–109, at pp. 97–8.

13. Martin Banham, 'Review of the *Trials of Brother Jero*', *The Horn*, 4:1 (1961), pp. 18–19, at p. 19.
14. Biodun Jeyifo, 'Wole Soyinka: In Person', in Biodun Jeyifo (ed.), *Conversations with Soyinka* (Jackson: University of Mississippi Press, 2001), pp. 13–18, at p. 13.
15. James Gibbs, 'The Masks Hatched Out', *Theatre Research International*, 7:3 (1982), pp. 180–207, at p. 196.
16. Collings to J. Rogers, British Council, Enugu, 25 February 1963, Three Crowns Series, 1967–71, LG29/221–1, AOUP.
17. Collings to Joan Littlewood, 14 February 1962, Soyinka: Lion and the Jewel, OP1619/12161, AOUP.
18. Joan Littlewood to Collings, 20 February 1962, in ibid.
19. See Amuta, *The Theory of African Literature*, p. 64 for an interesting reading of the play as a 'historical stock-taking on the eve of a great communal event and in an obvious attempt to negate the romantic image of the African past that is dominant in Senghorian Negritude. The verdict that emerges in this play about the African (Nigerian) past is simple: guilty.'
20. Bell to Collings, 19 July 1962, Soyinka: Lion and the Jewel, OP1619/12161, AOUP.
21. Gerald Moore to Collings, 2 August 1962, in ibid.
22. Bell to Collings, 19 July 1962, in ibid.
23. Collings to Neale, 4 July 1962, in ibid.
24. Collings to Solaru, 14 September 1962, in ibid.
25. Solaru to Burton, 28 June 1962, in ibid.
26. Burton to Solaru, 5 July 1962, in ibid.
27. Edgar Wright, 'Report on Two Plays by Wole Soyinka', Soyinka: The Road, OP1619/12163, AOUP.
28. Martin Banham, 'Theatre in West Africa: A Conversation between Wole Soyinka and Martin Banham' (undated, *c.* 1963), MS 1748, Leeds University Library Special Collections (hereafter LUL).
29. Soyinka to Collings, undated, received 30 April 1964, Soyinka: The Road, OP1619/12163, AOUP.
30. Toyne to Adam Butcher, 5 September 1968, Soyinka: Three Short Plays, OP1620/12167, AOUP. Note that although there are different endings to *A Dance of the Forests* in the 1963 individual OUP edition and in this 1964 *Five Plays* edition, as described by Robert Fraser, there is no archival record of these changes being made to the playscript. See Robert Fraser, 'Four Alternative Endings to Wole Soyinka's "A Dance of the Forests"', *Research in African Literatures*, 10:3 (1979), pp. 359–74.
31. Chester to Toyne, 2 April 1968, Three Crowns Series, 1967–72, LG29/221–3, AOUP.
32. Wole Soyinka, 'The Future of West African Writing', *The Horn*, 4:1 (1959), p. 13, LUL.
33. Wole Soyinka to Neale, 17 July 1966, Soyinka: Lion and the Jewel, OP1620/12164, AOUP.
34. Stallworthy, personal interview, 3 July 2002, Wolfson College, Oxford University.
35. See Soyinka, *Aké: The Years of Childhood; Season of Anomy* (London: Collings, 1981), *Ibadan* and *You Must Set Forth at Dawn* (New York: Random House, 2006).
36. See Chapter 7, p. 141 for a discussion of standard royalty rates for paperbacks at the time.
37. Heapy to Wole Soyinka, 7 May 1975, Soyinka: The Road, OP1619/12163, AOUP.

38. Chester to Mrs Soyinka, in ibid.
39. Wole Soyinka to Collings, 25 January 1965, Three Crowns Series, 1967–71, LG29/221–1, AOUP.
40. Neale to Collings, 16 June 1965, in ibid.
41. James Gibbs, 'Rex Collings – Obituary, 1925–1996', *Bellagio Publishing Network Newsletter*, 18 (November 1996), p. 22.
42. Henry Louis Gates, 'Henry Louis Gates, Jr., 1975', in Biodun Jeyifo (ed.), *Conversations with Soyinka* (Jackson: University of Mississippi Press, 2001), pp. 48–67, at p. 50.
43. Rex Collings, letter to *The Times*, 15 October 1968, Soyinka: Three Short Plays, OP1620/12167, AOUP.
44. Gibbs, 'Rex Collings – Obituary'.
45. There was, however, some confusion over the copyright arrangement for Soyinka's plays. While the contracts showed that OUP controlled the copyright for all the plays published, this was contradicted in the correspondence and the copyright notices for *The Lion and the Jewel, The Swamp Dwellers, The Trials of Brother Jero* and *The Strong Breed*, which suggest that Soyinka reserved the right to grant permission on these titles. See Toyne to Illinca Bossy, 29 January 1969, Three Crowns Series, 1967–71, LG29/221–1, AOUP.
46. Jonathan Crowther to Roger Houghton, 26 June 1975, Soyinka: Lion and the Jewel, OP1619/12161, AOUP.
47. Collings to Neale, 26 July 1962, Easmon: Dear Parent and Ogre, PB/ED8149/911066, AOUP.
48. Collings to Wole Soyinka, 2 October 1962, Soyinka: Lion and the Jewel, OP1619/12161, AOUP.
49. Wole Soyinka to Collings, undated, received 30 April 1964, Soyinka: The Road, OP1619/12163, AOUP.
50. C. C. Linnet to Jonathan Croall, 31 January 1969, Soyinka: Three Short Plays, OP1620/12167, AOUP.
51. Houghton to Croall, 13 February 1969, in ibid.
52. Brown to John F. Bell and Stallworthy, 12 November 1969, Three Crowns Series, 1967–71, LG29/221–1, AOUP.
53. Bell to PJS, 15 June 1973, Three Crowns Series, 1971–74, LG29/222, AOUP.
54. This is further discussed in Chapter 7, pp. 135–7.
55. *A Dance of the Forests*, publicity leaflet, Soyinka: Lion and the Jewel, OP1619/12161, AOUP.
56. *The Lion and the Jewel* publicity leaflet, undated, in ibid.
57. Three Crown Books publicity brochure, September 1964, Three Crowns Series, 1967–71, LG29/221–1, AOUP.
58. English, *The Economy of Prestige*, p. 310.
59. S. W. Smith to C. Lewis, April 1967, Three Crowns Series, 1967–72, LG29/221–3, AOUP.
60. Ibid.
61. 'UK Sales Expressed as a Percentage of Total Sales', Three Crowns Series, 1967–71, LG29/221–1, AOUP.
62. Brown to Bell and Stallworthy, 12 November 1969, in ibid.
63. Stallworthy, personal interview, 3 July 2002, Wolfson College, Oxford University.
64. Stallworthy to Bell, 3 March 1971, Three Crowns Series, 1967–72, LG29/221–3, AOUP.

65. Chakava, 'Kenyan Publishing', p. 128 and Rathgeber, 'Nigerian University Presses', p. 14.
66. Clement Abiaziem Okafor, 'Teaching African Literature in Zambian Schools', *Research in African Literatures*, 1:2 (1970), pp. 177–82.
67. 'Three Crowns Books Sales', 1971, Three Crowns Series, 1967–72, LG29/221–3, AOUP.
68. *The Lion and the Jewel*, handwritten note 2 October 1973, Soyinka: Lion and the Jewel, OP1620/12164, AOUP. This is also discussed in Chapter 2, p. 43.
69. Bourdieu, 'The Field of Cultural Production', p. 53.
70. Darnton, 'What is the History of Books', p. 127.
71. Robert Imbali Maviala, Musingu High School, Kakemega, Kenya, to R. Heaps (sic), undated (*c.* June 1972), Soyinka: Kongi's Harvest, OP1620/12165, AOUP.
72. Robert Maviala to Heapy, 30 July 1972, in ibid.
73. Heapy to Maviala, 20 September 1972, in ibid.
74. Solaru to the Publisher, 7 December 1966, Three Crowns Series, 1967–71, LG29/221–1, AOUP.
75. Toyne to OUP Ibadan, 16 December 1966, in ibid.
76. Mitchell to Houghton, 14 February 1975, OP1619/911083, AOUP.
77. Anon., 'Wole Soyinka – Africa's Own William Shakespeare', *Pretoria News*, 30 October 2006, http://www.cafeafricana.com/Tributes-Wole-Soyinka.html, and Tanure Ojaide, 'Teaching Wole Soyinka's *Death and the King's Horseman* to American College Students', *College Literature*, 20 (1993), pp. 210–14, in which Ojaide refers to Soyinka as 'our W. S.'. Further examples of tributes to Soyinka, including comparisons with Shakespeare, are included in: Anon., 'Between Soyinka and Those Who Came After', *The Guardian*, 19 June 2004, http://www.cafeafricana.com/Tributes-Wole-Soyinka.html. In addition, Babs Ajayi refers to 'Our own WS and Kongi', in Babs Ajayi, 'Kongi: Giving Honour to a Literary Giant', *Nigeria World*, 9 February 2004, http://nigeriaworld.com/feature/publication/babsajayi/020904.html.
78. The association of Soyinka with Shakespeare has continued in recent critical studies: Antony Johae's reading of Soyinka's poem, *Hamlet*, concludes that Shakespeare's tragedy is the 'archetypal template for Soyinka's Sonnet', in Antony Johae, 'Wole Soyinka's "Hamlet": The Rotten State of Denmark Revisited', *Research in African Literature*, 38:4 (2007), p. 61, and Abiole Irele's tribute to Soyinka notes his 'manipulation of English' and the 'special effects he rings upon the language of Shakespeare', in Abiole Irele, 'The Achievement of Wole Soyinka', *Philosophia Africana*, 2:1 (2008), p. 9. Biodun Jeyifo argues, in relation to *A Dance of the Forests*, that 'it is one of his extraordinary accomplishments in this play that he was able to successfully absorb the influence of no less a towering, canonical figure of English theatre history and world literature than Shakespeare', Biodun Jeyifo, 'Forget the Muse, Think Only of the (Decentred) Subject?', *Tydskr. Letterkd* (online), 48:1 (2011), pp. 51–63.

9 Publishing Athol Fugard

1. Anon., *South Africa: Time Running Out – A Report on the Study Commission on the US Policy towards Southern Africa* (Berkeley: University of California Press, 1981), p. 131.
2. Athol Fugard, *Notebooks, 1960–1977*, ed. Mary Benson (New York: Alfred A. Knopf, 1984), pp. 150–1.
3. Ibid., pp. 78, 226 and 172.

4. Stephen Gray (ed.), *Athol Fugard* (Johannesburg: McGraw Hill, 1982), p. 26.
5. Dennis Walder, '*Athol Fugard* by Stephen Gray', *Research in African Literatures*, 15:3 (1984), pp. 461–4.
6. Hilary Seymour, '"Sizwe Bansi is Dead": A Study of Artistic Ambivalence', *Race and Class*, 21:3 (March 1980), pp. 273–89, at p. 282.
7. André Brink, '"No Way Out": Sizwe Bansi is Dead and the Dilemma of Political Drama in South Africa', *Twentieth-Century Literature*, 39:4 (1993), pp. 438–54, at p. 439.
8. Albert Wertheim, *The Dramatic Art of Athol Fugard* (Bloomington: Indiana University Press, 2000), pp. viii and xi.
9. Harry Garuba, 'The Island Writes Back: Discourse/Power and Marginality in Wole Soyinka's *The Swamp Dwellers*, Derek Walcott's *The Sea at Dauphin*, and Athol Fugard's *The Island*', *Research in African Literatures*, 32:4 (2001), pp. 61–76, at p. 71.
10. Dennis Walder, *Athol Fugard* (Tavistock: Northcote House Publishers, 2003), p. 57.
11. See Amuta, *The Theory of African Literature*, p. 3.
12. Ibid., p. 108.
13. Green to Lewis, 25 June 1968, Fugard: Hello and Goodbye, OP2005/15116, AOUP.
14. Philip to Stallworthy, 26 November 1968, in ibid.
15. Buckroyd to Stallworthy, undated (*c*. January 1969), in ibid. Buckroyd was an editor in the House Books department – the general publishing editorial department of OUP.
16. Ibid.
17. Ron Heapy, report on *People Are Living There*, 22 November 1968, in ibid.
18. Letter from Stallworthy, 13 November 1968, Fugard: People Are Living There, OP2007/15137, AOUP.
19. Ron Heapy, report on *People Are Living There*, 22 November 1968, Fugard: Hello and Goodbye, OP2005/15116, AOUP.
20. Fugard, *Notebooks*, p. 166.
21. Letter from A. R. M. to Stallworthy, 8 January 1970, Fugard: Hello and Goodbye, OP2005/15116, AOUP.
22. Ibid.
23. Ibid.
24. J. W. Cornwell to Stallworthy, 31 December 1968, in ibid.
25. Cannon to Stallworthy, 25 February 1970, in ibid.
26. Stallworthy to Fugard, 3 July 1970, in ibid.
27. Stallworthy to Brain, July 1970, in ibid.
28. Brain to Bell, 20 July 1970, Fugard: Boesman and Lena, OP2007/15136, AOUP.
29. Fugard, *Notebooks*, p. 201.
30. See Chapter 4, pp. 78–80 for further details.
31. See Chapter 1, p. 28 for further discussion of this point.
32. Fugard to Stallworthy, 5 April 1969, Fugard: People Are Living There, OP2007/15137, AOUP.
33. Publishing Agreement for 'People Are Living There', 25 November 1969, in ibid. This agreed terms of 10 per cent royalty, rising to 12.5 per cent after the first 10,000 copies were sold, and a £100 advance.
34. Fugard to Stallworthy, undated (received on 19 October 1970), Fugard: Hello and Goodbye, OP2005/15116, AOUP.
35. Fugard to Brain, 11 January 1971, in ibid.
36. Brain to Sheil, 6 March 1971, in ibid.

37. Brain to Sheil, 8 March 1971, Fugard: Boesman and Lena, OP2007/15136, AOUP; Brain to Dieter Pevsner, 20 August 1971, Penguin books, Fugard: Hello and Goodbye, OP2005/15116, AOUP; and Brain to Sheil, 22 October 1971, Fugard: People Are Living There, 2007/15137, AOUP.
38. Sheil to Brain, 10 March 1971, Fugard: Hello and Goodbye, OP2005/15116, AOUP.
39. Brain to Sheil, 8 March 1971, in ibid. This document sets out the initial offer of a £150 advance on royalties of 10 per cent rising to 12.5 per cent after 5000 copies sold. This was subsequently changed to a £200 advance on royalties of 10 per cent rising to 12.5 per cent after 3000 copies sold.
40. Brain to Sheil, 4 April 1972, Fugard: Hello and Goodbye, OP2005/15116, AOUP.
41. Brain to Gracie, March 1972, Fugard: Boesman and Lena, OP2007/15136, AOUP.
42. Brouillette, *Postcolonial Writers*, p. 4.
43. Genette, *Paratexts*, pp. 16–36.
44. Stallworthy to Fugard, 3 January 1970, copied with PS to Richard Brain, Fugard: Hello and Goodbye, OP2005/15116, AOUP.
45. Brain to the Publications Committee, 16 March 1972, in ibid.
46. Brain to Sheil, 22 October 1971, Fugard: Hello and Goodbye, OP2005/15116, AOUP. It was not until October 1971 that Stallworthy managed to get the contracts signed. The contract specified an advance of £100 against royalties of 10 per cent for the right to publish in the series for the 'British Traditional Market', excluding Canada.
47. Heapy to Production, 16 February 1972, in ibid.
48. *Boesman and Lena*, undated, in ibid.
49. Fugard to Heapy, 2 April 1973, in ibid.
50. Fugard to Heapy, 18 February 1975, in ibid.
51. Fugard to Kariara, undated (*c.* February 1975), in ibid.
52. Heapy to Houghton, 12 February 1975, in ibid.
53. Vandenbroucke, *Truths the Hand Can Touch*, p. 14.
54. Brain to Bell for the Delegates, 6 October 1970, Fugard: Boesman and Lena, OP2007/15136, AOUP.
55. Brain to Sheil, 22 October 1971, Fugard: Hello and Goodbye, OP2005/15116, AOUP. The terms agreed for the hardcover trilogy were an advance of £200 against royalties of 10 per cent, rising to 12.5 per cent after 3000 copies were sold.
56. In 1970 Oxford University Press was restructured. It was divided into three separate divisions. The Clarendon Press was the Academic division, and the London Publishing activities were divided into the General division (general trade publishing, including the Music department and Children's Books) and the Education division (School Books, English Language Teaching and Tutorial Books department). See Sutcliffe, *The Oxford University Press*, pp. 280 and 284–8.
57. Athol Fugard, 'Introduction', in *Three Port Elizabeth Plays* (Oxford: Oxford University Press, 1974), p. xxiv.
58. Brain to Fugard, 20 April 1972, Fugard: Boesman and Lena, OP2007/15136, AOUP.
59. Athol Fugard, quoted in letter from Richard Brain to Mrs Egan, Viking Press, New York, 8 May 1972, in ibid.
60. Brain to Ann A. Hancock, Viking Press, New York, 22 October 1971, Catherine Dittemore, Viking Press to Brain, 2 November 1971, and Brain to Catherine Dittemore, 8 November 1971, in ibid.
61. Brain to Fugard, 20 April 1972, and 9 May 1972, Fugard: Hello and Goodbye, OP2005/15116, AOUP.

62. Dennis Walder, email interview, 18 August 2008.
63. See Currey, *Africa Writes Back*, p. 12, for a discussion of the significance of hardback publication in relation to the African Writers Series.
64. Derek Cohen, 'A South African Drama: Athol Fugard's "The Blood Knot"', *Modern Language Studies*, 7:1 (1977), pp. 74–81, at p. 74.
65. Robyn Swett to C. C. Linnett, 18 January 1978, New York OUP, Soyinka: Four Plays, 015019, AOUP.
66. Fugard, *Notebooks*, pp. 150–1.
67. Dennis Walder, *Township Plays* (Oxford: Oxford University Press, 1993), p. xxviii.
68. Vandenbroucke, *Truths the Hand Can Touch*, p. 127.
69. See Walder, *Athol Fugard*, pp. 20–1, 55–6 and 65–70 for a discussion of the first performances of these plays, and their reception, in South Africa.
70. *A South African Season*, Royal Court Theatre programme (1974), p. 1.
71. *Daily Telegraph*, 13 October 1976, p. 4. Athol Fugard correspondence and newspaper articles donated by Mary Benson, File: 97.15.4.1, NELM.
72. John Kani and Winston Ntshona to the Royal Court Theatre, 2 November 1976, in ibid. It should be noted at this point that there are no references in the OUP archive to this event and evidently OUP played no part in this protest.
73. Brain to Fugard, 20 April 1972, Fugard: Hello and Goodbye, OP2005/15116, AOUP.
74. Heapy to Fugard, 9 March 1973, Fugard: Boesman and Lena, OP2007/15136, AOUP.
75. Brain to Fugard, 16 August 1973, in ibid.
76. Fugard to Heapy, 19 February 1974, Fugard: Statements, 211385–2, AOUP.
77. Heapy to EAK, Ely House, 29 August 1973, Fugard: Boesman and Lena, OP2007/15136, AOUP.
78. Sheil to Brain, 29 April 1974, Fugard: Statements, 211385–2, AOUP.
79. Brain to Buckroyd, 3 March 1974, Fugard: Statements, 211385–2, AOUP.
80. As discussed in Chapter 4, pp. 81–3.
81. Neville Gracie to Buckroyd, 19 February 1974, Fugard: Statements, 211385–2, AOUP.
82. New publications notice, March 1974, Fugard: Statements, 211385–2, AOUP.
83. Heapy to Fugard, 27 February 1974, in ibid.
84. Bourdieu, *Rules of Art*, pp. 37 and 99–101.
85. Bourdieu, 'The Market of Symbolic Goods', in *Field of Cultural Production*, p. 115.
86. Fugard, 'Introduction', in *Statements*, p. vii.
87. Peter Wilhelm, 'Athol Fugard at Forty' (interview), *To the Point* (1972), reprinted in Gray (ed.), *Athol Fugard*, p. 111.
88. 'Statements', Correspondence and typescript, File: 89.2.6, NELM.
89. Fugard to Buckroyd, 12 March 1974, Fugard: Statements, 211385–2, AOUP.
90. Heapy to Fugard, 21 May 1973, Three Crowns Series, 1971–74, LG29/222, AOUP.
91. Brain to Benson, 6 February 1974, Fugard: Statements, 211385–2, AOUP.
92. Buckroyd to Benson, 5 July 1974, Fugard: Statements, 211385–2, AOUP. Carol Buckroyd did, however, consult Mary Benson's advice over the proofs.
93. Brain to Buckroyd, 3 March 1974, in ibid.
94. Brink, '"No Way Out"', p. 439.
95. Bourdieu, 'The Market of Symbolic Goods', p. 118.
96. Gray (ed.), *Athol Fugard*, p. 21.

97. Dennis Walder, 'Crossing Boundaries: The Genesis of the Township Plays', *Twentieth Century Literature: A Scholarly and Critical Journal*, 39:4 (1993), pp. 409–22, at p. 417.
98. Fugard, 'Introduction', in *Statements*, p. xi.
99. Vandenbroucke, *Truths the Hand Can Touch*, p. 118.
100. Ibid., p. 126.
101. Sheil to Buckroyd, 8 May 1974, Fugard: Statements, 211385–2, AOUP.
102. Buckroyd to Sheil, 13 May 1974, in ibid.
103. Gardiner, 'Recuperating the Author', p. 263.
104. Buckroyd to Kani and Ntshona, 14 May 1974, Fugard: Statements, 211385–2, AOUP.
105. Buckroyd to Fugard, 14 May 1974, in ibid.
106. Genette, *Paratexts*, pp. 38–9.
107. Ibid., p. 26.
108. Fugard, *Statements: Three Plays*, back cover.
109. New publications notice, undated, Fugard: Statements, 211385–2, AOUP.
110. Sales figures for *Statements*, undated (*c.* July 1976), in ibid. See also letter from Sheila Fugard to Ad Donker, 2 September 1977, File: 2007.12.1.10.31, NELM.
111. Robyn Swett to C. C. Linnet, 18 January 1978, Soyinka: Four Plays, 015019, AOUP.
112. Unsigned letter, 16 January 1978, Fugard: Statements, 211385–2, AOUP.
113. Gracie to Adam Sisman, 3 August 1977, in ibid.
114. Walder, '*Athol Fugard* by Stephen Gray', p. 461.

Conclusion

1. Said, *Culture and Imperialism*, p. 158.
2. Bourdieu, *Rules of Art*, p.142. This issue is explored above, in particular on pp. 42–3 in relation to the Nigeria branch, pp. 56–7 in relation to the Eastern Africa branch, and also in Chapter 5, p. 99.
3. Casanova, *World Republic of Letters*, p. 40.
4. Ibid., p. 115.
5. Bourdieu, 'The Production of Belief', pp. 78–9.
6. Said, *Culture and Imperialism*, p. 80.
7. Bourdieu, 'The Production of Belief', p. 78.

Bibliography

Primary sources

Three Crowns series (African literature), 1962–76, Oxford University Press

Al-Hakim, Tewfik, *The Tree Climber*, trans. Denys Johnson-Davies (1966).
Benson, Mary, *Chief Albert Lutuli of South Africa* (1963).
Clark, John Pepper, *Three Plays* (1964).
—— *Ozidi* (1966).
de Graft, Joe C., *Sons and Daughters* (1964).
—— *Through a Film Darkly* (1970).
Easmon, Raymond Sarif, *Dear Parent and Ogre* (1964).
Egbuna, Obi B., *The Anthill* (1965).
—— *Daughters of the Sun and Other Stories* (1970).
Fugard, Athol, *People Are Living There* (1970).
—— *Boesman and Lena* (1973).
—— *Hello and Goodbye* (1973).
Gabre-Medhin, Tsegaye, *Oda-Oak Oracle* (1965).
Kimenye, Barbara, *Kalasanda* (1965).
—— *Kalasanda Revisited* (1966).
Mtshali, Oswald Mbuyiseni, *Sounds of a Cowhide Drum* (1972).
Nicol, Davidson, *The Truly Married Woman and Other Stories* (1965).
Nkosi, Lewis, *The Rhythm of Violence* (1964).
Rotimi, Ola, *The Gods are Not to Blame* (1971).
Senghor, Léopold Sédar, *Prose and Poetry*, selected and translated by John Reed and Clive Wake (1965).
Soyinka, Wole, *A Dance of the Forests* (1963).
—— *The Lion and the Jewel* (1963).
—— *Five Plays* (1964).
—— *The Road* (1965).
—— *Kongi's Harvest* (1967).
—— *Three Short Plays* (1969).

Other OUP publications

Hunter, N. B., *A First Course in Geography and History for African Schools* (London: Oxford University Press, 1931), vol. 1 and vol. II.
Mellor, Mabel, *A Practical Modern Geography*, West African Edition Book II (London: Oxford University Press, 1934).
Mofolo, Thomas, *Chaka the Zulu* (London: Oxford University Press, 1949).
Pohl, Victor, *Farewell the Little People* (Cape Town: Oxford University Press, 1968).
Williams, J. Grenfell, *Moshesh, the Man on the Mountain* (London: Oxford University Press, 1950).

Archival sources

Archives of Oxford University Press Archive (AOUP)

Africa and India Branch Books (1927–35), File: IB/14.
Benson: Chief Albert Lutuli, 12031.
Chaucer Pkt 86 1962 CG11/CPGE/54.
Clark: Ozidi, OP1620/12168.
Clark: Three Plays, OP1619/12157.
CPGE, File: 000069 CGB, Pkt 91(7).
Das: Larins Sahib, OP2005/15120.
Easmon: Dear Parent and Ogre, PB/ED8149/911066.
East Africa/Nairobi Branch Accounts, 1966–75.
Eastern Africa Branch Accounts, 1964–73.
Egbuna: Daughters of the Sun, OP9/8138.
Fugard: Boesman and Lena, OP2007/15136.
Fugard: Hello and Goodbye, OP2005/15116.
Fugard: People Are Living There, OP2007/15137.
Fugard: Statements, 211385–2.
Gabre-Medhin: Oda-Oak Oracle, 2006/15128.
Gubegna: Defiance, 1943/911093.
Kimenye: Kalasanda, OP2006/15131.
Macmillans in Africa: 1967–8, File: 8380.
Mtshali: Sounds of a Cowhide Drum, OP1619/12159.
New Oxford English Course for East Africa, Books I–VI, Pupils and Teachers Notes, CA48/LOCA002512–23.
New Oxford English Course for Nigeria, Books 1–VI, Teachers and Pupils Notes, CA48/LOCA002494–250.
Nigeria Branch Accounts.
Nkosi: The Rhythm of Violence, OP2005/15123.
Oxford Paperbacks Misc., 1962–1974, LG25/195.
Raja Rao: The Policeman and the Rose, OP1620/12172.
Senghor: Selected Poems, OP1103/211248.
South Africa Branch Accounts, Cape Town.
South Africa Branch File, 165 (1) May 1928–July 1975.
Southern African Branch, Oxford Packet 165 (2), LOGE 96, LG12, Packet 88 (2), Cape Town (General).
Soyinka: Four Plays, 015019.
Soyinka: Kongi's Harvest, OP1620/12165.
Soyinka: Lion and the Jewel, OP1619/12161.
Soyinka: Lion and the Jewel, OP1620/12164.
Soyinka: The Road, OP1619/12163.
Soyinka: Three Short Plays, OP1620/12167.
Three Crowns Series, 1967–71, LG29/221–1.
Three Crowns Series, 1967–72, LG29/221–3.
Three Crowns Series, 1967–72, LG29/223.
Three Crowns Series, 1971–74, LG29/222.
Wake (ed.): Prose and Poetry, OP1947/775.
West Africa Branch, Ibadan, Nigeria Misc., 286/322.

Documents cited

Hart, Riette, 'Cape Town Branch: The Story of Oxford University Press Southern Africa' (1992), South Africa Branch File.

Oxford House, Ibadan (Oxford: Oxford University Press, 1954), West Africa Branch, Ibadan, Nigeria Misc., 286/322.

Cape Town Archives Repository (CTAR)

Cannon, F., to J. Kruger, Publications Control Board, 18 March 1970, File: BCS 100 41/70.

Objectionable Literature: Various Publications Published by Oxford University Press Southern Africa, BCS 100, 41/70.

Van Wyk, A., to the Secretary for Customs and Excise, 17 March 1964, File: Lewis Nkosi, 201/64 BCS 41.

Cape Town University Libraries (CTU)

Leo Marquard Papers: correspondence files

Leo Marquard Papers, BC587.

Leo Marquard Papers, E22.1–E22.23.

Leo Marquard Papers, Letters from Friends and Associates, C.125.1–C.136.7.

Leo Marquard Papers: documents cited

Marquard, Leo, 'Memorandum on Native Education, Evidence before National Education Committee', Senate Select Committee (Abolition of Passes and Coordination of Documents) Bill 1952, January 1950, E22.1–E22.23.

Marquard, Leo, 'Writing under Permit', Rhodes University, 30 August 1962, H2.25.55.

'Marquard Tells of the Raid on his House', *Cape Argus*, 12 May 1964, BC587.

'Graaff Questions Police Raids', *Cape Times*, 2 July 1964, BC587 A6.42.

Leeds University Library Special Collections (LUL)

Banham, Martin, 'Theatre in West Africa: A Conversation between Wole Soyinka and Martin Banham' (undated, *c.* 1963), MS 1748.

Soyinka, Wole, *A Dance of the Forests* typescript, File: BC MS 20C.

—— 'The Future of West African Writing', *The Horn*, 4:1 (1959).

—— 'Letter to Rex Collings with "Prisonettes"'.

—— *The Road*, typescript, File: BC MS 20C.

National English Literary Museum, Grahamstown (NELM)

Correspondence files

Correspondence between Ad Donker and Sheila Fugard, File: 2007.12.1.10.45.

Fugard, Athol, correspondence and newspaper articles donated by Mary Benson, File: 97.15.1.1–97.15.5.5.

Mtshali, Oswald Joseph, Correspondence relating to Oswald Mtshali from Guy Butler, File: PL086–PL089(2).

OUP CTB after 1969, Correspondence of David Philip relating to OUP Cape Town branch, File: 2006.30.2.

Paton to Brown, 6 November 1973, File 2002.33.6.1: Paton and Alexander: Campbell: Selected Poems (Donker) 1982.
'Statements', Correspondence and typescript, File: 89.2.6.

Documents cited

Daily Telegraph, 13 October 1976, File: 97.15.4.1.
Hart, Riette, 'Cape Town Branch: The Story of Oxford University Press Southern Africa' (1992), OUP CTB after 1969, File: 2006.30.2.12.

University of Witwatersrand Library

Richards, Charles Granston, 'No Carpet on the Floor: Recollections and Reflections on the Work of Forty Years, 1935–1975, in the Development of Literature and Publishing', unpublished memoir (1991).

Oral sources and correspondence

Attwooll, David, personal interview, 16 February 2003, Oxford Brookes University.
Cannon, Paul, email correspondence, 14 September 2011.
Currey, James, personal interview, 6 November 2003, Oxford Brookes University.
Heapy, Ron, personal interview, 3 July 2002, Oxford University Press.
Philip, David and Marie Philip, personal interview, 5 April 2007, Cape Town.
Stallworthy, Jon, personal interview, 3 July 2002, Wolfson College, Oxford University.
Walder, Dennis, email interview, 18 August 2008.

Published sources

Abu-Jamal, Mumia, 'Soyinka's Africa: Continent of Crisis, Conflict and Cradle of the Gods', *Black Scholar*, 31:1 (2001), pp. 31–42.
Ahmad, Aijaz, *In Theory: Class, Nations, Literatures* (London: Verso, 1992).
Alden, Patricia, 'Competing Interpretations: Charles Mungoshi's "The Accident"', *Zambezia*, 21:2 (1994), pp. 107–22.
Altbach, Philip (ed.), *Publishing and Development in the Third World* (London: Hans Zell, 1992).
Amuta, Chidi, *The Theory of African Literature: Implications for Practical Criticism* (London: Zed Books, 1989).
Anon., 'Black Writers and Harold Bloom's Literary Canon', *Journal of Blacks in Higher Education*, 6 (1994–95), pp. 24–5.
Anon., *South Africa: Time Running Out – A Report on the Study Commission on the US Policy towards Southern Africa* (Berkeley: University of California Press, 1981).
Arnove, Anthony, 'Pierre Bourdieu, the Sociology of Intellectuals, and the Language of African Literature Author(s)', *NOVEL: A Forum on Fiction*, 26:3 (1993), pp. 278–96.
Aseidu-Akrofi, A., 'Education in Ghana', in A. Babs Fafunwa and J. U. Aisiku (eds), *Education in Africa: A Comparative Survey* (London: George Allen & Unwin, 1982).
Balabkins, Nicholas, *Indigenization and Economic Development: The Nigerian Experience* (Greenwich, CT: JAI Press, 1982).
Bandele-Thomas, Biyi, 'Wole Soyinka Interviewed', in *Wole Soyinka: An Apparisal* (Oxford: Heinemann, 1994), pp. 142–60.
Banham, Martin, 'Review of the *Trials of Brother Jero*', *The Horn*, 4:1 (1961), pp. 18–19.

Barnhisel, Greg and Catherine Turner, *Pressing the Fight: Print Propaganda and the Cold War* (Amherst and Boston: University of Massachusetts Press, 2010).
Biersteker, Thomas, *Multinationals, the State and Control of the Nigerian Economy* (Princeton, NJ: Princeton University Press, 1987).
Birmingham, David, *The Decolonization of Africa* (London: UCL Press, 1995).
Bloom, Harold, *The Western Canon: The Books and School of the Age* (London: Macmillan, 1994).
Boehmer, Elleke, *Colonial and Postcolonial Literature* (Oxford: Oxford University Press, 1995).
Bourdieu, Pierre, *Distinction* (London: Routledge, 1984).
—— *The Field of Cultural Production*, ed. Randal Johnson (Cambridge: Polity Press, 1993).
—— 'The Field of Cultural Production, or: The Economic World Reversed', in *Field of Cultural Production*, pp. 29–73.
—— 'The Market of Symbolic Goods', in *Field of Cultural Production*, pp. 112–44.
—— 'The Production of Belief', in *Field of Cultural Production*, pp. 74–111.
—— *The Rules of Art: Genesis and Structure of the Literary Field*, trans. Susan Emanuel (Cambridge: Polity Press, 1996).
Brink, André, '"No Way Out": Sizwe Bansi is Dead and the Dilemma of Political Drama in South Africa', *Twentieth Century Literature*, 39:4 (1993), pp. 438–54.
Brouillette, Sarah, *Postcolonial Writers in the Global Literary Marketplace* (Basingstoke: Palgrave Macmillan, 2007).
Bukenya, Austin S., 'East and Central Africa', *Journal of Commonwealth Literature*, 7:2 (1972), pp. 15–25.
Burton, Antoinette (ed.), *Archive Stories: Facts, Fictions and the Writing of History* (Durham, NC: Duke University Press, 2005).
Cain, P. J. and A. G. Hopkins, *British Imperialism: Crisis and Deconstruction* (London: Longman, 1993).
Carlin, Murray, *Not Now, Sweet Desdemona* (Nairobi: Oxford University Press, 1969).
—— *The Thousand* (Nairobi: Oxford University Press, 1969).
Casanova, Pascale, *The World Republic of Letters*, trans. M. B. Debevoise (Cambridge, MA: Harvard University Press, 2004).
Chakava, Henry, 'East and Central Africa', *Journal of Commonwealth Literature*, 13:3 (1978), pp. 10–17.
—— 'A Decade of Publishing in Kenya', *African Book Publishing Record*, 14:4 (1988), pp. 235–42.
—— 'Kenyan Publishing: Independence and Dependence,' in Philip Altbach (ed.), *Publishing and Development in the Third World* (London: Hans Zell, 1992), pp. 119–50.
Chatterjee, Rimi B., *Empires of the Mind: A History of the Oxford University Press in India under the Raj* (Delhi: Oxford University Press, 2006).
Chinweizu, Jemie Onwuchekwa and Madubuike Ihechukwu, *Toward the Decolonization of African Literature: African Fiction and Poetry and their Critics* (London: KPI, 1980).
Christie, Pam and Colin Collins, 'Bantu Education: Apartheid Ideology or Labour Reproduction', *Comparative Education*, 18:1 (1982), pp. 59–75.
Clarke, Becky, 'The African Writers Series – Celebrating Forty Years of Publishing Distinction', *Research in African Literatures*, 34 (2003), pp. 163–74.
Cohen, Derek, 'A South African Drama: Athol Fugard's "The Blood Knot"', *Modern Language Studies*, 7:1 (1977), pp. 74–81.

Cook, David, 'East and Central Africa', *Journal of Commonwealth Literature*, 4 (1969), pp. 9–18.

Currey, James, 'African Writers Series: 21 Years On', *African Book Publishing Record*, 11 (1985), pp. 11–13.

—— *Africa Writes Back: The African Writers Series and the Launch of African Literature* (Oxford: James Currey, 2008).

Darnton, Robert, 'What is the History of Books', in *The Kiss of Lamourette: Reflections in Cultural History* (New York: W. W. Norton, 1990).

Davis, Caroline, 'Postcolonial Publishing: Oxford University Press and the Three Crowns Series 1962–1976', *Book History* (2005), pp. 227–8.

Davis, Geoffrey V. and Holger G. Ehling, 'Levelling the Playing Fields: An Interview with David and Marie Philip', in Geoffrey V. Davis (ed.), *South African Writing: Voyages and Explorations* (Amsterdam: Rodopi, 1994).

Delegates of the University Press, 'Annual Report, 1 April 1975–31 March 1976', *Oxford University Gazette* (Oxford: Oxford University Press), November 1976, Supplement no. 1.

—— 'Annual Report, 1 April 1976–31 March 1977', *Oxford University Gazette* (Oxford: Oxford University Press), December 1977, Supplement no. 1.

—— 'Annual Report, 1 April 1977–31 March 1978', *Oxford University Gazette* (Oxford: Oxford University Press), November 1978, Supplement no. 1.

—— 'Annual Report, 1 April 1978–31 March 1979', *Oxford University Gazette* (Oxford: Oxford University Press), November 1979, Supplement no. 1.

de Villiers, G. E. (ed.), *Ravan: Twenty-Five Years (1972–1997): A Commemorative Volume of New Writing* (Randburg: Ravan Press, 1997).

Dodson, Don and Barbara Dodson, 'Publishing Progress in Nigeria', *Scholarly Publishing*, 4:1 (1972), pp. 61–72.

Donker, A., 'English-Language Publishing in South Africa', *English in Africa*, 10:1 (1983), pp. 29–35.

Dubow, Saul, 'Introduction', in S. Dubow and A. Jeeves (eds), *South Africa's 1940s: Worlds of Possibilities* (Cape Town: Double Storey Books, 2005).

English, James, *The Economy of Prestige: Prizes, Awards and the Circulation of Cultural Value* (Cambridge, MA: Harvard University Press, 2005).

Essery, Isabel, 'Politics and Publishing in South Africa: Interviews with Two Pioneers', *Logos*, 17:3 (2006), pp. 151–6.

Fafunwa, A. B., *History of Education in Nigeria* (London: George Allen & Unwin, 1974).

Finkelstein, David and Alistair McCleery (eds), *The Book History Reader* (London: Routledge, 2002).

Fraser, Robert, 'Four Alternative Endings to Wole Soyinka's *A Dance of the Forests*', *Research in African Literatures*, 10:3 (1979), pp. 359–74.

—— *Book History through Postcolonial Eyes: Rewriting the Script* (London: Routledge, 2008).

—— 'War and the Colonial Book Trade: The Case of OUP India', in Robert Fraser and Mary Hammond (eds), *Books without Borders*, vol. II: *Perspectives from South Asia* (Basingstoke: Palgrave Macmillan, 2008).

Fraser, Robert, with Nourdin Bejjit, 'The Tiger that Pounced: The African Writers Series (1962–2003) and the Online Reader', *Chadwyck Healey's African Writers Series Online*, September 2005.

Friedman, G. and R. Blumenthal (eds), *A Writer in Stone: South African Writers Celebrate the 70th Birthday of Lionel Abrahams* (Cape Town: David Philip, 1998).

Fugard, Athol, John Kani and Winston Ntshona, *Statements: Three Plays* (Oxford: Oxford University Press, 1974).

—— *Three Port Elizabeth Plays* (Oxford: Oxford University Press, 1974).
—— *Notebooks, 1960–1977*, ed. Mary Benson (New York: Alfred A. Knopf, 1984).
Gardiner, Juliet, 'Recuperating the Author: Consuming Fictions of the 1990s', *Papers of the Bibliographical Society of America*, 94:2 (2000), pp. 255–74.
—— 'What is an Author? Contemporary Publishing Discourse and the Author Figure', *Publishing Research Quarterly*, 16:1 (2000), pp. 63–76.
Garuba, Harry, 'The Island Writes Back: Discourse/Power and Marginality in Wole Soyinka's *The Swamp Dwellers*, Derek Walcott's *The Sea at Dauphin*, and Athol Fugard's *The Island*', *Research in African Literatures*, 32:4 (2001), pp. 61–76.
Gates, Henry Louis, 'Henry Louis Gates, Jr., 1975', in Biodun Jeyifo (ed.), *Conversations with Soyinka* (Jackson: University of Mississippi Press, 2001), pp. 48–67.
Gedin, Per I., 'Private Enterprise Publishing in Africa: Why and How it Should be Fostered', *Logos*, 2:3 (1991), pp. 133–9.
Genette, Gérard, *Paratexts: Thresholds of Interpretation* (Cambridge: Cambridge University Press, 1997).
Gibbs, James, 'The Masks Hatched Out', *Theatre Research International*, 7:3 (1982), pp. 180–207.
—— 'Rex Collings – Obituary, 1925–1996', *Bellagio Publishing Network Newsletter*, 18 (November 1996), p. 22.
—— 'Soyinka in Zimbabwe: A Question and Answer Session, James Gibbs 1981', in Biodun Jeyifo (ed.), *Conversations with Wole Soyinka* (Jackson: University Press of Mississippi, 2001), pp. 82–109.
Gray, Stephen (ed.), *Athol Fugard* (Johannesburg: McGraw Hill, 1982).
Green-Simms, Lindsey, '"No Danger No Delay": Wole Soyinka and the Perils of the Road', *Journal of Postcolonial Writing*, 46:1 (2010), pp. 53–64.
Griffiths, Gareth, *African Literatures in English: East and West* (Harlow: Pearson Education, 2000).
Griswold, Wendy, *Bearing Witness: Readers, Writers and the Novel in Nigeria* (Princeton, NJ: Princeton University Press, 2000).
Gupta, Suman, 'Samuel Becket, *Waiting for Godot*', in David Johnson (ed.), *The Popular and the Canonical* (Abingdon: Routledge, 2005), pp. 210–61.
Hench, John, *Books as Weapons: Propaganda, Publishing, and the Battle for Global Markets in the Era of World War II* (Ithaca, NY: Cornell University Press, 2010).
Hill, Alan, *In Pursuit of Publishing* (London: John Murray, 1988).
Hofmeyr, Isabel, *The Portable Bunyan: A Transnational History of the Pilgrim's Progress* (Princeton, NJ: Princeton University Press, 2004).
Horrell, Muriel, *A Decade of Bantu Education* (Johannesburg: South African Institute of Race Relations, 1964).
Huggan, Graham, *The Postcolonial Exotic: Marketing the Margins* (London: Routledge, 2001).
Hyslop, Jonathan, *The Classroom Struggle: Policy and Resistance in South Africa 1940–1990* (Pietermaritzburg: University of Natal Press, 1999).
Indire, Filomina, 'Education in Kenya', in A. Babs Fafunwa and J. U. Aisiku (ed.), *Education in Africa: A Comparative Survey* (London: George Allen & Unwin, 1982), pp. 115–39.
Irele, Abiole, 'The Achievement of Wole Soyinka', *Philosophia Africana*, 2:1 (2008), pp. 5–19.
Jeyifo, Biodun, 'Realms of Value in Literature Art: Interview with Wole Soyinka, 1985', in Biodun Jeyifo (ed.), *Conversations with Wole Soyinka* (Jackson: University Press of Mississippi, 2001), pp. 117–21.

—— 'Wole Soyinka: In Person', in Biodun Jeyifo (ed.), *Conversations with Soyinka* (Jackson: University of Mississippi Press, 2001), pp. 13–18.

—— *Wole Soyinka: Politics, Poetics, and Postcolonialism* (Cambridge: Cambridge University Press, 2004).

—— 'Forget the Muse, Think Only of the (Decentred) Subject?', *Tydskr. Letterkd* (online), 48:1 (2011), pp. 51–63.

Johae, Antony, 'Wole Soyinka's "Hamlet": The Rotten State of Denmark Revisited', *Research in African Literature*, 38:4 (2007), pp. 61–9.

Johanson, Graeme, *Colonial Editions in Australia, 1843–1972* (Wagga Wagga: Elibank Press, 2000).

Johnson, David, *Shakespeare and South Africa* (Oxford: Oxford University Press, 1996).

—— 'From the Colonial to the Post-colonial: Shakespeare and Education in Africa', in Ania Loomba and Martin Orkin (eds), *Post-Colonial Shakespeares* (London: Routledge, 1998), pp. 218–34.

Johnson, Walton, 'Education: Keystone of Apartheid', *Anthropology & Education Quarterly*, 13:3 (1982), pp. 216–37.

Jones, Thomas Jesse, *Education in Africa: A Study of West, South, and Equatorial Africa by the African Education Commission, under the Auspices of the Phelps-Stokes-Fund and the Foreign Mission Societies of North America and Europe* (New York: Phelps-Stokes Fund, 1922).

—— *Education in East Africa* (New York: Phelps-Stokes Fund, 1925).

Joshi, Priya, *In Another Country: Colonialism, Culture and the English Novel in India* (New York: Columbia University Press, 2002).

Kallaway, Peter, *Apartheid and Education: The Education of Black South Africans* (Johannesburg: Ravan Press, 1984).

—— *The History of Education under Apartheid, 1948–1994* (Cape Town: Pearson, 2002).

—— 'Welfare and Education in British Colonial Africa and South Africa during the 1930s and 1940s', *Paedagogica Historica*, 41:3 (2005), pp. 337–56.

Kant, Immanuel, *Critique of Judgment*, rev. edn (New York: Cosimo, 2007).

Kenyatta, Jomo, *My People of Kikuyu* (Nairobi: Oxford University Press, 1966).

Küster, Sybille, '"Book Learning" versus "Adapted Education": The Impact of Phelps-Stokesism on Colonial Education Systems in Central Africa in the Interwar Period', *Paedagogica Historica*, 43:1 (2007), pp. 79–97.

Larson, Charles, *The Ordeal of the African Writer* (London: Zed, 2001).

Lee, Jenny, 'Exploiting the Imprint', in David Carter and Anne Galligan (eds), *Making Books: Contemporary Australian Publishing* (St Lucia, Queensland: University of Queensland Press, 2007), pp. 17–33.

Lefevere, André, 'The Historiography of African Literature Written in English', in Bill Ashcroft, Gareth Griffiths and Helen Tiffin (eds), *Key Concepts in Post-Colonial Studies* (London: Routledge, 1998), pp. 465–70.

Lindfors, Bernth, 'Amos Tutuola: Debts and Assets', *Cahiers d'Etudes Africaines*, 10:38 (1970), pp. 308–34.

—— 'Bibliography: Africa Western', *Journal of Commonwealth Literature*, 20:2 (1985), pp. 6–18.

—— *Long Drums and Canons: Teaching and Researching African Literatures* (Trenton, NJ: Africa World Press, 1995).

—— *The Blind Men and the Elephant and Other Essays in Biographical Criticism* (Asmara, Eritrea: Africa World Press, 1999).

Lizabarre, Camille, *Something Else Will Stand Beside It: The African Writers Series and the Development of African Literature* (Ann Arbor: University of Michigan Press, 1998).

Low, Gail, 'In Pursuit of Publishing: Heinemann's African Writers Series', *Wasafiri*, 17 (2002), pp. 31–5.

—— 'The Natural Artist: Publishing Amos Tutuola's *The Palm-Wine Drinkard*', *Research in African Literatures*, 37 (2006), pp. 15–33.

—— *Publishing the Postcolonial: West African and Caribbean Writing in the UK, 1950–1967* (Abingdon: Routledge, 2011).

Makotsi, Ruth and Lily Nyariki, *Publishing and the Book Trade in Kenya* (Nairobi: East African Educational Publishers, 1997).

McClintock, Ann, '"Azikwelwa" (We Will Not Ride): Politics and Value in Black South African Poetry', *Critical Inquiry*, 13:3 (1987), pp. 597–623.

McDonald, P., *The Literature Police: Apartheid Censorship and its Cultural Consequences* (Oxford: Oxford University Press, 2009).

McGann, Jerome, *The Textual Condition* (Princeton, NJ: Princeton University Press, 1991).

McKenzie, D. F., *Bibliography and the Sociology of Texts* (London: British Library, 1986).

Merrett, Christopher, *A Culture of Censorship: Secrecy and Intellectual Repression in South Africa* (Cape Town: David Philip, 1995).

Mosha, Herme Joseph, 'A Reassessment of the Indicators of Primary Education Quality in Developing Countries: Emerging Evidence from Tanzania', *International Review of Education*, 34:1 (1988), pp. 17–45.

Moss, Glenn, 'The Life and Changing Times of an Independent Publisher in South Africa', *Logos*, 4:3 (1993), pp. 144–6.

—— 'Publishing in Post-Apartheid South Africa', *Logos*, 4:3 (1993), pp. 140–3.

Mpe, Phaswane, 'The Role of the Heinemann African Writers Series in the Development and Promotion of African Literature', *African Studies*, 58 (1999), pp. 105–22.

Mpe, Phaswane and Monica Seeber, 'The Politics of Book Publishing in South Africa: a Critical Overview', in Nicholas Evans and Monica Seeber (eds), *The Politics of Publishing in South Africa* (London: Holger Ehling Publishing, 2000), pp. 15–42.

Mungoshi, Charles, *Coming of the Dry Season*, rev. edn (Harare: Zimbabwe Publishing House, 1981).

Murray, A. V., *The School in the Bush: A Critical Study of the Theory and Practice of Native Education in Africa* (London: Longmans, Green, 1929).

Ndegwa, R. N., 'Africa: East and Central', *Journal of Commonwealth Literature*, 16:2 (1982), pp. 9–11.

—— 'Africa: East and Central', *Journal of Commonwealth Literature*, 17:2 (1982), pp. 2–8.

—— 'Africa: East and Central', *Journal of Commonwealth Literature*, 21:2 (1986), p. 2.

Newell, Stephanie, *Ghanaian Popular Fiction: 'Thrilling Discoveries in Conjugal Life' and Other Tales* (Oxford: James Currey, 2000).

—— *Literary Culture in Colonial Ghana: 'How to Play the Game of Life'* (Manchester: Manchester University Press, 2002).

—— *West African Literatures: Ways of Reading* (Oxford: Oxford University Press, 2006).

Ngaboh-Smart, Francis, 'Re-narrating the Nation: Soyinka's *The Interpreters*', *Journal of Postcolonial Writing*, 46:1 (2010), pp. 42–52.

Ngũgĩ wa Thiong'o, *Decolonising the Mind: The Politics of Language in African Literatures* (Oxford: James Currey, EAEP, Heinemann, 1986).

—— *Moving the Centre: The Struggle for Cultural Freedom* (Oxford: James Currey, 1993).

—— *Penpoints, Gunpoints and Dreams: Towards a Critical Theory of the Arts and the State in Africa* (Oxford: Oxford University Press, 1997).

Ngwane, Z., 'Apartheid under Education: Schooling, Initiation, and Domestic Reproduction in Post-Apartheid Rural South Africa', in Peter Kallaway (ed.), *The History of Education under Apartheid 1948–1994: The Doors of Learning and Culture Shall Be Opened* (Cape Town: Pearson, 2002), pp. 270–85.

Nottingham, John, 'Establishing an African Publishing Industry: A Study in Decolonization', *African Affairs*, 271:68 (1969), pp. 139–44.

Nwankwo, Victor, 'Nigeria', in Philip G. Altbach and Edith S. Hoshino (eds), *International Book Publishing: An Encyclopedia* (London: Routledge, 1995).

Nyerere, Julius, 'Africa and the Debt Crisis', *African Affairs*, 84:337 (1985), pp. 489–97.

Ojaide, Tanure, 'Teaching Wole Soyinka's *Death and the King's Horseman* to American College Students', *College Literature*, 20 (1993), pp. 210–14.

Okafor, Clement Abiaziem, 'Teaching African Literature in Zambian Schools', *Research in African Literatures*, 1:2 (1970), pp. 177–82.

Okpaku, Joseph O. O., 'Publishing and Public Enlightenment in Africa', in Edwina Oluwasanmi, Eva McLean and Hans Zell (eds), *Publishing in Africa in the Seventies* (Ife: University of Ife Press, 1975), pp. 233–7.

Okunoye, Oyenlyi, 'Captives of Empire: Early Ibadan Poets and Poetry', *Journal of Commonwealth Literature*, 34:2 (1999), pp. 105–23.

Oluwasanmi, Edwina, Eva McLean and Hans Zell (eds), *Publishing in Africa in the Seventies* (Ife: University of Ife Press, 1975).

Onibonoje, G. O., 'Wanted! A Cultural Revolution, Not a Dialogue', in Edwina Oluwasanmi, Eva McLean and Hans Zell (eds), *Publishing in Africa in the Seventies* (Ife: University of Ife Press, 1975).

Onyerisara, Ukeje and J. U. Aisiku, 'Education in Nigeria', in A. Babs Fafunwa and J. U. Aisiku (eds), *Education in Africa: A Comparative Survey* (London: George Allen & Unwin, 1982), pp. 210–39.

Peires, Jeffrey, 'Lovedale Press: Literature for the Bantu Revisited', *History in Africa*, 6 (1979), pp. 155–75.

Philip, David, 'Book Publishing under and after Apartheid', in *Book Publishing in South Africa for the 1990s: Proceedings of a Symposium Held at the South African Library, Cape Town, 22–23 November 1990* (Cape Town: South African Library, 1991).

Radway, Janice, *A Feeling for Books: The Book-of-the-Month Club, Literary Taste, and Middle-Class Desire* (Chapel Hill: University of North Carolina Press, 1997).

Rathgeber, Eva-Maria McLean, 'Nigerian University Presses: Problems and Prospects', *The African Book Publishing Record*, 5:1 (1979), pp. 13–18.

'Rebusoajoang', 'Education and Social Control in South Africa', *African Affairs*, 78:311 (1979), pp. 228–39.

'Report of the Committee on the University Press', *Oxford University Gazette*, 100 (1970), Supplement no. 7 (cited as the Waldock Report).

Rich, Paul B., *White Power and the Liberal Conscience: Racial Segregation and South African Liberalism, 1921–1960* (Manchester: Manchester University Press, 1984).

—— *Hope and Despair: English-Speaking Intellectuals and South African Politics, 1896–1976* (London: British Academic Press, 1993).

Rowell, Charles H., '"With Bloodstains to Testify": An Interview with Keorapetse Kgositsile', *Callaloo*, 2 (1978), pp. 23–42.

Said, Edward W., *Culture and Imperialism* (London: Vintage, 1994).

—— *Orientalism*, rev. edn (London: Penguin, 2003).
Schmidt, Nancy J., 'The Writer as Teacher: A Comparison of the African Adventure Stories of G. A. Henty, Rene Guillot, and Barbara Kimenye', *African Studies Review*, 19:2 (1976), pp. 69–80.
Seymour, Hilary, '"Sizwe Bansi is Dead": A Study of Artistic Ambivalence', *Race and Class*, 21:3 (March 1980), pp. 273–89.
Smith, Richard C., *Teaching English as a Foreign Language, 1912–1936: Pioneers of ELT* (London: Routledge, 2003).
Soyinka, Wole, *Collected Plays: Volume 1* (London: Oxford University Press, 1973).
—— *Collected Plays: Volume 2* (London: Oxford University Press, 1974).
—— *Ibadan: The Penkelemes Years – A Memoir, 1946–65* (London: Methuen, 1994).
Spender, Lynne, *Intruders on the Rights of Men: Women's Unpublished Heritage* (London: Pandora Press, 1983).
Squires, Claire, *Marketing Literature: The Making of Contemporary Writing in Britain* (Basingstoke: Palgrave Macmillan, 2007).
Stec, Loretta, 'Publishing and Canonicity: The Case of Heinemann's African Writers Series', *Pacific Coast Philology*, 32 (1997), pp. 140–9.
Stoler, Ann Laura, 'Colonial Archives and the Arts of Governance: On the Content in the Form', in Francis X Blouin Jr. and William G. Rosenberg (eds), *Archives, Documentation, and Institutions of Social Memory: Essays from the Sawyer Seminar* (Ann Arbor: University of Michigan Press, 2006), pp. 267–79.
Sutcliffe, Peter, *The Oxford University Press: An Informal History* (Oxford: Oxford University Press, 1978).
Thompson, John, *Merchants of Culture: The Publishing Business in the Twenty-First Century* (Cambridge: Polity Press, 2010).
Thompson, Leonard, *A History of South Africa* (New Haven, CT: Yale University Press, 1990).
Towheed, Shafquat, 'Two Paradigms of Literary Production: The Production, Circulation and Legal Status of Rudyard Kipling's Departmental Ditties and Indian Railway Library Texts', in Robert Fraser and Mary Hammond (eds), *Books without Borders*, vol. II: *Perspectives from South Asia* (Basingstoke: Palgrave Macmillan, 2008), pp. 125–36.
Trump, M. (ed.), *Rendering Things Invisible: Essays on South African Literary Culture* (Johannesburg: Ravan Press, 1990).
Vandenbroucke, Russell, *Truths the Hand Can Touch: The Theatre of Athol Fugard* (New York: Theatre Communications Group, 1985).
van der Vyver, J., 'General Aspects of the South African Censorship Laws', in T. Coggin (ed.), *Censorship: A Study of Censorship in South Africa* (Johannesburg: South Africa Institute of Race Relations, 1983).
—— *Liberals against Apartheid: A History of the Liberal Party of South Africa, 1953–1968* (London: Macmillan, 1997).
Visser, Nicholas, 'Drama and Politics in a State of Emergency: Athol Fugard's My Children! My Africa!', *Twentieth-Century Literature*, 39:4 (1993), pp. 486–502.
Walder, Dennis, '*Athol Fugard* by Stephen Gray', *Research in African Literatures*, 15:3 (1984), pp. 461–4.
—— 'Crossing Boundaries: The Genesis of the Township Plays', *Twentieth Century Literature: A Scholarly and Critical Journal*, 39:4 (1993), pp. 409–22.
—— *Athol Fugard* (Tavistock: Northcote House Publishers, 2003).
Wallis, Philip, *At the Sign of the Ship* (Harlow: Longman, 1974).
Wanjala, Chris, 'East and Central Africa', *Journal of Commonwealth Literature*, 8:2 (1973), pp. 14–22.

Welbourn, Hebe, 'Village Gossip: *Kalasanda* by Barbara Kimenye', *Transition*, 24 (1966), p. 56.
Wertheim, Albert, *The Dramatic Art of Athol Fugard* (Bloomington: Indiana University Press, 2000).
Wilhelm, Peter, 'Athol Fugard at Forty' (interview), *To the Point* (1972), reprinted in Stephen Gray (ed.), *Athol Fugard* (Johannesburg: McGraw-Hill, 1982), pp. 111–14.
Wright, Edgar, 'East and Central Africa', *Journal of Commonwealth Literature*, 2 (1967), pp. 10–14.
Yesefu, Abdul R., 'Mbari Publications: A Pioneer Anglophone African Publishing House', *The African Book Publishing Record*, 8 (1982), pp. 53–7.
Zell, Hans, 'Publishing in Africa', unpublished paper, Oxford Brookes University Library, Special Collection on African Publishing, *c.* 1992.
—— *African Publishing Companion: A Resource Guide* (Lochcarron: Hans Zell, 2002).
Zell, Hans M. and Helene Silvers, *A Reader's Guide to African Literature* (London: Heinemann Educational Books, 1972).

Digital sources

Ajayi, Babs, 'Kongi: Giving Honour to a Literary Giant', *Nigeria World*, 9 February 2004, http://nigeriaworld.com/feature/publication/babsajayi/020904.html.
Anon., 'Between Soyinka and Those Who Came After', *The Guardian*, 19 June 2004, http://www.cafeafricana.com/Tributes-Wole-Soyinka.html.
Anon., 'Wole Soyinka – Africa's Own William Shakespeare', *Pretoria News*, 30 October 2006, http://www.cafeafricana.com/Tributes-Wole-Soyinka.html.
Chancellor, Masters and Scholars of the University of Oxford v. *Commissioner for Inland Revenue, Republic of South Africa Cape Provincial Division*, 31 March and 13 June, 1994, before J. Berman, Tax Cases, volume 57, SATC 231; also cited as 1995 (3) SA 258, http://www.btinternet.com/~akme/berman.html.
Corbett, C. J., 'Judgement in Case no. 385/94 in the Supreme Court of South Africa (Appellate Division), in the matter between The Chancellor, Masters and Scholars of the University of Oxford and the Commissioner for Inland Revenue', 30 November 1995, p. 9, http://www.safii.org/za/cases/ZASCA/1995/157.pdf.
Gyllensten, Lars, 'Nobel Prize in Literature Presentation Speech 1986', http://nobelprize.org/nobel_prizes/literature/laureates/1986/presentation-speech.html.
Howatt, A. P. R., *Warwick ELT Archive Launch Lecture*, paper read at the Centre for English Language Teacher Education, University of Warwick, 7 May 2005, to mark the official opening of the Warwick EL Archive, http://www2.warwick.ac.uk/fac/soc/celte/research/elt_archive/launch/lecture/.
Krog, E. W., 'The Progress of Shona and Ndebele Literature', http://www.mazwi.net/essays/the-progress-of-shona-and-ndebele-literature.
Mitchell, L. G., 'Bowra, Sir (Cecil) Maurice (1898–1971)', *Oxford Dictionary of National Biography*, Oxford University Press, online edn, May 2005, http://www.oxforddnb.com/view/article/30841.
Quigly, Isabel, 'Obituary: Rex Collings', *The Independent*, 8 June 1996, http://www.independent.co.uk/news/people/obituary-rex-collings-1335987.html.
Richardson, George B., to Inland Revenue for Exemption Status from Corporate Tax, 24 March 1977, http://www.btinternet.com/~akme/75dcm2.html.
—— (full application) to Local Inspector of Taxes, 2 August 1977, Oxford University Press Application for Exemption from Corporation Tax http://www.btinternet.com/~akme/75gbr2.html.

Statement by the African National Congress GA/5498, 26 October 1976, http://www.anc.org.za/un/pr/pr1026–76.html.

United Nations, Resolution A/RES/31/6, A General Assembly of the United Nations, 42nd Plenary meeting, 26 October 1976, http://www.un.org/documents/ga/res/31/ares31.htm.

Vigne, Randolph, 'David Philip: Publisher who Resisted Apartheid', *Independent on Sunday*, 10 March 2009, http://www.independent.co.uk/news/obituaries/david-philip-publisher-who-resisted-apartheid-1641047.html.

Theses

Bejjit, Nourdin, 'The Publishing of African Literature: Chinua Achebe, Ngũgĩ wa Thiong'o and the Heinemann African Writers Series 1962–1988', unpublished Ph.D. thesis, Open University (2009).

Index

Notes:
The abbreviation OUP (Oxford University Press) is used in subheadings.
Bold entries refer to illustrations or tables.

Printed in Great Britain
by Amazon

57717814R00153